The Arts and Events

Cultural heritage and contemporary arts benefit from being showcased in events. Arts-related events are each unique in reflecting local culture; they may be spontaneous (street art and so on) or planned (i.e. studio tours or arts festivals).

The Arts and Events explores the nature and complexity of managing arts events and fills a significant gap in the available literature. It investigates the history, development and management of arts events to offer much more than purely economic benefits. It therefore contributes to a greater understanding of how arts events can create a beneficial experience for the individual and the community as well as their future sustainable development. The title explores a broad range of events from around the globe including: inspirational events for building creative (social, cultural and human) capital; affirming events for encouraging links to cultural identity or heritage; pleasurable events that offer enjoyable recreational, leisure and touristic experiences; enriching events that create opportunities for personal growth and/or to sell products or experiences; and finally, celebratory events that enhance cultural diversity.

This significant volume is a valuable source for researchers, policy-makers and managers of arts events around the globe.

Hilary du Cros is an Honorary Research Fellow, University of New Brunswick, Canada. She has a unique perspective on arts, heritage and tourism management. Books include the popular textbook *Cultural Tourism: The Partnership between Tourism and Cultural Heritage Management* (2002; second edition forthcoming 2014, which will be titled *Cultural Tourism*) and *Cultural Heritage Management in China* with Y.S.F. Lee (Routledge, 2009).

Lee Jolliffe is a Professor of Hospitality and Tourism at the University of New Brunswick, Canada, and has a research interest in culture and tourism. Her previous books include *Sugar Heritage and Tourism in Transition* (Channel View Publications, 2013) and *Mining Heritage and Tourism* with Michael V. Conlin (Routledge, 2011).

Routledge Advances in Event Research Series

Edited by Warwick Frost and Jennifer Laing
*Department of Marketing, Tourism and Hospitality,
La Trobe University, Australia*

Events, Society and Sustainability
*Edited by Tomas Pernecky and
Michael Lück*

Exploring the Social Impacts of Events
*Edited by Greg Richards, Maria deBrito
and Linda Wilks*

Commemorative Events
Warwick Frost and Jennifer Laing

Power, Politics and International Events
Edited by Udo Merkel

Event Audiences and Expectations
Jo Mackellar

**Event Portfolio Planning and
Management**
A Holistic approach
Vassilios Ziakas

Conferences and Conventions
A research perspective
Judith Mair

Fashion, Design and Events
*Edited by Kim M. Williams, Jennifer Laing
and Warwick Frost*

Food and Wine Events in Europe
*Edited by Alessio Cavicchi and
Cristina Santini*

Event Volunteering
*Edited by Karen Smith, Leonie Lockstone-
Binney, Kirsten Holmes and Tom Baum*

The Arts and Events
Hilary du Cros and Lee Jolliffe

Forthcoming:

The Future of Events and Festivals
*Edited by Ian Yeoman, Martin Robertson,
Una McMahon-Beattie, Elisa Backer and
Karen Smith*

Sports Events, Society and Culture
*Edited by Katherine Dashper,
Thomas Fletcher and Nicola McCullough*

**Exploring Community Events and
Festivals**
Edited by Allan Jepson and Alan Clarke

Event Design
*Edited by Greg Richards, Lénia Marques
and Karen Mein*

**Rituals and Traditional Events in the
Modern World**
*Edited by Warwick Frost and Jennifer
Laing*

The Arts and Events

Hilary du Cros and Lee Jolliffe

Routledge
Taylor & Francis Group

LONDON AND NEW YORK

First published 2014
by Routledge
2 Park Square, Milton Park, Abingdon, Oxon OX14 4RN

and by Routledge
711 Third Avenue, New York, NY 10017

Routledge is an imprint of the Taylor & Francis Group, an informa business

British Library Cataloguing in Publication Data
A catalogue record for this book is available from the British Library

Library of Congress Cataloging in Publication Data
A catalog record for this book has been requested

ISBN: 978-0-415-83394-3 (hbk)
ISBN: 978-0-203-79282-7 (ebk)

Typeset in Times New Roman
by HWA Text and Data Management, London

Printed and bound by CPI Group (UK) Ltd, Croydon, CR0 4YY

Contents

Plates

Figures

Tables

Boxes

Acknowledgements

A number of arts, tourism and event management professionals and others have contributed to this book. They have helped by talking to us about their situations or by giving advice generally. In particular, the authors would like to thank, first of all from Hong Kong: Samuel Leong, Kin Cheung, Josephine Do, John Batten, Robert Rogers, Lawrence Wood, and Brian King. From Australia, we would like to express thanks to Angie McGowan, Dominique du Cros, and Barry Hiern. From Canada, Diana Alexander and Rebecca Millar were extremely helpful with their comments. Finally, from Northern Ireland, Paula McFetridge deserves a special mention.

We would also like to thank the University of New Brunswick, the Hong Kong Institute of Education and the National University of Singapore for providing institutional support in the course of preparing the manuscript.

Abbreviations

AAF	Asian Contemporary Art Fair
ADKSL	Association for the Development of Keur Serigne Louga
AE	Arts Ecologies
AHAF	Asia Hotel Art Fair
AIA	American Institute of Architects
ANZ	Australia and New Zealand
BBC	British Broadcasting Corporation
BLF	Bookworm (International) Literary Festival
CCFS	Celtic Colours Festival Society
CCIF	Celtic Colours International Festival
CSIV	Children's International Summer Villages
EFF	Edinburgh Fringe Festival
EIF	Edinburgh International Festival
FAP	Federal Art Project
FESFOP	Festival International de Folklore et de Percussion de Louga
HKIEd	Hong Kong Institute of Education
ICH	Intangible Cultural Heritage
IOC	International Olympics Committee
KDA	Kalbarri Development Association
MOMA	Museum of Modern Art
NEA	National Endowment for the Arts
NOHJF	New Orleans Heritage and Jazz Festival
PAP	People's Action Party
PIA	Performing Industry Association (Ltd)
PWAP	Public Works of Art Project
RAF	Reykjavik Arts Festival
RLCCE	Research in Local Culture and Creativity in Education
SAF	Sharjah Art Foundation
SAR	Special Administrative Region
SCA	Sustainable Creative Advantage
SISS	Schoodic International Sculpture Symposium
SOCO	Society for Community Organization
SOCOG	Sydney Organizing Committee for the Olympic Games

SXSINC	Sculpture by the Sea incorporated
TTCSI	Trinidad and Tobago Coalition of Service Industries
UNESCO	United Nations Educational Scientific and Cultural Organization
UNWTO	United Nations World Tourism Organization
VIP	Very Important Person
WKCD	West Kowloon Cultural District
WKCDA	West Kowloon Cultural District Authority
WPA	Works Progress Administration

1   Introduction

The twentieth and twenty-first centuries have seen an explosion of arts events in every corner of the world. Many of these events are successful first time round and some have even repeated on a regular basis because of this success, particularly in regard to benefits they bring the community in which they are anchored. However, these benefits cannot always be guaranteed every time an event is repeated. This book wants to move beyond vague views of social and cultural good that are generated by successful arts events by applying new concepts and terms to events presented in case studies in this book in ways which could also be emulated or improved upon by other authorities.

The new approach presented here includes drawing together relevant aspects of arts management, cultural policy, urban planning, tourism, economic and leisure concerns for assessing the success of particular arts and cultural events and their contribution to a community's creative capital. An interdisciplinary understanding of creative capital in terms of how it creates an advantage for the community is an important aspect of describing and analysing the benefits that arts events can bring. This new approach is also accompanied by a new classificatory system or nomenclature to bring more precision to the analysis.

Successful arts events

Five key types of arts events have been identified for this book: *inspirational events* that are catalysts for building creative (social, cultural and human) capital; *affirming events* for encouraging links to cultural identity or heritage; *pleasurable events* that offer enjoyable recreational, leisure and touristic experiences; *enriching events* that create opportunities for personal growth and/or to sell products or experiences, and finally, *celebratory events* that celebrate cultural identity and diversity. Affirming and celebratory events are subtly different from each other, because the former is an exercise in affirming interest and support for arts by a particular community and the latter aims at celebrating arts more broadly. The arts featured in all these event categories can be contemporary or heritage-based and they can be visual (painting, sculpture, mixed media, film, installations and so on) or performing (music, dance, singing, live theatre and any combinations of these activities). It is not uncommon for some types of events to feature contemporary, heritage, visual and performing arts all together, while others may be highly focused on a particular period, activity, artist or performer.

The types of events to which this classification can also be applied include those such as festivals, fairs and expositions, temporary and travelling exhibitions, studio and gallery related events and community and/or arts education events. Of these, festivals are often the largest and most closely analysed category of arts events given they have a long history and there are many popular ones that bring a number of different benefits to organizers and communities. However, as will be described in Chapter 2, especially some of the earliest internationally successful arts events connected with fairs and expos. Meanwhile, many museums and galleries rely on temporary and travelling exhibitions as important supplements to their permanent exhibitions. The fourth category of studio and gallery related events include that which focuses on a cluster of studios or galleries as a particular site of activity. In this way, studios or galleries might be bundled together for art walks or hops or host events individually that fulfil another need, such as a rapid series of pop-up exhibitions. Community and/or arts education events are more often the result of public arts education policies or corporate social responsibility visions, so deserve a category of their own.

Past arts and events research

The previous work on integral concepts regarding arts events has occurred in a number of disparate disciplines and will be grouped thematically below for a more logical flow under the following headings: global/local; urban/rural; arts management, community involvement and cultural policy; tourism/host benefits; public consumption and participation. This section will start with some of the spatial themes, because most events are heavily place-based, for instance they often use a city's or town's name in their title.

Significance of global/local context of events

Relevant to this section are works on the 'glocalization' of arts and events, mobile creative class and other ideas that have broadened the spectrum on context of events.

The *glocal* concept has been used to describe the adaptive activity of communities' re-localization of the global trends in interaction with their local context. Boaventura de Sousa Santos identifies two forms of this process:

> The first one I would call *globalized localism.* It entails the process by which a given local phenomenon is successfully globalized ... The second form of globalization I would call *localized globalism.*
>
> (Santos in Ganga n.d:327)

Globalized localism would manifest in the case of events that have proved remarkably successful in one location in fulfilling a particular need and where this need is also to be found elsewhere it can be repeated with local trimmings (e.g. fringe festivals that were established after the Edinburgh Fringe Arts Festival in 1947 and most blockbuster travelling art exhibitions). Alternatively, *localized globalism* would inspire an event that starts off as a more amorphous concept, such as that of hosting an outdoor music festival, and that can incorporate overseas' artists, but still be themed to be a uniquely local event (e.g. the Fuji Rock Festival in Japan and the New Orleans Heritage and Jazz Festival have little in common other than experiencing outdoor music performances). In this sense, this second kind of glocal event is rarely conceived of as an abstract understanding of the role of art, its display and interpretation. Indeed, the cultural organizations and individuals behind them are conditioned by the local social, political and economic pattern of development and by the existing policies and initiatives within which they need to integrate often taking a more pragmatic approach.

Some authorities have been particularly concerned about the global/local balance in relation to promotion of local arts in the face of growing commodification of arts events for greater commercial exploitation. Jepson, Wiltshier and Clarke (2008) have argued that the results of commercialization and commodification in regard to some arts festivals, which originated as a community enterprise first, has removed them from this local nexus to become 'placeless festivals'. If numerous local artists and performers (some of whom may only have limited local appeal) have been passed over in favour of more popular performers with a known reputation, then the event loses its local focus.

Urban/rural juxtaposition

Much that relates to an event's appeal can be related back to a diversity of place-based planning approaches and attitudes to 'place-making'. It is possible that there is an urban/rural juxtaposition on this issue that influences the ultimate development and perception of an event. First, consideration of this position will be discussed for urban planning policies that have been tried to provide the right conditions towards the transformation of cities into international cultural cities, then there will be a consideration of approaches taken in rural contexts.

Miles (2005) has observed that destinations promoted as 'cultural cities' have 'flagship' cultural institutions (e.g. Bilbao's Guggenheim Museum), post-industrial entertainment zone (e.g. revitalized waterfront areas), strong private-sector tourism investment and a historic quarter with small to medium-sized enterprises (which usually includes arts-related businesses). Richards and Palmer (2010) have taken this further and argued that in order to be 'eventful' many cities also require flagship events for which they are uniquely known. Evans (2009) has also completed a comprehensive international study of creative industry policies and strategies that surveyed public sector creative city initiatives and their underlying rationales. He looked at examples from Europe, North America, Africa and southeast Asia. A list of interventionist types of policies was discussed including those that put emphasis on start-up and small and medium-sized enterprises (SMEs) and those that favoured the encouragement of the larger creative sectors. His findings raised the question of whether such policies need to concentrate on 'growth' and 'arts cluster' models or target theoretical frameworks for building creative capital for the community. He also noted that how these policies emphasize social regeneration and revitalization objectives differed from city to city with reference to its place in each one's eco-historic cycle (a cycle of development where arts and creative industries have reanimated older districts).

Examples of historic quarters or post-industrial zones with arts clusters are also important in research on European cities of culture undertaken by authorities such as Avery (2007) for Liverpool, Maitland (2007) for London, and by Ali-Knight and Robertson (2003) for Barcelona, Edinburgh, and Glasgow. Hence, examples of cultural cities that have also become genuinely 'creative' and are generating cultural consumption (as in studies by Mommaas 2004, Evans 2007 and Galligan 2008) are of interest, although arts and culture should not be seen as 'the magic substitute for all the lost factories and warehouses (or) a device that will create a new urban image' (Hall 2000:40). Other work investigates the synergies derived from clustering of activities in creative clusters such as Drake (2003), Evans (2009), and Stolarick and Florida (2006). Much of the social and cultural capital accumulated with the clustering is also claimed to assist with urban regeneration where arts have developed organically (without public intervention), or alternatively, as a result of integrated planning by public authorities that has enhanced this process. Urban regeneration, culture and local identity are also key concerns of Orbaşli (2000) who is concerned about the superficiality of some post-industrial historic urban environments and their utility for tourism. In addition, if conservation for a commercial reason is promoted foremost, is it unlikely to satisfy deeper yearnings for a 'sense of identity and pride of place' for those concerned? Her perspective is coming from studying European historic towns, many of which have undergone extensive post-war or post-industrialism rebuilding and are witnessing an increase in tourism. It has been also observed by several authorities that grand government-led revitalization projects using the arts as a focus have stifled or been unsuccessful in enhancing the local character of art production (Page and Hall 2003; Smith 2007). Because they lack a grassroots up foundation, they enhance the feeling of 'placelessness' or the 'every city looks the same' syndrome (Relph in Smith 2007) rather than the opposite.

Where tourism has been promoted as a substitute for loss of other industries, showcasing culture and art in events and otherwise has become increasingly important for the dual reasons of destination branding and benchmarking. Page and Hall (2003) indicate exploiting culture for tourism purposes is a social process linked closely with identity construction that usefully includes a commercial product that can be consumed. Some cities are strongly branded or are internationally known as having arts as their centrepiece attraction, such as Paris and Vienna. In Asia, there seems to be a case for art clusters and heritage enhancing a place's touristic appeal. Where creative industries and historic businesses exist together, urban heritage activists can lobby for a more sympathetic regeneration of the urban fabric, if this is failing to occur (Murray 2007; Chang and Teo 2009; Designing Hong Kong 2013). Finally, Richards and Palmer (2010) state that many cities hunger to be 'eventful' in terms of transforming themselves into major stages for a constant series of events that may lead to a 'festivalization' of the city. The benefits this can bring a city is that events can enhance the growth of the symbolic and experience economies that allow for greater place-based cultural consumption (Pine and Gilmore in Richards and Palmer 2010).

In terms of useful urban studies, Brooks and Kusher (2001) sought to define important characteristics of a metropolitan region's arts economy and arts environment in a comparative analysis of 20 American cities. They looked specifically at the level of arts activity for visitors and residents, the financial health of the arts sector, the quality of the arts and the potential for growth. They then analysed the relationship among the different measures and found additional measures of potential utility (Brooks and Kusher 2001). Even so, they concluded that such studies, whether the results were favourable or not to a particular city, would be used in ways that might not give a clear idea of creative capital by city authorities and other stakeholders in their aim to benchmark their city above others.

Many studies relating to arts events or community arts development and creative capital have either an urban or rural context with the balance tipped towards those conducted in urban environments. For instance, one of the best frameworks for analysing creative capital came from a study of a rural community in Australia by Mitchell and Fisher (2010) and an equally interesting one for drivers of cultural value for host communities from Italy by Campetta, Manzoni and Salvemini (2010). Accordingly, dynamic arts environments with the capital suitable for a foundation for arts events are not only found in cities. Harvey, Hawkins and Thomas (2012) demonstrate in their study of rural clusters in West Cornwall that this context can also yield suitable conditions for successful arts events. They focus on the relationships between the key cluster and its surrounding area together with the spatial linkages and temporalities of the relations that occur across and beyond the cluster. It examined the dynamics and durability of cluster's key stakeholders, while also paying attention to the disconnections.

Critically, the clustering of artistic talent, whether in an urban or rural context, is often a pre-condition for many events that require some kind of bundling such as those mentioned earlier, particularly festivals, studio and gallery hops or walks. McKercher and du Cros (2002:112) have already recognized bundling as an important strategy within cultural tourism 'combining a variety of similar themed products and experiences and promoting their collective consumption to visitors'. It is also important for the local sustainability of many arts events that they do not just target tourists as their key market, as noted earlier by Jepson *et al.* (2008).

The arts, community involvement and cultural policy

Event planners and managers that actively seek to fulfil some kind of societal need either develop their events as non-government or government initiatives or policies. The latter occurs as a result of a conscious public sector attempt at arts management. Arts management authority Derik Chong (2009) notes that discussion of this topic often includes the complementary term 'cultural management' between which there is much overlap, particularly as many public institutions tend to deal with both. There is also much overlap in events, which have a number of aims beyond that of displaying artistic creativity. Hence, where positive benefits of events are discussed it can often be in relation to community awareness, education and creative development. Such benefits are often sought after by the public sector and housed in public policies on arts and/or culture. Examples of such events would include community arts festivals with activities that invite participation by families, the elderly, schools or community service organizations.

Chong (2009) looked in depth at the relationship between cultural and arts policies and relative returns for the United Kingdom and the United States in his latest book on arts management. He argues that public subsidies for the arts have been traditionally considered to be useful because they promote overall public benefits (such as encouraging civilizing influences, national pride and collective identity), while they can be exploited for their extrinsic worth for expanding local job opportunities (with some economic spillover effects) and promoting tourism. An additional equity argument holds that policies should ensure the arts be made available to all in a way that may help address social inequalities and promote cultural diversity. However, American neoliberalist views of subsidies for arts suggest that such policies just provide conditions for mediocrity rather than excellence and even some complacency about the true value of art. By creating an environment where tax incentives and indirect subsidies are in place, it is thought by neoliberalists that artistic creativity will be encouraged and that artists and performers need not spend their time in the constant search for government grants and related bureaucratic procedures. This claim on these creative individual's time is indeed perceived as a problem by New York's mayor, Michael Bloomberg. In 2012, he told his administration staff to loosen up the bureaucratic process for arts subsidies and 'get out of the way' of artists and arts organizations so that emerging artists could benefit and enrich the city's reputation as a creative city (UNESCO Observatory 2013a).

Much of this kind of rhetoric is based in the historical-cultural conditions of different countries with most public policies around the world falling somewhere in between the two positions. For instance, Singapore's arts funding (including that for events) is still strongly linked to public arts policy and related social engineering goals (Lee 2010; Chong 2011), while Australia and Hong Kong have been experimenting with some neoliberalist elements in their policies (Radbourne 2002; du Cros and Leong 2011). Cultural differences in the approach to arts policy have been notable in Singapore, since independence from the United Kingdom was granted in 1965. During the establishment of People's Action Party (PAP) at this time most of the politicians ignored their original cultural leanings in order to gain influence with the conservative elements within the Chinese ethnic majority. Their party line of anti-colonial and anti-Western liberalism was designed to please this sector and beat the leftists in the first elections. Aspects of the autocratic Confucian/Asian values philosophy continued after the 1980s. For instance, government and community leaders continue to view activists and politically themed artworks and performances negatively, as they are seen to threaten harmony and social cohesion (Velayutham 2007; Lee 2010).

The Singapore government realized in the 1990s that it had to embrace more global trends for fear of being left behind developmentally and in international exercises aimed at benchmarking cities. It responded to this concern by encouraging a greater diversity of artistic endeavours and events than was possible previously, particularly with public sector funding. However, fear of leftist and liberalist ideology was still evident between 1989–2001, especially in relation to media control issues and with some artists being investigated by the police as suspected communists and arts organizations losing public funding and recognition. The government still requires all arts events to apply for a license, especially exhibitions. This government measure is supposedly aimed at preventing racial/cultural discord (Chong 2004; Velayutham 2007; Lee 2010).

Despite being a majority ethnic Chinese society, Hong Kong has taken a different approach from Singapore to arts policy. In Hong Kong, public directives for the arts are buried within an extremely brief and vague cultural policy generated by the Hong Kong Special Administrative Region (SAR) government (Home Affairs Bureau 2013). Hong Kong has been a SAR of China since the handover of sovereignty to China by the United Kingdom in 1997. This postcolonial society is still more concerned about sustained economic development than encouraging the right conditions for greater local artistic development, despite branding itself as 'Asia World City'. Even so, given this orientation and competition from around the region, Hong Kong has a growing arts scene, possibly due to its cosmopolitan social values.

The Hong Kong government has largely ignored local arts clusters in organically developing cultural districts to fund an architect-designed cultural and arts hub that will become the West Kowloon Cultural District (WKCD), to fulfil economic and cultural goals. As a strategic investment to turn Hong Kong into a global city, the government has had to grapple with the long-term infrastructure needs of the arts and cultural sector. The recently formed West Kowloon Cultural District Authority (WKCDA) has been allocated a one-off government funding of HK$21.6 billion for construction and operation and it would see to the planning, designing and building of a range of performing arts and visual arts facilities on a 100-acre site that would also include commercial, residential and other components. Even so, the primary motivation for the Hong Kong SAR government to fund such a huge project as WKCD is to provide a greater diversity of arts and cultural activities for tourists. There are also a host of opportunities in synergizing with CreateHK (a dedicated agency established under the Commerce and Economic Development Bureau in 2009) to develop creative industries in Hong Kong. It is also proposed that new glocal arts events that would appeal to both local and international participants will be held in the facilities of WKCD, when completed. Even so, the fraught project has been criticized by the community, arts, public policy and urban planning experts, since it was mooted by the Chief Executive in his annual policy address in 1998 after Hong Kong's own handover to the People's Republic of China in 1997 (Hui 2006; du Cros and Leong 2011). The government is still adamant that WKCD will be successful in achieving its goals.

Tourism/host benefits

Compared to most tourist attractions at destinations, events can only be relied upon to draw or retain tourists for a short duration. Authorities with a focus on the management of such events for tourism classify them in relation to their size, scope, purpose, and specialist appeal in terms of the markets they address, such sports or arts/culture (Hede, Jago and Deery 2003; Shone and Parry 2004; Tum, Norton and Wright 2006; Getz 1997, 2009 and 2010). Arts events are a natural part of the 'experience economy', as promoted by Pine and Gilmore (1999), as they showcase the cultural rhythms or creative synergies of a particular place. The definition of such experiential encounters is still being developed in the literature in relation to creative industries, events and arts experiences in a tourism context (Kay and Polonsky 2010).

The economic impact of tourists attending arts events, particularly festivals, has been well explored by research (O'Sullivan and Jackson 2002; Chabra, Sills and Cubbage 2003; Maughan and Bianchi 2004). Social and cultural impacts of tourism at such events have also been dealt with occasionally, such as in studies by Quinn (2006:289). She described arts festivals, in particular, as 'socially significant cultural practices', which deserve consideration beyond their contributions to economic and tourism development 'as a product to enliven a destination' (Quinn 2006:301). One danger identified in the study is that by running a 'model tourism' event that highlights internationally known headliners, local arts can be marginalized and alienated. Sustainability of the event is compromised, because with 'no host community, there could be no festival' (Getz in Quinn 2006:304). A detailed analysis of the needs of host and arts communities that support arts-based community tourism can also be found for two case studies from the US by Aquino, Phillips and Sung (2012). However, little has been explored of the social and cultural aspects of arts events that have fostered change and community development. Even so, work such as Campetta, Manzoni and Salvemini (2010) and Mitchell and Fisher (2010) have managed to identify value drivers for host communities of arts events. These studies have elements that will be built upon by case studies examined in Chapters 3 to 6 in this book.

Campetta *et al.* (2010) analysed two major Italian arts events, Fuorisalone and Salone del Gusto, in Milan and Turin respectively, and differentiated connected value dimensions that were symbolic, social, intellectual and economic. They then highlighted specific value drivers of these dimensions: differentiation of the stakeholders (cross-sectionality); links with the authentic roots of the urban setting (local competency, authenticity and identity); passion to produce something new and different from other similar events (innovation); and the dynamics of competition and cooperation among the stakeholders (co-operation/ competition). However, tourism management issues for host communities, such as traffic congestion during peak periods, were observed but not accommodated in this assessment framework.

An Australian study by Mitchell and Fisher (2010) over a three-year period examined the potential for arts events to impact on a community using an approach

Table 1.1 Criteria for understanding how an event might contribute creative capital to a community (based on Mitchell and Fisher, 2010:192)

Key criteria	Questions checklist for assessing contributions
Creativity	What are the special arts resources in this community that can assist in creating this event? How is the event encouraging creativity in the community?
Clusters	What are the community networks helping the event? Is the event a point of connection? What connections are being made at the event?
Critical mass	Does the event create or feed off a critical mass of art activities?
Flow on effect	Does the event provide benefits that flow onto the community and other sectors?
Multiple pathways	Does the event provide multiple ways to engage the community and allow them to participate?
Experience economy	'Experiences are replacing goods and services, because they stimulate our creative faculties and enhance our creative capacities' (Florida in Mitchell and Fisher, 2010:192). What is unique about this community's culture and what does this event add to an experience of the community for a visitor?
Job and wealth creation	Who does the event partner with in order to create a critical mass of job opportunities and income for the community?
Favourable conditions/ supportive environment	What makes things happen in this community? What is its structural/institutional capital?
Knowledge/ intellectual property	What do we know about the setting of the event? It's people, history, successes, failures and its aspirations? What knowledge, new ideas, skills and pathways can the event generate?
Social, human and cultural capital	What groups or events are important to the way things are done around the community that have a bearing on the event? How does the event maintain linkages in the community and its arts and heritage? How does it enhance individual's and the community's arts development potential?

that tried to measure changes in branding and connectivity in relation to creativity and innovation. In doing so, the researchers asked a series of specific questions (see Table 1.1).

While this checklist of questions was by no means exhaustive as criteria for understanding the contribution of creative capital, it provided the authors with a framework for investigating the annual *Kenilworth Celebrates!* festival in terms of community support and benefits. However, should festivals be considered a special class of arts event in relation to social and cultural impacts of tourism? Jepson *et al.* (2008), who have also examined community festivals in terms of involvement and inclusion, observed that in relation an event they studied:

if stripped to their bare bones, festivals and moreover community festivals are a public themed celebration which can act as a catalyst for demonstrating community values and culture. This is what the local community festival under examination here aimed to encapsulate; a demonstration of local cultural events at both permanent and semi-permanent venues presenting the locality, a festival for the community, by the community. A festival cannot provide the heart to a community unless its organizers ensure it has culturally inclusive blood flowing through it.

(Jepson *et al.* 2008:10)

Similarly Falassi's (1987) view that festivals achieve a sense of community and well-being by renewing the life stream of a community is only possible if the life stream is inclusive of local communities' cultures, and it is fed by the tributaries from within those communities. These are aspects, which are identifiable to those communities, particularly when they are promoted in the festival.

However, an extra special case might be fringe arts festivals. Much has been written regarding the activities of the 'Creative Class', first by Florida (2002:8) who identified them as a group of innovative professionals 'whose economic function is to create new ideas, new technology and/or a new creative content'. Frequently, these individuals are also a key tourism market for and participants in fringe festivals where they seek inspiration, stimuli and outlets for their work. In view of this spotlight, fringe festivals intended to be open to all-comers to display their artistic wares have been under pressure to aim for greater quality and include more recognized artists. Initially begun in Edinburgh as an event with local or regional appeal and lofty ideals about equity of access, balance is starting to shift to global over the local in some cases. In order to do this more successfully, some fringe festivals have developed a selection process and are now juried (with a selection committee) like mainstream arts festivals. Others still try to continue unjuried, but with lesser access to sponsors and government funding in many cases. Artists and performers have a mixed reaction to the benefits of juried versus unjuried festivals, depending how many benefits or resources are available at each, the spontaneity allowed and how much promotion they might expect (Mulcahy 2005; Frew and Ali-Knight 2010).

Finally, heritage arts festivals can have special significance to a community in a rapidly changing world. This significance can be either as an internal affirmation of cultural identity, or as both an internal and external statement of that identity. That is, it is a statement made to tourists and overseas residents (diaspora) as well as those living where the festival is held. Safeguarding the intangible cultural heritage values associated with festive events also has become a particular concern of intergovernmental agencies, such as UNESCO and the United Nations World Tourism Organization in the context of the economic exploitation of these events for tourism and other commercial activities (UNWTO 2012). A new category was identified, i.e. that of 'intangible cultural heritage' (ICH) in the 1970s. By 1989, it was further promoted by adoption at the UNESCO General Conference that endorsed the *Recommendation on the Safeguarding of Traditional Culture and Folklore* (UNWTO 2012). This document drew the attention of the world's decision-makers to the importance of intangible cultural heritage in enabling different cultural groups to assert their cultural identity, allowing humanity to maintain its cultural diversity. In 1999, UNESCO established a listing and award system for intangible heritage 'Masterpieces of Oral and Intangible Heritage' to honour the most popular and traditional cultural activities or popular and traditional forms of expression, which includes heritage arts festivals.

The recommendation and the declaration were largely replaced later on by the Convention for the Safeguarding of the Intangible Cultural Heritage, 2003. It was adopted on 17 October 2003 by UNESCO General Conference in Paris and put into implementation in 2006. It was proposed with the intention of protecting ICH by encouraging an integrated approach to heritage as being 'traditional, contemporary and living at the same time', and inclusive so that individuals might feel part of the same or different communities, representative of cultural elements globally and in community-based arts activities (UNESCO Observatory RLCCE 2013a). More recently, the UNWTO sponsored a study of tourism and ICH, which featured examples of best practice heritage arts events such as processions, festivals, exhibitions and workshops that tourists could attend and whose presence would also benefit the host community (UNWTO 2012).

Consumption/participation and public support

Arts events are often organized and funded against a background of tension between neoliberalism and social interventionist policies from public administrations that require empirical evidence of successful implementation. Radbourne's (2002) work on this issue looked at the literature on relationship marketing, cultural economics and value measurement, and an analysis of the long-term outcomes of Australian government strategies for the funding of arts marketing. She then created a hypothesis that

> while social intervention is acceptable (even desirable and necessary), and achieves the social goals of governments, market intervention (by the public sector) reduces the benefits of relationship-building and the exchange of values between arts organizations and their audiences.
>
> (Radbourne, 2002:50)

This is a very similar observation to that of Chong (2009) who documented a rise of Harvard-type of business management practice entering arts administration in the UK from the late 1990s onwards, which he calls 'managerialism', which did not sit well with many of the artists and cultural critics of the time. Their chief concern was that the creative process or even an environment that enables art to happen would be more difficult to achieve, if there was too much concentration on purely administrative functions, such as, constant data collection about arts consumption.

The countries with a history of consistent public funding include the UK, Canada, USA, and Australia. For instance, in the United Kingdom alone there are the Arts Councils of England, Scotland, Wales and Northern Ireland, with funding often devolved to Regional Arts Boards, and a Lottery Fund to provide capital funding. The Canada Council for the Arts funds companies and projects, alongside foundations, sponsors and provincial governments. In the United States, grant funding is allocated by the National Endowment for the Arts (NEA), and state and municipal governments; however, support comes mostly from philanthropy, foundations and private sponsorship (Radbourne 2002).

Meanwhile, McNicholas (2004) holds that view that postmodern effects of globalization, such as a diffusion of barriers, borders and boundaries, have paved the way for revolution in arts and business relationships in relation to sponsorship. The parameters of the field of study have been extended with the complexities of postmodern influences and cross-disciplinary interconnectedness. Maturation of the field, incorporating information technology, public relations, marketing and human resources management, has concurrently brought an expansion in the field from within and can been seen to be having an impact of the appeal of arts events with international as well as local. Support for the arts events created within this context is likely to vary. At the pinnacle, will be those events with business partnerships that are more intermeshed, two-way, mutually involved and mutually affecting and which will include the development of highly customized activities that provide stronger value and image associations over time (McNicholas 2004). How this affects events that have been traditionally part of corporate social responsibility agendas, such as community arts/education activities, requires further research.

Social inclusiveness is only possible within local communities with a history of participation in arts activities. Governments cannot develop or sustain the kind of interdependence between artists/organizations and consumers that fosters the dialogue and shared values of relationship marketing. Relationship marketing is a practice where the value of the product is co-produced by the customer or patron and the arts organization, leading to a greater likelihood of mutual satisfaction. Radbourne (2002:59) notes 'such interdependence is possible only when a situation of mutual trust and commitment between the organization and its patrons has been cultivated'. It may also have a role to play in new social media initiatives, such as Kickstarter and Fringebacker, which are new forms of patronage currently known as 'crowdsourcing'. The latter uses a specially designed website to collect small amounts of funding from a lot of private sponsors from the general public for artistic projects (Fringebacker 2013).

Another view is held regarding participation advanced by Bourdieu (1984) in that social-class influences consumer behaviour and sponsorship. He argues that people typically consume certain products and adopt certain consumption and patronage styles as a means of creating distinction and declaring their social status, particularly in relation to the performing arts. While most arts organizations have been actively removing distinctions between high-brow and low-brow arts in promotion of events, arts consumers have continually restored them, according to Bourdieu (1984). Accordingly, a study from Spain by Sintas and Alvarez (2005) looked at three competing hypotheses about this symbolic role played by consumption: the distinction, the boundary-effacement, and omnivore effects with the suspicion that all these were working simultaneously, but to differing degrees. They found instead that in regard to the Spanish performing arts, arts consumers had four modes of consumption: sporadic, popular, snob, and omnivorous, with weak evidence for a few popular performing arts events that were liked by everyone (and not all were lowbrow performances). Alternatively, strong evidence favoured the hypothesis that consumers from the highest social class consume all arts at higher rates than everyone else does, and that there was some evidence that all social classes use the performing arts' consumption to symbolize status differences (Sintas and Alvarez 2005:1454).

Empirical analyses of arts consumption have also consistently discovered that gender is an essential determinant (such as Cheerbo and Peters 1995; Bihagen and Katz-Gerro 2000; DiMaggio 2004). In particular, women are significantly more likely than men to seek out what they identify as high-status cultural activities. One recent study by Christin (2012) for the United States investigated the effect of (1) early socialization in the arts and status; (2) involvement by gender in the labour force; and (3) the influence of marriage status on women's and men's cultural participation. The study revealed that the gender gap in consumption of high status cultural activities can be traced partly to differences in early socialization in the arts for women and men. This difference was reinforced by several employment-related differences in cultural participation.

Sustainable creative advantage: a new concept

A few common terms should be more closely examined before launching into the next section and an explanation of the heart of this book. First of all, 'creativity', 'creatives' and the 'creative process' are all terms that get bounced around in discourse without much close attention to their actual meanings at the time. Most dictionaries tend to define 'creativity' as a noun that describes the ability to go beyond traditional ideas and devise meaningful new ones as well as forms, methods, interpretations and so on with emphasis on originality and imagination. The 'who' element associated with this ability are increasingly describing themselves as more than just artists, inventors, communications or IT types, becoming 'creatives' in some debates and literature. These are often people who have absorbed the message of Florida's (2002) work on the 'Creative Class' and want to be acknowledged as part of that group. Accordingly, the creative process was first described by creatives, such as, artists and performers who undertook some self-reflection on how they found inspiration, much of which was not under conscious control. How much is conscious and subconscious is still the subject of experimental psychological studies, however, what is more relevant here is what factors support the process and enable breakthroughs and artistic activities to come into being.

One last term that is current in arts management, urban studies and tourism literature is 'art ecologies' (see Chong 2011; Hager and Sung 2012). Speaking to art critic and journalist, John Batten, in Hong Kong, it appears that this term is becoming increasingly popular with the arts community too, in terms of

Plate 1.1 Evidence of creative spark and freshness each time an arts event is held is important for maintaining sustainable creative advantage (New Orleans Heritage and Jazz Festival: du Cros 2011)

describing the health of linkages and interdependent relationships between key stakeholders in similar way to the health of natural ecologies. One of the uses of the term is in presenting the relationships between an arts-funding body and its funded organizations, artists and society in general. However, it brings a little more to the table in that the relationships can be mapped in regard a healthy spread and growth of benefits, so that the ecology can be productive as a whole to maintain and enhance that vibrancy. How the movement of money, skills, access to resources and other factors occurs could also be mapped to make it a useful concept for arts and cultural planners and policy makers (Robinson 2010).

Knowing more about the nature and health of arts ecologies is important for understanding the enabling conditions for achieving sustainability in relation to arts events. Such conditions are also important for establishing a sustainable advantage that is place-based and makes the most of available creative capital (creativity, creatives, creative processes and arts ecologies). Overall, there is a need for an arts event to maintain a 'sustainable creative advantage', (SCA) which is not as simple as a sustainable competitive advantage (and completely different), in order to be considered to have characteristics of some or all of the above.

What is a sustainable creative advantage really? Building different kinds of capital for and beyond the community is a short answer, but a holistic concept such as SCA is more appropriate in this context than applying separate concepts of creative, cultural or social any other type of capital, particularly as most artists and arts academics do not warm to the word 'capital' – it is too closely associated with purely financial benefits in their minds. The term tries to encompass at least four kinds of capital (social, cultural, human and economic) under this umbrella term as well as that creative spark that makes a really good arts event appeal to participants.

How to use this book

By taking this new approach, this book offers readers a bridge over the divide between the more conceptual world of the artists and arts academics, and that of the more pragmatic events and tourism managers and other academics. This is a key aspect of the book and one that has required an interdisciplinary approach in order to address adequately. Chapter 1 has reviewed the relevant literature from arts management, cultural policy, urban planning, tourism and events management, economic and leisure disciplinary authorities in order to provide a sound basis for analysing key aspects of arts and events. Likewise, Chapter 2 looks at the influences through time on the creation, development and management forms and styles of arts events, particularly for the ancient, modern and contemporary periods from early music and ritualistic festivals through to pop-up exhibitions and hotel art fairs.

Chapter 3 will look more closely at understanding what kinds of benefits and impacts different kinds of events can offer in terms of being inspirational, affirming, pleasurable, enriching and/or celebratory in terms of their key orientation or market. It will deal with a broad range of modern (and postmodern) arts events including festivals, fairs and expos, temporary and traveling exhibitions, studio- and gallery-related events, professional and community arts events and specifically tourism-inspired arts events. Case studies of best practice examples from diverse locations representing different *types* of art events will be interspersed through the chapter (e.g. USA, Canada, Croatia, Senegal, United Arab Emirates, Australia, Israel, Argentina and Macau).

Planning, development and implementation measures for successful arts events will be presented in Chapters 4 and 5. Examples will be used throughout to guide the reader and suggest a range of ideas for innovative and sustainable events. Chapter 6 will assist event managers and researchers in measuring performance of events by proposing an assessment tool to gauge sustainable creative advantage with several in-depth examples. A conclusion to the book is provided in Chapter 7 that will outline directions for future research and key points such as the significance of applying new perspectives on arts events in context of understanding and safeguarding cultural diversity, encouraging links to cultural identity or heritage; offering enjoyable recreational, leisure and touristic experiences; and in creating opportunities for personal and economic growth.

2 Historical context of arts events

This brief history of how arts events and their management have developed around the world, since ancient times, includes some of the earliest and most controversial international exhibitions and those in museums and galleries. In particular, how different eras in the development of arts events are a reflection of society and its view of the role that artists play. Case studies will be mainly drawn from the history of city branding, museums and events (for example, from London, Edinburgh, New York and Paris). For instance, the longest continuously running arts events and the first ones with a regional or global reach include the Edinburgh Arts Festival and Great Exhibitions of the nineteenth century. This section will discuss trends and changes over time, for instance, from fixed events to pop-ups, from single arts to multiple arts-focused events, and the hybridization of the arts in its linkages with hallmark sports events (e.g. London Cultural Olympiad).

The origin of arts events: the ancient and pre-modern world

The ancient world did not begin with celebrating arts for arts' sake or segment arts into different areas for any special attention initially, particularly as most artists and performers were not professional or were considered to be of low status. Rites of passage, annual rituals and agricultural celebrations were often supported by or depicted by the arts in many early cultures. Middle East, Mexico, Europe and much of the rest of the world loosely organized festivals with religious associations, social or religious focus, usually with strict boundaries on who were able to participate as artists. Foreign talent and artists who had not closely studied the artistic performances suitable to accompany certain religious events would not have been welcome. For instance, a particular type of ritualistic dance was important to the female believers of the cult of Dionysus as a way to reach the emotional elevation needed to attain the religious ecstasy required for the festive worship of the Greek god. It was only taught to members of the Dionysian cult not outsiders (Papaioannou and Lykesas 2012).

Even so, the professional status of artists was often quite low or perhaps they were viewed as practitioners of a craft with little emphasis on originality or much incentive to compete or innovate to attract accolades. Until cities became more established with larger economic support bases for specialist occupations, artist or artisan quarters for the visual arts and the infrastructure and audience for the performing arts were impossible and that meant sporadic folk arts and religious arts performances were more often the norm. Such practitioners did not dedicate all their time to their art, whilst the most proficient were better than most hobbyists today, there were no events designated solely to valorise such arts and provide encouragement. Where this situation started to change was with the rise of a belief amongst the wealthiest urban citizens that their status would be enhanced by patronage of the arts and of quality professional artists and their productions. Along with this patronage, some incentives for artistic improvement would grow from formal and informal criticism associated with competitions and likely from greater financial rewards from patrons for providing a type of reflected glory for their artists being publicly acclaimed. While ancient Greek arts events were often linked to religious and seasonal festivals, such as the Eleusinian and Dionysian festivals, patronage of the arts was seen by ancient Greek and Roman elites as adding to their personal or family prestige. In the competitions associated with such festivals, each poet[1] would require a patron to commission the work and the theatrical performance could be enjoyed by a wider audience than just the patron (Hornblower and Morgan 2007).

Box 2.1 Athens City Dionysia Festival: performances and competitions

In the Classical period of Greece in the fifth and fourth centuries BC, theatre festivals started to be held as public events. De Cauter and Dehaene (in Ioannidou 2011:390), note that theatre in classical Athens:

> suspended the usual distinction between the political *agora* (place of assembly) and the private *oikos* (household): During the *City Dionysia*,[2] for example, the rules of in- and exclusion adopted within the political realm were explicitly suspended. The whole community was free to participate in these theatre festivals, not only the citizens of the *polis* but also ambassadors of other (colonized) cities, women, the foreigners living in Athens and even slaves. The issue of ownership—private or public—is often simply irrelevant for the heterotopian character of these places.
>
> (De Cauter and Dehaene in Ioannidou 2011:390)

The City Dionysia, also known as the Great Dionysia, (including the feast of Dionysus Eleuthereus), was considered in ancient times to be far the most splendid of the Bacchic festivals. Dionysus was one of the more popular Greek gods, because his worship allowed the opportunity for a holiday from everyday cares and behaviour, even to the point of reaching ecstatic states for some in the more esoteric rituals, such as the Mysteries already mentioned (such as the cult of Dionysus) (Athenian Agora Excavations 2013).

The Great Dionysia was held within the city precincts, in the sacred enclosure of Dionysus Eleuthereus on the south slope of the Acropolis, where the remains of the great Athenian theatre are still visible. This is distinct from the Anthesteria and the Lenaea dramatic festivals, which were generally celebrated in a district outside the walls. The date of the festival can be fixed with a fair amount of certainty as within the last half of March and the first half of April when the weather was much more favourable for witnessing outdoor performances and festivities. It was approximately five days in duration with a packed schedule of performances and celebrations (Haigh 1898; Hart 2010).

Timing of the event

It was both a seasonal festival celebrating Spring, and one that symbolized the supremacy of the Athenian state in arts and culture to those visiting from elsewhere in Greece. The calmer weather in the Mediterranean meant that visitors could more comfortably sail to Athens for this festival than others held during winter (Hart 2010). With the streets filled with strangers, the city also presented an animated appearance in contrast to the calm of the more locally focused winter festival of the Lenaea. The Athenians during the height of the Athenian empire enjoyed the opportunity to display the magnificence of their city before these domestic Greek tourists and ambassadors. The various religious ceremonials, the sacrifices to the gods, the poetry, the tragedies, and the comedies were impressive in terms of their statement about the wealth, public spirit, theatrical and literary accomplishments of the Athenians. This point was also brought home to visitors before the commencement of the performances in the theatre when the tribute collected from the allies was solemnly deposited in the orchestra in the presence of the audience.

However, in the fourth century BC, after the fall of the Athenian empire, these political overtures ceased to be part of the City Dionysia. Visitors still arrived from all parts of Greece to enjoy the festival (Haigh 1898).

Performances and competitions

The festival's performances also included those that were part of competitions. At the City Dionysia, there were two types of choral competitions, one between choruses of boys, and the other between choruses of men. The choruses were known as 'cyclic choruses', because a circle of 50 participants was made to perform. Records show that there were five choruses of boys and five choruses of men, and each chorus was supplied by one of the ten tribes[3] of Attica (Haigh, 1898). In this way, all ten tribes took part in one or other of the two competitions. In the dramatic competitions, the rivalry was confined to individual playwrights/poets and *choragi* (conductors of the chorus). The choruses and *choragi* were selected indiscriminately from the whole population, although the *choragi* with the most resources no doubt had an advantage as leaders of the chorus they were expected to bear the costs of its participation. They were also earmarked annually to present liturgies or some public arts enterprise on behalf of Athens to enhance its artistic reputation and their own civic standing. Meanwhile, playwrights could be commissioned by one of these individuals, supplied with a chorus and any other production needs. The city authorities that coordinated the festival activities usually paid the actors. As the event became more competitive over the years, additional prizes were awarded to dramatists and later actors, a move which led to an improvement in professionalism (Hart 2010). The judges (representing the ten tribes) were responsible for choosing the winners.

While the name of the winning tribe to which the chorus belonged was always given a prominent position, the records of dramatic victories give only the names of the poet and the principal actor for dramatic contests indicating a more sophisticated approach to artistic judgment that made tribal affiliations irrelevant.

Of the dramatic performances at the City Dionysia, the tragedies received the greatest attention. The City Dionysia was the founding home of the tragic drama and its earliest public competitions in tragedy with the first contest held in the year 535 BC (Haigh 1898). The regulation of the City Dionysia was either first instituted by Athenian political leader, Pisistratus (sixth century until 528/7 BC), or reorganized by him, and later enhanced by the addition of the tragic competitions (Goldhill 1987). It is possible that these were regulated from the first on the same system, which prevailed in the records of the fifth century (Haigh 1898). Poets, even such as Aeschylus, were limited to not more than four plays and some of the more famous plays that have been performed in recent times come from this period.

Ancient Middle Eastern societies rarely celebrated artists individually or in specific arts events, before the advent of invasions by the Greeks and Romans. Some local events then started to take on influences from these societies and later elites (Dvorjetski 2012). Later, storytelling and poetry started to be celebrated more for their own sakes with all classes and some dedicated events arose with individual artists receiving some valorization. Poetry in Arabic literature dates from the sixth century AD with oral traditions of poetry originating sometime before that. It was a natural part of pre-Islamic festivities and reached a new height in the later courts of the Islamic leaders. Meanwhile, Bedouin oral poetry traditions were celebrated at their annual festivals. Words in praise of the tribe (*qit'ah*) and lampoons denigrating other tribes (*hija*) seem to have been some of the most popular forms of early poetry. The *sha'ir* represented an individual tribe's prestige and importance in the region, and mock battles in poetry or *zajal* would often substitute for real wars. Ukaz, a market town not far from Mecca hosted a regular poetry festival, where the craft of the *sha'irs* would be exhibited in pre-Islamic times (Arab Cultural Trust 2013; UNESCO 2013).

China and later Japan also adopted poetry and painting competitions as a form of leisurely pursuit of the elite and the imperial courts. In these rigidly hierarchical societies, the gentry that dabbled in the arts had raised the status of painting by the Song dynasty in China (Heian period in Japan), in particular, to that of a higher art form than that of a decorative art commissioned by them previously (Ebrey 1999). The suppression of Confucianism during the following Yuan dynasty (established by Kublai Khan) meant that more animated and publicly accessible theatrical performances were encouraged. As well, Chinese playwrights mocked and satirized the hierarchical nature of society for the first time for larger audiences of around a thousand per theatre. Performances were also given in vernacular Chinese with sumptuous costumes, makeup, singing and acrobatics, unlike previously, and this practice led to the later development Chinese opera. Cities often had a theatrical district with more than a dozen of these buildings making bundled arts events such as, theatrical festivals and competitions possible, although none are evident in the literature (Liu 1972). The Mongols of the Yuan dynasty also raised the status of artisans. The Mongols traditionally did not have their own artisan class, because they migrated from place to place and could not carry with them the art supplies needed by artisans. They were thus dependent upon the more sedentary world for crafts, and they prized artisans highly. For example, artisans throughout the Mongol domains were offered tax benefits and were freed from *corvée* labour (unpaid labour), and their products were highly prized by the Mongol elite (Rossabi 2013). This recognition led to a golden age of arts production, which had an impact beyond the region as Chinese artworks and handicrafts became highly prized and publicized beyond China's shores.

Meanwhile private arts events such as, family poetry and painting competitions of the mandarin class in China, are described in almost ethnographic detail in the classical novel *The Dream of the Red Chamber* by Cao Xueqin from the Qing dynasty (1644 –1911). Across the water, Japanese poets and painters synthesized local and imported influences to produce a diverse range of genres and styles celebrated at court, in the theatre and the pleasure quarters. Artisans were also well regarded in Japan in the pre-modern period of the Edo Shogunate, but gained even more recognition during the modernization of the Meiji Restoration (of the emperor) in the late nineteenth century, when they were expected to join the intellectual classes and be more erudite and literate. Arts events, however, tended to be divided into those arts that still supported agricultural or religious festivals and those which were enjoyed solely by the elite, until the Japanese began following the European passion for major industry and arts expositions by establishing their own for a domestic audience (Guth 2004).

In early pre-modern Europe, however, mystery and miracle plays are frequently cited as a popular arts annual event in the early medieval literature of all the Catholic countries of Europe, especially Spain, Germany, France and Italy. These works were performed at seasonal festivals for a largely illiterate public. For example, the title, the subject, and the arrangement of Dante's famous poem were closely connected with dramatic representations of Hell, Purgatory, and Paradise, when performed in the festivities in Florence, to ensure that the audience was clear what might await them in the afterlife as a consequence of their actions. These plays were written, produced and acted by monks; the cathedral was transformed briefly into a theatre; the stage was a type of graduated platform in three divisions rising one above the other (placed near or over the altar), and the costumes were provided by the well patronized vestry of the church (Shaw 1867).

Eventually, the establishment of city-states and a number of influential merchant towns meant that secular events arose to celebrate their establishment and cultural identity. Some arts even became solely associated with such events, for instance, the creation of masks for the Venice Carnival and special effigies for the foundation days of various French towns. The Venice Carnival can be documented as originating in the eleventh century. By the eighteenth century, it had become a lavish event with transnational fame characterized by masquerades, licentiousness, masked balls and feasts in contrast to the street parades of effigies and other activities mentioned earlier, such as Mysteries and miracle plays (Smith 2003). The effigies first appeared in urban religious processions at the end of the fourteenth century in many European towns and continue to serve as emblems of identity for these towns, where they remain part of the living culture. The giants and dragons are large-scale models measuring up to nine metres in height and weighing as much as 350 kilos. They represent mythical heroes or animals, contemporary local figures, historical, biblical or legendary characters or trades. Processions usually occur once per town during summer or autumn. One key example is the Tarasque Dragon Festival in Tarascon (France) in June (UNWTO 2012). Versions of both types of events still continue in their host cities and towns, however, with a strong recognition of their importance for tourism and involvement by non-local participants.

The events have become more secular as they have become linked to concerns about local city and cultural identity within each country and the European Union. The knowledge transfer process of the local symbolism and skills needed to create the effigies to the next generation of artisans in particular has continued as an important aspect of city authorities funding and maintaining this arts event form. The continuance of the intangible cultural heritage behind each procession gives it its own unique quality.

From the local to the global in arts events: the modern world

The period from the mid-nineteenth century until the advent of postmodernism embodied a belief in progress and a simplistic desire to feature the arts in new kinds of events, many of which could be inspirational, affirming, pleasurable, enriching, or celebratory events or could be one of mixture of these aims. This is also the time where some events moved from being place-based and of primarily local significance to having a global reach. It also sees more interest in arts education and the rise of the amateur artists as participants; recognition of artists as professionals or sometimes celebrities; events that provoke controversy, and also ones that due to their scale and complexity require a more professional approach to management.

However, Frith *et al.* (2013) argue that the term 'festival' did not come into common use, until the European cities started to put on special public music events that were initially celebrations of classical music. The Edinburgh Music Festival, which was first held between 30 October and 5 November 1815, was one such city festival dedicated to only one area of the arts. It initially featured seven concerts in two venues with 150 performers. The event must have received some kind of publicity, possibly through newspaper reports as it brought in a 'concourse of strangers' to Edinburgh who filled up all the available accommodation (Frith *et al.* 2013; Miller 1996). It also became such an important annual event looked forward to by the local community that appreciated such music, it shows a disposition amongst them that would prove a good foundation for making their city of focus of influential international festivals later in its development. How and why this occurred is described in reference to the case studies in Box 2.2.

Box 2.2 Edinburgh Arts Festivals (International Arts, Fringe, and Film) case study

First of all, why has Edinburgh become such a centre for the arts and arts festivals? Unlike many cities today, which see offering arts experiences and events as an add-on for tourism marketing, Edinburgh has a long-standing relationship with the arts from the pre-modern period.

This is more than its city authorities wanting to make a distinction between its urban cultural experiences and that of the rural area around it as suggested by some (Richards and Palmer 2010). For instance, it is the location of one of the world's oldest universities, University of Edinburgh, since 1593, and one of the United Kingdom's oldest arts colleges, Edinburgh College of the Arts, since 1760. The university's musical society was established in 1867, which helped the community to support the musical arts and later assisted Edinburgh to become a base for national orchestras and choirs, such as the Royal National Orchestra of Scotland.

Edinburgh College of the Arts offered courses in the visual arts, such as drawing, from 1760 onwards, and then established the Reid School of Music in 1839 with a bequest from General John Reid, who died in 1807. He was from a longstanding, influential Edinburgh family and an accomplished flute player and composer of military band music. He also asked that an annual concert be organized in his name, which still occurs every February. The Reid Chair professors from the School of Music were active in building arts development in the city over the nineteenth century setting up musical events and in developing programmes for musicians. The school became a faculty in 1893 and offered the first Bachelor of Music degree in the UK.

The current site for the college was donated by City of Edinburgh in 1906, and it merged with the University of Edinburgh in a controversial move in 2011 (Edinburgh College of the Arts 2013). Both establishments are located in the picturesque old town area in sight of the castle.

Another factor in Edinburgh's focus on the arts also dates back to the nineteenth century, when it became associated with some of Scotland's leading figures of the Enlightenment. Edinburgh, with its universities, colleges and influential thinkers developed a highly educated population and was also seen as a leading light in innovation, even before it became dubbed 'Athens of North' and one of Europe's most festive cities.

Edinburgh International Arts Festival

The Edinburgh International Festival (EIF) was established in 1947. The founders comprised Rudolf Bing (general manager of Glyndebourne Opera), Henry Harvey Wood (Head of the British Council in Scotland), and a group of Edinburgh civic leaders. Despite the mood of post-war Britain, the organizers had big ambitions to host a festival that would someday inspire the cultural life of the region by providing a platform for an inspiring arts event. These founders also hoped that, if successful in its artistic ambitions, the Festival would create a major new source of tourism revenue for Edinburgh and for Scotland. As the key festival for the city, it receives the most funding with a breakdown in 2012 of 49 per cent of the Festival's total income generated through earned income including ticket sales, sponsorship and donations, with 51 per cent coming from public sector grants (EIF 2013).

The programme is also the most diverse with all areas of the arts represented. However, it is distinct from the Fringe Festival and Comedy Festival in that it is a curated event with the director researching and inviting acts and artists to attend. Accordingly, some resources may be provided, such as free venue hire and stage management for the well-known works that are in demand (Mulcahy 2005). The Director also has to be careful to include a number of headliners both from the local and global arts scene (Quinn 2006).

Edinburgh Fringe Festival or Edinburgh Festival Fringe

The city is home of the world's first fringe festival, which started with eight bands of radical play producers who wanted access to Edinburgh Arts Festival in 1947, but were told there was no room on the schedule for them. They then found their own facilities by discovering and booking some of the festival's more remote stages without access to the bigger audiences. They also had to do their own public relations, mostly by word of mouth without access to the festival's box office, and marketing. During the first attempt, word spread that the works were worth seeing and houses gradually filled. A year later a newspaper critic, Robert Kemp, endorsed a repeat of the event by the playmakers. Even without attending, he was the first to dub them 'fringe' to describe their location on the edgy outskirts of the Edinburgh arts scene. One unusual measure to attract audiences to Edinburgh was for students involved in the festival to promote their university dorms as low-cost accommodation. The minimalist and more frugal nature of these theatrical productions also meant tickets were more affordable in comparison with the mainstream festival (Mulcahy 2005).

University students continued to assist with administering bookings for university dorms, ticketing and refreshments until 1954, when the festival adopted a more professional approach to management. Its constitution was officially endorsed in 1958, when it already had garnered some imitators in the UK and overseas.

Finally, a freer association of the International Arts Festival with the Edinburgh Fringe Festival (EFF) occurred under John Drummond, Festival Director for Edinburgh International Arts Festival, who wanted to broaden the appeal of that festival by attracting a younger, less conservative audience from the Fringe to International festival events by narrowing the divide between the events. The International Festival organizers felt they still had to make sure content of the Fringe Festival was up to the International Festival's standards, if it was going to be cross-promoted and the publicity improved for both events. The International Festival is a curated event and the Fringe is open to all comers. Drummond also needed to get the International Festival's council to agree to this new initiative. In 1981, Edinburgh authorities set up a multi-space facility that could be used by participants of both festivals, however, Fringe performers could undertake sub-lets while IF participants were resourced in the usual way. This faith in its drawing capacity was rewarded when the first Fringe Sunday events attracted an audience of 30,000 (Miller 1996).

The Fringe Festival is still held in August and follows its 'all comers policy' and much of its original vision. Some performers have complained that it is becoming too elephantine in scale to provide them with much useful experience or exposure and that it has become a victim of its own success.

Comic Liam Mullone observed in an interview that it is a 'tortuous month of walking about with a handful of soggy fliers ... reminding people over and over to see acts that don't have their own TV series' and that the organizers were less than helpful (Simpson 2012:11). More recently, the organizers have made the claim online that it is the largest arts festival on the planet, and if true it would mean that naturally problems would result.

In 2012, it hosted 2,695 different shows; staging 42,096 performances in 279 venues by 22,457 performers (EFF 2013), which could give credence to their claim given its incredible popularity and that most works are of a small and modest nature to reduce costs to the unfunded participants.

Edinburgh International Film Festival

The first eight years of this festival showed the influence of Edinburgh as a centre for intellectualism. Not content to establish a typical curated film festival, organizers deliberately went against the grain, to give it a platform to film theory, experimental film, new European and world cinema, maverick film-makers and American exploitation movies between 1969 and 1977. This approach created a paradox with a organizing committee linked closely to the UK arts establishment working as an instrument of resistance towards the dominant culture. Accordingly, the Festival became notorious for its provocations and critiques of film culture. Stanfield (2008) has observed 'uniquely among film festivals, the EIFF maintained not only a dialogue with film theory, but was also a primary platform for its dissemination'.

It also included special features or segments, such as, retrospectives of famous filmmakers, which in turn attracted others both new and old to the event. The organizers were keen to fill obvious gaps in the film festival landscape such as greater valorization of female filmmakers.

The festival was the first to host a European women's film segment, and was the first international film festival to be directed by a woman, Linda Myles. Programming innovations included a diverse mix of low-budget American movies, avant-garde cinema and non-English language films. EIFF also published a series of pioneering auteur studies and for a while published magazine dedicated to film criticism (Stanfield 2008). Once again, this approach became a model to other events especially those directly aimed at an auteur or well-informed audience.

Overview of all three festivals

Edinburgh's festivals have often acted as models to others (Mulcahy 2005). Its offerings have become one continuous year-long festival or a 'festivalization of the city' (Richards and Palmer 2010:28). Even with the economic downtown in recent years, these festivals still continue to be successful, particularly with their background and openness to innovation and re-invention. Recent research has shown such a strategy is no less important for sustainability during challenging economic conditions (Devine and Devine 2012). It certainly does not hurt either that the city has a historic streetscape that makes striking backdrop for summer street performances and that the arts still enjoy royal patronage.

The expositions and world fairs over the 1851–1939 period were often the only occasions that ordinary citizens would come into contact with unusual, avant-garde or spectacular artworks, and early arts and communication technologies. For instance, parts of New York's Statue of Liberty were featured at two such international events, Philadelphia in 1876 and Paris in 1878. Also, the first talking films were shown at the Exposition Universale in Paris in 1900, while the first time that modular and pre-fabricated structures were used on a huge scale was for the Crystal Palace for the Great Exhibition of the Works of Industry of all Nations in London in 1851 (Nelson-Atkins Museum of Art 2012).

Auerbach (2008) has observed that expositions along with museums and art collections were potent mechanisms in the construction and representation of power relationships. In addition, there was an unavoidable 'cultural text' or subtext apparent in what was created, chosen and displayed. In particular, these events also allowed the opportunity for countries to show off to exhibition visitors their supremacy in a particular field. The Great Exhibition in London in 1851, while the first of these events, concentrated more on Britain's scientific innovations than its arts. Meanwhile, Paris' first event of this kind, the Exposition Universelle in 1855 made the arts far more central (L'Art Nouveau 2013a). The third edition of this event, in 1889, attracted around 32 million visitors, 61,700 displays, and was held over 50 hectares in urban Paris (L'Art Nouveau 2013b).

In some ways, the rationale for expositions in the nineteenth century was not that different to that of the Great Dionysia where Athens displayed its artistic sophistication to those who were trading partners or the colonized. Hence, in some respects the early exhibitions were not really very different to the more permanent displays in public museums of the time (for example, the British Museum in London) with overt nationalistic narratives and a strong modernist view of the differing cultural and technological evolution of diverse participating countries. This led to some of these countries holding their own events as well as still sending exhibits to key expositions, perhaps to even the score and show that they were also part of the 'modern world'.

One such event was in the city of Nanyang in China in 1910. Fernsebner (2006) has investigated the materiality and mobilities of objects and subjects on display in this first official exposition supported by the Chinese imperial government. The way the exposition was framed was examined within the context of national survival at a time when Qing dynasty China had lost substantial ground in commerce and trading. Goods and items were sourced from all over China to be displayed for both domestic and a global audience. Such movements of materiality and governed subjects should be seen within the context of burgeoning work in the role of mega-events and nation-building in capitalistic societies (Roche 2003:100). Also, on display were exposition workers who were trained to be practical, efficient and dedicated. The expo workers were encouraged through training for expo work to aspire to being integral to the task of ushering in a new globally competitive and strong China (Fernsebner 2006).

Accordingly, Hobsbawm (1992) has suggested the long-lasting appeal of these events and their popularity derive from their functions in marking time and history in a society characterized by incessant intergenerational change during this period. Roche (2003) approaches these mega-events by relating them to the interpersonal and public experience, and structuring of time in contemporary global society. This previous research portrays expos as iconic displays of modernity and as international chronological markers of time, history and 'progress'. For instance, the first prototypes of new mass transport and communications technologies were featured (e.g. planes, cars, telephones, radio, film and television). In the arts and social sciences, controversial and avant-garde works sometimes made an appearance alongside the more spectacular examples of architecture (e.g. the Eiffel Tower) (Roche 2003). An example of one of the more unusual artistic exhibits of its time was the first photographic exhibit organized by African Americans of African Americans that was held at the Great Paris Exhibition of 1900. It was seen as an unexpected highlight for visitors interested in sociology backed by the power of photography (du Bois 1900).

During this period, the performing arts also began to develop new art forms that have yielded some very long-running events. One example of a type of music festival that has evolved over the many years since its inception is The Proms, originally known as the 'Robert Newman Promenade Concerts'. It has been a fixture of the London classical music calendar since 1895. Promenade-style events were not uncommon at the time. However, the funding from entrepreneur Dr George Cathcart and the involvement of concert organizer Robert Newman boosted this one above the rest, along with the mission to make it a repeatable event with a strong focus on bringing classical music within the financial reach of the general public and present it in a pleasurable way. The first conductor he hired (who stayed with the event until his death in 1944) was Henry Woods, who also made sure the programme content was attractive to a broad audience and included many high-quality performances (Jacobs 2004; Mullens 1995).

The 'Proms' in the event's name is short for 'promenade' as around one fifth of the capacity of the venue is left free of seats to allow the attendees to walk around during the performance. This unique concept for the presentation behind the appeal to the event perhaps harks back to Elizabethan times when standing room was allowed near the stage and seating in the stalls (as has been faithfully reproduced in the new Shakespeare's Globe theatre more recently). The other feature that enhances the event's popularity, particularly with younger patrons, is that the standing room tickets are substantially cheaper than those for seats, but only available on the day of the concert. Over the years, this has meant that this ten-week-long summer festival draws a lot of students on summer holidays. They usually attend as small groups of friends and make each concert a social event as well. Up until recently, these have mainly been local students who wait for hours and sometimes even overnight for tickets to popular concerts. Affirmation of the event's role in celebrating British culture is most evident on the last night and in featuring local popular acts and celebrities, as well as international performers, during the event. For instance, 2013 saw the inclusion of British New Wave rock band, The Stranglers and a number of pop groups from the urban music genre that is well established in the UK as well as classical music performances (Silverman 2013). There have also been special appearances by British celebrities, such as Matt Smith (actor who played Dr Who at the time) and the Team GB 2012 Olympic medalists (see Beechey 2012).

Another different kind of event is the periodic international art fair or exhibition that only deals with the arts, especially visual arts. The first of these (and still ongoing) is the Venice Biennial International Art Exhibition first held in 1895. It is the oldest periodic contemporary art exhibition in the world, and one of Italy's most prestigious cultural events. It is also one of the first arts events to develop commercial practices still used by many international exhibitions, arts fairs and biennales elsewhere today.

Meanwhile, the growing interest in establishing periodic contemporary arts events brought about huge changes in the arts world. For instance the Exhibition of Modern Art, held in New York's Armory of the National Guard, 1913, held over 1,000 works of 300 avant-garde artists and also caused a storm of criticism and controversy (Paglia 2012). The public had not had much exposure to modern art prior to this time. The need to raise awareness and create a more sophisticated culture of art appreciation amongst the general public is possibly what spurred concerned cultural authorities to found the US Museum of Modern Art (MOMA) in 1929. The first public exhibition opened in 1939 in New York (Bazin 1967).

The visual arts events go through an immense change after the end of the nineteenth century.

From around the turn of the century, significant periodic contemporary art exhibitions were established in many countries, including the United States, Brazil and Germany. These events have played a fundamental role in connecting art markets and museums. Most of these events work by selecting artists and works, from among countless proposals, with a view to disseminating a greater appreciation of contemporary art amongst the public (Bagdadli and Arrigoni 2005).

The twentieth century also saw a huge and rapid development of new techniques of display (away from the salon style of 'skied' paintings[4] and casually displayed sculptures to sparsely spaced ones in neutral settings); new values (aims of exhibitions had changed under the influence of individual curators, researchers and artists involved); influence of new museums (e.g. the Guggenheim Museum and MOMA in New York); new technologies (new arts, new ways of displaying arts and organizing content) and new diplomatic realities (cultural institutes, traveling exhibitions, cultural exchanges, arts and the beginning of soft relationships between countries). New techniques in display and global ambitions began turning one-off temporary exhibitions into circulating ones and eventually in some cases into international arts blockbuster extravaganzas. The first global traveling exhibition that could also be termed an ancestor of the current blockbusters was the 'Family of Man' photographic exhibition. It was curated by the Museum of Modern Art initially in New York in 1955, and then travelled around the world to be installed in various locations until well into the 1960s.

At the same time that contemporary arts were discovering a more global reach, local tensions also began to emerge given the rate of cultural change in many places as the twentieth century progressed. While there were many authorities also lauding the importance of progress through scientific and technological

Box 2.3 Venice Biennale case study

Developmental context

The city of Venice, like Edinburgh, has a specific background that made it a natural and successful location for a major arts event. Already known throughout Europe for hosting the Carnivale, by the time of the first Biennale in 1895, it had been trading on past glories by being part of the Grand Tour for wealthy tourists and a unique cultural landscape that attracted extensive literary attention – not all of it positive (France 2011). This negative criticism was heaped on Venice as it was no longer the mercantile power it had been. Its political and economic influence had become tarnished by the invasion of Napoleon in 1797 and the city's later annexation by Austria making it impoverished and in places dilapidated. However, while recognizing its decay, city authorities saw an opportunity. Ironically, they worked to use this image of Venice as a means to regenerate the city and position it within the modern realities of Europe, in an early example of destination brand positioning. Hence 'its poetic qualities contained the universalism which opened the city up for international consumption' (West, 1995:406). West (1995) also argues that Venice was a logical choice out of all the cities on the Italian peninsula for a major international arts event, because it was neutral territory in terms of not being overwhelmed by religious and secular associations (like Rome), and had not industrialized (like Milan) spoiling its landscape and reputation for artistic tolerance.

The first Biennale ran between April and October 1895, after a series of false starts and abortive efforts as authorities worked to build the demand for a major arts event in the city.

A rationale to launch it successfully was finally found by the mayor, Richardo Selvatico, who used the wedding anniversary of King Umberto I and Queen Margherita (19 April) as a reason to start the Biennale in April. In addition to this tenuous excuse, it was also argued that the event could be used for cultural exchange, to educate Italian artists and the public from all over the new nation during the post-unification of Italy. West (1995) has concluded that throughout the early history of the event, a tension was clearly evident, between national and international ambitions in the organization and selection ratios of Italian and non-Italian artists and artworks.

An enduring event

The Biennale nevertheless survived this tension and became an important international event on the arts calendar. How it did that is of particular interest to this book and is rooted in the economic and cultural conditions of Venice at the time. Also, the location of the cultural space within the city opened Venice up to a new style of promotion, as its gardens pleasurable qualities were fully recognized in arts criticism and event marketing for the first time. Establishing pavilions to display artworks in the Castello Gardens, as well as displays in the adjacent civic halls, meant that the event had an indoor/outdoor feeling that bridged that of the expositions of the nineteenth century and the cultural theme parks of the twentieth century. The other gardens and important cultural landmarks were also included in the opening pages of catalogues and accompanying information for tourists from the earliest times. The positive image this presented was also supported by arts critics' reviews, whose expenses were financed by the astute Biennale organizers. However, the critics' premium (a prize for the best piece of journalism about the event) was not the only benefit they received.

The first instance of a VIP area at an arts event was, according to West (1995), in 1903 at the fifth Biennale. It was known as the 'Sala'. It comprised a reception room, a library, a smoking room and a post/telegraph office in line with advances in media and communications technology, in order to further publicize the event during its almost six-month run. The Biennale also kept with the times by instituting electric lighting in 1901 for interior spaces. Also, pleasing for tourists was the addition of a restaurant designed in the 'Byzantine-Venetian Style' to the garden area in 1907.

The financial structure of the first Biennale is interesting – like most international exhibitions of the period – it offered prizes known as 'premiums'. Funding for this aspect came from private and public sources, in particular Venice's own and other Italian city museums, which were also seeking items for their modern art collections that had received some kind of critical acclaim and public exposure at the event. Premiums were granted to artists and critics (such as for reviews) at the Biennale initially, and then later only to critics as an early form of marketing and promotion for the event and for the works recognized. Advertising space was also included in its arts catalogues for the first time and that went a long way to providing private sponsorship for event. West (1995) also notes this was the first time that items normally considered 'high art' were depicted in a publication with mundane consumer goods and services in the catalogues and pamphlets available to visitors.

Initially, visitor numbers grew from 224,327 in 1895 to 457,960 visitors in 1909 with a major dip as World War I approached. Organizers also noticed similar trends in the artwork sales over this period. In general, earnings increased from 240,000 lire for the first event to 420,000 at the second. This growth also mirrored the changes in space occupied, which went from 14 rooms to 31 rooms for the two events (West 1995). However, the financial benefit for the event from tourism would have been worth the early teething problems pre- and post-1895 in terms of establishing a model that worked and attracting a critical mass of artists, artworks, critics, curators and visitors to make it viable over the long term.

More recent issues for the event

The event is still trying to apply innovative business and marketing practices in the early twentieth-first century. In 2004, a market positioning problem was identified by the organizers as the Biennale appeared to be losing its cultural hegemony and market appeal, because of a series of changes in its competitive environment. The internal changes in the art world and the growing complexity of the marketplace in the early twenty-first century have provided various challenges, which have made the Biennale consider its strategic marketing research as extremely important. Accordingly, Bagdadli and Arrigoni (2005) conducted a strategic positioning evaluation in 2005 to determine the current marketing position of the Biennale and help its organizers "'better understand" the competitive environment, define and control their current position, and affirm and strengthen their function and prestige'. At the time, there had been very little research into strategic position of these kinds of events and the survey had to use an exploratory approach with a strong emphasis on qualitative data collection.

The survey found that direct competition came from other traditional periodic exhibitions, such as, Kassel's Documenta and from new ones, such as, the Havana Biennial in Cuba and the Qwangju Biennial in South Korea. The latter two events (which are comparatively low budget) are promoted as a better alternative to the established model, because they appear to be more receptive to novel or experimental artistic contexts, particularly those far from the Western market circuits. Bagdadli and Arrigoni (2005) suggested that the Biennale was paying too much attention to the art market and not enough to the artists and critics. On the other hand, it was also found that indirect competition had emerged as the way of developing and promoting artistic values and trends had fallen under the influence of international art marketers, with the complicity of museums, in a way that diminished the ability of periodic exhibitions in carrying out their traditional role of connecting art markets with art institutions.

The study recommended that the Biennale's organizers consider appointing more authoritative international curators capable of presenting a coherent artistic panorama. The selection process would need special care with the director allowed the time available to travel to the world's art centres in order to choose artists of the highest quality. A similar approach has been common for some key city performing arts festivals for a while. Also, it was recommended that it should draw up a long-term strategic plan, one that allows for periodic marketing assessments. More attention should be paid to identifying its role in the art world and to selecting the ideal measures for fulfilling that role (Bagdadli and Arrigoni 2005).

Box 2.4 Family of Man Photographic Exhibition (MOMA) case study

Background

This exhibition was hailed at the time as 'the most ambitious and challenging project photography has ever attempted' and it was compared with the Grand Canyon, because the feeling of having stepped into something monumental. It even became integral to Roland Barthes critique of modern culture and its favourite myths in his collection of essays, *Mythologies* (Barthes 1972). MOMA had undertaken large-scale photographic exhibitions since 1942 and so this event allowed its curator to perfect many of the new techniques trialled in these earlier war-related efforts, while making the images accessible to a wider audience as it was traveling nationally and internationally. 'The Family of Man' also circulated under the auspices of the Museum's new International Program. This initiative was built on a national programme that had been in existence since the 1930s and was founded with federal government post-war funding in 1952 to develop and tour circulating exhibitions that also included arts events, such as United States representations at international exhibitions and festivals, one-person shows, and group exhibitions. The International Program funding still assists MOMA art exhibitions to travel around the world (Staniszewski 1998; MOMA 2013).

The exhibition theme, display and contents

Prior to this exhibition MOMA had run 'The Road to Victory' (1942), 'Airways to Peace' (1943) and 'Power in the Pacific' (1945) nationally circulating photographic exhibitions which with heavy government funding came a patriotic message.

It was once observed that during this period that the museum was 'a minor war industry, and like other such enterprises, entered into contracts with the procurement bureaus of the central government. Its product was cultural' (Lynes in Staniszewski 1998:224). The chief curator for 'The Family of Man' in 1955 was Edward Steichen, who also had been involved in some of the earlier events. So it is likely that visitors loyal to the museum over the years would recognize that some of the underlying themes and display techniques of the latter exhibition from those before, in particular the exhibition's vision of greater individual and human freedom was very strong, whilst the nationalistic and wartime agendas had given way to a more universalist and right-wing religious message.

The photographs included in the exhibition focused on the commonalties that bind people and cultures around the world. The exhibition served as an expression of humanism in the decade following World War II, in line with the values of its initial target audience of a 1950s middle-class American family. First impressions of the exhibition prepared the visitor who passed a 'prologue' of images meant instil an uplifting and thoughtful mood. These images included a mix of natural scenes with that of human figures that were either nude or in a traditional costume of some kind. One of the first captions read 'Let there be Light, Genesis 1:3' and was paired with images of a nude headless pregnant female figure dwarfed by an image of a landscape of a stream flowing into the sea. The rest of exhibit held images selected by Steichen and his assistant Wayne Miller. These included ones that represented the cultural diversity of the world's societies but with the sub-text of the accompanying quotations being principally Christian (as in the earlier example). Significantly, as crowds of visitors were expected to attend the exhibition, images of crowds were also included within it.

The most common image featured in press and media reports of the time was that of a young Peruvian flute player by photographer Eugene V. Harris. It was thought to encapsulate the symbolic side of the exhibition and the importance of the arts to human experience. Paul Rudolph, who directed the installation's design, commented,

> The Family of Man was a very important thing for me because I had never really considered the idea of heightening the experience one has in an exhibition in relation to what the exhibition is intended to say and tell ... Exhibition design can deal very much with storytelling.
>
> (Rudolph in Staniszewski 1998:238)

This was possibly the first time that some self-reflection about how the interplay between the form, content and layout of arts exhibitions could subliminally influence the visitors' experience. Curators and designers had been aware for many years that technical changes in the way artworks were displayed obviously had an impact on mood, but had rarely considered how the choice of artworks, their display mode and their contextualization with text (and with proximity to other images) would enhance or influence the mood and message. In this revelation, Rudolph was close to leaving modernism behind for the concerns of postmodernism in terms of analysing the value of arts events for visitors and how personal biases of their creators might shape their overall message.

Controversy

The images chosen, when viewed today, would be considered an interesting mix of cheesy, mundane, challenging and thoughtful. Fortunately, the more cloying images never overwhelmed the more challenging ones of subjects such as illness, death, or disturbed children. However, the way the curators dealt with a controversy in the first two weeks of the event's run is quite telling. The image that caused it in 1955 was one titled 'Death Slump in Mississippi' from 1937 by an unknown photographer that depicted an African American corpse tied to a tree after a lynching. Although it was not a large image, it was observed to interrupt the visitor flow, as people clustered around it to examine it more closely and/or discuss it. Staniszewski (1998) notes that at the time the United States was still heavily racist and the post-war civil rights movements were also just starting to make an impact. Another photo of positive race relations caused little comment in comparison. However, the death slump image was not targeted negatively in the media, because it appeared near the 'inhumanities section', which also contained wartime death squad shootings and an image of the atom bomb exploding. Steichen was the one who considered it a discordant note that pushing event experience too much towards a disturbingly squawk rather than a balanced harmony (as evinced in part by the constant and regular flow of visitors through the exhibit), as if the event's narrative could be considered a piece of music. Nevertheless, the image was removed from exhibition, and it only ever appeared in an early hard-cover copy of the catalogue.

Statistics

The event scored record-breaking attendance figures possibly due to its geographical reach and length of circulation. However, well-handled publicity and word of mouth ensured a high turnout wherever it went. Even so, in its first two weeks it attracted 35,000 visitors and the first edition of the catalogue priced at one dollar sold 250,000 copies (for the first edition of the event). There were ten different editions of the event, which in all made for 150 exhibitions at 37 countries over six continents. The final number of pictures used in these editions over the period it was in circulation numbered 503 images from 68 countries (Staniszewski 1998; MOMA 2013).

Overall impact

The few rare negative reviews of the exhibition came from critics who viewed its experience as more like what one would have from natural science or ethnology museum not MOMA, and that it was too heavily skewed towards some type of 'visual morality play' (Kramer in Staniszewski 1998). Looking back from the twenty-first century, it is hard to imagine what kind of impact it had at the time. These days, it feels as if social media and widespread access to digital photography have just about killed photography as a profession. However, these trends may also have created something on a greater scale than this exhibition to which anyone with a

camera, phone or computer has two-way access. Significantly, a version of
the exhibition was held at Clervaux Castle, Luxembourg, in 2009 for a few
months. It is possible that it may be about make a come-back, so that people
can make up their own minds about its legacy (see News 352 2009 for some
idea of the exhibit's redux).

The Pulitzer Photography Exhibition featured later in Chapter 5 has also
drawn on this format, so it is still in current use.

innovation, some were concerned for the first time about the survival of folk
traditions and heritage arts from the less industrialized pre-modern period. For
the modern period in developed countries, it almost seems like for every new type
of arts event created there is one that is the result of reviving or restoring an event
from previous times, for instance, various folk music festivals. Many of these
revived/revival heritage arts events also worked to celebrate and affirm cultural
identity in post-conflict and/or post-agricultural contexts.

In Europe, both large and small events were revived in the post-war period
by city authorities, as they perceived a need to celebrate and affirm their own
distinct traditions. An example of a small event that was revived and which has
since grown in popularity is one based on the rich baroque tradition of music
in Varaždin, a city in Croatia. The Varaždin Baroque Evenings was founded as
a small city music event in 1968, which then became a festival in 1971. It re-
started the baroque tradition of concerts being held between the autumn months of
September and October for the populace of the town. The music is also enhanced
for tourists by the ambience of the well-preserved city architecture of that period
that comprises town houses, castles and churches.

In summary, the current program for Baroque Evenings is focused on both
European and Croatian baroque music with a clear emphasis on the music genre
of Varaždin. In later years, it has also included a combination of visual arts, poetry
and cuisine from the baroque period. Steadily the popularity of the festival has
grown to up to 30 concerts annually. The festival is financed by the Croatian
State Government, the City of Varaždin and a few private sponsors. The event
enjoys both local participation and support from within and without the music
community, which has made it sustainable beyond its initial revival (Rojnik 2011;
Bobić 2011).

Pluralism in arts events: the contemporary world

Again just before the turn of a century, new ideologies started to take root that
have affected the development, display and celebration of the arts in events.
The postmodern dogma of pluralism meant that as there was greater support for
cultural diversity occurring so that some arts previously considered 'high arts'

were steadily losing their pre-eminence. A multiplicity of other cultural forms was emerging that were highly differentiated, although not in a hierarchical fashion as before (DiMaggio, 1991). This restructuring allowed more and different kinds of arts events to emerge, also that the arts were now required to work with other activities to source more resources and for a greater freedom of thematic structure (e.g. Cultural Olympiads of the last 15 years).

The commercial side has been strengthened in response to the professionalization of arts events and the growth in popularity of some as sites for commerce. However, for the visual arts the proliferation of contemporary art fairs is the clearest evidence of the increasing importance of market structures (Bagdadli and Arrigoni 2005). Originating in the 1960s, these fairs have been the commercial rivals of the great periodic exhibitions. Contemporary art fairs, such as, Art Basel

---

Box 2.5 Cultural Olympiad case study

Background

As noted earlier in the chapter, dramatic competitions and music performances were often associated with ancient Greek festivals (Hornblower and Morgan 2007). This tradition was revived by the Greek themselves in late nineteenth century to assist with nation-building (Sanada, 2009; Ioannidou, 2011). However, it took Baron Pierre de Coubertin to suggest that contemporary arts and festival activities could be linked to the twentieth-century revival of the Olympic Games from 1906. He outlined to a special congress in Paris in that year the principle of 'Olympic Art Competitions' and they appeared in the first official program in the 1912 Stockholm Olympic Games. Another common name for this associated arts event was the 'Pentathlon of the Muses' with its key objective of attracting artists to present works and compete for 'art medals' across five main art forms: architecture, literature, music, sculpture and painting (Sanada, 2009). The competitive aspect of the associated festival was dropped later in the twentieth century. The establishment of the International Olympics Committee's (IOC) Cultural Commission not long after saw more expansive displays of cultural and artistic practice being underwritten by host countries, in the new programme segment known as the Cultural Olympiad.

The institutionalization of the Olympiad as an integral part of the Olympics gathered pace after the first International Sport-Culture Forum, organized in 1997 by the IOC and its Cultural Commission. It stressed the moral mission of Olympianism 'which is to develop a collective respect and understanding between different cultures' and not to allow commercialization, pursuit of personal interests to dominate (He in IOC 2000:5).

Another forum was organized in March 2000 that directly addressed the creation of a new cultural policy and the restructuring of the Cultural

Commission as the Commission for Culture and Olympic Education to implement it. Very much at the heart of the discussion at the 2000 Forum was the essence of what de Coubertin was trying to achieve in the early twentieth century and how much of his vision was still relevant to the cultural policy to which the Commission would adhere. In particular, debate was undertaken on whether events, such as the World Art and Sport Contest 2000, would continue in the same form (IOC, 2000). Cartalis observed that:

> The Cultural Olympiad can support effectively the harmonious interaction between the physical and intellectual functions, provided that a number of preconditions are met and that its forces resist ... commercialization and drive towards the reduction of cultural and educational inequities as well as towards the convergence of sport and education.
>
> (Cartalis in IOC 2000:27)

The concern at the international level about arts, education and equity has also led to other initiatives, such as the Seoul Agenda for Quality in Arts Education 2010, which aims to see arts education made available more widely and used as force for social good (UNESCO Bangkok 2013).

Cultural Olympiad, London 2012

The most extensive program for a Cultural Olympiad in the years since the 2000 IOC Forum was at the recently held London Olympics. It was hoped by many that it would enhance the cultural capital over 2012 beyond the normal selection of activities and performances. Arts Council England, Olympics Lottery Distributor (money was entailed away from many regular arts and heritage activities) and the Legacy Trust UK (an independent charity formed to create a cultural and sports legacy from the Games) received £97m between them. Special funding was allocated to the 2012 London Festival create a highpoint around the time of the Games. The programme of over 500 events ran over four years with more than 16 million people participating or attending them. Key programmes associated with the Olympiad included: Artists Taking the Lead, Discovering Places, Film Nation: Shorts, New Music 20×12, Stories of the World, and World Shakespeare Festival was undertaken in cooperation with the Royal Shakespeare Company and other arts organizations throughout the UK. Many of these activities involved public participation, for example Film Nation targeted young filmmakers, and Stories of the World allowed young people to carry out voluntary work in 50 museums across the UK. A large number of eminent artists and performers from around Britain were featured in events (London Cultural Olympiad 2012).

Overview of impact

Overall, the Olympiad was hailed a great success by the IOC and UK government. However, it was not without its critics. Some arts organizations found their funding boosted for events in a way that was not sustainable beyond the Olympiad period.

Bailey (2012) also noted that before the actual games had even started that entire program 'was underfunded, poorly managed and without a strong artistic focus'. Early implementation of the program was compromised by the resignation of Keith Khan in 2008 as head of Culture for the London Organizing Committee. Another director did not take over until nearly two years later when Ruth MacKenzie took up the role in February 2010. Other comments from art critics and others (Bailey 2012) centred on the over-reliance on social inclusion as against artistic quality that was dictated by the Labour government policy of the time even though this is supported to some extent by the spirit of Olympianism. Hence, events of this type will always walk a tightrope between the two in the way that many smaller community arts events often do too.

(in Switzerland, Miami and Hong Kong) and the Dubai Art Fair are now fixed dates on the international art calendar, and herald the latest trends for the market. In addition to the conventional offering of participating galleries and their works, these fairs are now offering various ancillary events, which are more cultural than commercial to build up the loyalty of private collectors and art critics in particular. For example, Art Basel Hong Kong included public lectures given by renowned figures in the art world in a programme that also allowed opportunities for industry networking and cross-cultural discussions in sessions titled 'conversations' and 'salon', which harks back to those similarly named activities in early biennales. The appearance of extensive review sections in international specialty publications, such as, *The Art Newspaper, Flash Art International* (published in New York and Milan, respectively) and *artasiapacific* (originally published in Sydney, now New York), testifies to the growing importance of this kind of event for collectors, critics, curators, gallery owners/managers and artists. Some events also dedicate special attention to the media such as whole areas set aside for these publications to attract more subscribers at Art Basel events.

Most indicative of how the art market and art tourism are driving the creation of new events is that many major hotel chains are now leasing several floors at a time to art fair organizers. Since 2010, each five-star hotel chain represented in Hong Kong has hosted a hotel art fair with the JW Marriot Hotel in Admiralty signing up with a local organizer in 2012 to host the Asian Contemporary Art Fair (ACAF) twice a year on three of its floors (ACAF 2013). The first hotel art fair held in Asia was the 2008 Tokyo Asia Top Gallery Hotel Art Fair. It was initiated by Asia Art Net and operated by the Asia Hotel Fair Committee, both based in

Seoul, Republic of South Korea (Asia Hotel Fair Committee 2013). It has proved effective in Asia at a time of growing interest in regional artists that has allowed galleries exposure to new collectors through the use of a hotel's own publicity resources, as well as the added benefit of a reduction of venue hire costs (renting individual rooms for display cost less than stalls at a traditional art fair).

Another new arts event form that has taken root in Asia and which seems popular is the Affordable Art Fair. It is a concept first developed in 1996 in Battersea, London and the first fair was held there in 1999 (Affordable Art Fair 2013). Again, some of this popularity is based on an emerging market of new art collectors who have disposable income for this activity for the first time, however, it is also a concept that encourages entrepreneurism from smaller organizations as operation costs are much lower. Like the hotel fairs, this event form avoids high-cost venues and provides activities to encourage new art buyers to have confidence in their selections. It differs from the former in that there is more community arts involvement and not-for-profit arts organizations and artists' collectives can present works alongside existing private galleries.

The role of museums in this context has been rapidly developing as well. Caldwell (2000) has observed that contemporary art museums enhance and diffuse contemporary culture by sharing the institutional mission of biennials. In the contemporary art system, museums either manage collections or mount exhibitions, with the aim of presenting the most representative artists and works. Though museums possess fewer resources than biennials, in recent years they have increasingly been acquiring works by young artists. Today, they are considered key players in the marketplace, especially by galleries and the artists themselves (Caldwell 2000). Museum directors have become more influential in the art world due to the greater professionalization of their area, more careful and far-sighted interlocutors, capable of making intelligent choices regarding their collections without the guidance of the most prominent periodic exhibitions (Scott 2000). Hence, art fairs, museums and new periodic exhibitions are able to compete with the traditional biennials and fairs with respect to their ability to present, disseminate and make the most of the latest artistic trends and artists. However, not all artists have waited passively on the sidelines to have their work featured by a curator in an event. The 1980s saw the rise in popularity of self-curated, entrepreneurial exhibitions after one which launched by the key artists of the Young British Artists movement. The first of these events to catch the attention of critics and peers was *Freeze* in 1988, where artist Damien Hirst showcased his fellow Goldsmith College students' work in a radical new way (Altschuler 2013).

Another innovation for both museums and the arts in terms of travelling museum-based exhibitions has been in the area of establishing linkages with other sectors in order to broaden the appeal of some themes in a more interdisciplinary way for the purposes of engaging younger audiences. An interesting example of this postmodernist pluralism stems from the television documentary *Wallace and Gromit's World of Invention* (Aardman Animations/BBC TV 2010) that was based on Aardman's popular stop-motion animation movies of fictional inventors, Wallace and Gromit. The documentary that was produced by Aardman Animations

Ltd for the BBC became a museum exhibition at the Science Museum of London before the documentary was aired, which was set up by Aardman's special events arm SGA in 2009 (Science Museum 2009). It then travelled to Australia and was localized a little in content to include examples of Australian inventions. The exhibition then toured the Powerhouse Museum of Arts and Sciences in Sydney (2012–13) and Scienceworks in Melbourne (2013) (Powerhouse Museum 2013). What did not change was how the nature of animation and aspects of the creative process behind it was interwoven with themes of technological inventions, environmental management and even the creativity behind marketing (see Plates 2.1–2.4). This approach allowed the travelling exhibition to include a large number of arts-based interactive displays and activities that were aimed at getting children to think about the nature of creativity and inventiveness (and not to forget about protection of intellectual property too, as this was a private-sector initiative with strong concerns in that direction).

In the performing arts, events such as open air rock festivals in large cities are becoming more of a commercial concern with numerous events competing for headline acts, while those in rural settings can have more of a community or not-for-profit focus as they work hard to draw visitors to these areas. However, much has changed since the early days of Woodstock (original 1969) and Glastonbury (1970 onwards), two classic examples from the United States and United Kingdom, respectively. Some of the current challenges for the sustainability of this arts event form are more complex, as it evolves over time, contextualizes itself within glocal influences and that of its supporting cultural/arts ecology. How these events (which were initially non-profit) have led to the development of large outdoor music events in numerous kinds of venues and a variety of operational formats is worthy of a book on its own. However, it is noticeable that some successful annual events of this kind have gone beyond their original locus to become part of the corporate music business world.

Of note, are breakout events that try something not attempted before, such as WOMAdelaide, a world music festival in the Australian city of Adelaide. It is a four-day outdoor festival for music, arts and dance from anywhere in the world, with most emphasis on acts or art forms not featured commonly at other events in Australia (WOMAdelaide 2013). Prior to the establishment of the festival in 1992, Adelaide society had no specific interest in the genre of 'world music', but became quite involved as the event proved successful. City arts festivals and events have more competition from each other in a shrinking world with some so concerned that they are losing their position that they have completely reworked their signature events, as in the case of Singapore, in 2014 after an extensive review.

Economic concerns and those of greater access for new and emerging talent and art forms mean that key places for small arts events in cities, namely private galleries have developed new strategies. Two new types of art forms include; the 'bundled event', such as a gallery hop or art walk, and a very transient arts event known as a 'pop-up exhibition'. The latter appears to be a New York idea initially and dates from 2007.[5] Thought to originally be more about minimizing the impact

Plate 2.1 Wallace and Gromit Model at Sydney Powerhouse Exhibition (du Cros 2012)

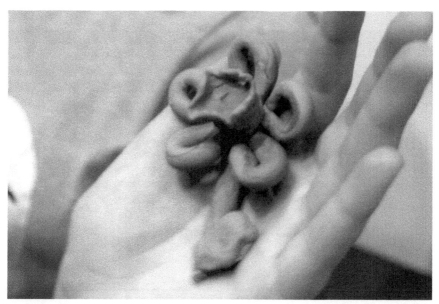

Plate 2.2 Result of a children's claymation participatory activity themed around the films and the environment at the Sydney Powerhouse Exhibition (du Cros 2012)

Plate 2.3 Wallace and Gromit paint blasters make a point about creativeness and fun (du Cros 2012)

Plate 2.4 A simple arts activity that introduces an awareness of basic arts and marketing concepts to children (du Cros 2012)

of high rents, they actually allow more freedom of form and content than traditional private gallery exhibitions of artists' work. For instance, Gallery 151's first exhibit was wall graffiti, uncovered during a renovation for the gallery, that were an early example of a collaborative effort encouraged by former resident Edith DeAK. It led to a mission being adopted by the gallery to spring surprising exhibits on the public for brief periods, which has continued to the present day (Gallery 151 2013). Although, pop-up galleries and exhibitions have spread around the world, they are not a well-researched phenomenon. They do seem to be becoming increasingly popular in cities with high rents or not enough venues to showcase emerging artists.

New arts event forms have also emerged in Asia in the twenty-first century. Artists in Tokyo came up with the PechaKucha concept. The word was chosen because in Japanese it means 'chit chat'. Expatriate artists, Astrid Klein and Mark Dytham, created the event in response to a need to have more meeting places and venues around the city that were affordable and accessible. Sometimes it uses industrial space and encourages participants to bring their own folding chairs and refreshments. Klein and Dytham still monitor and encourage the use of the concept internationally and run PechaKucha Night Tokyo. They allow new adopters and organizers to make a simple 'handshake agreement' to run four events a year and only one agreement is offered per city to avoid awkward competition. Essentially, the event offers the opportunity for new and well-known artists alike to give a simple presentation of 20 images for 20 seconds each (20 × 20). The images advance automatically and presenters talk along with the slides about recent projects or new ideas. It has become immensely popular as it gives everyone equal time and exposure with opportunity for feedback afterwards whilst socializing and drinking. Hence, the events are sometimes held in bars, restaurants, clubs, homes, and outdoors in beer gardens, at the beach and even at a quarry (PechaKucha 20 × 20 2013a; PechaKucha Barnsley 2013).

Following on from such inspirational events, there are changes occurring in how the means for implementation are found. In the current economic climate, many artists and performers are finding public or private funding hard to find, so are appealing to the public for small donations. This is sometimes carried out through website-based crowdsourcing for a number of arts projects including arts events (UNESCO Observatory 2013a). Kickstarter.com has been successfully helping fringe theatre and other projects this way by acting as a platform for creative artists and groups or 'creatives' to find private patrons. Its founders argue that it is just following on from earlier patronage traditions where

> Mozart, Beethoven, Whitman, Twain, and other artists funded works in similar ways – not just with help from large patrons, but by soliciting money from smaller patrons, often called subscribers. In return for their support, these subscribers might have received an early copy or special edition of the work.
>
> (Kickstarter.com 2013)

Kickstarter is supported by the inclusiveness and far-reaching nature of the web. How this might play out for repeatable events is unclear, except that new events could use it as seed funding which might then be matched by government arts agencies or corporate sponsors to kick off an inaugural event with the ambition to be on-going.

Trends in arts events: lessons from the past for the future

Overall, the arts and events prosper most when there are the conditions for a healthy cultural/arts ecology to support them. The most spectacular and/or long-running annual events occur when there was public and private goodwill, respect for the arts and artists, opportunities for knowledge transfer, practice and training, and bold creative people to attempt new event forms or revive and replicate others in a new way. In the twenty-first century, there are now new forms of arts events emerging that are more affordable, accessible and inclusive than those in the past. There is more of a 'bottom-up' than 'top-down' approach as different communities (real and cyber) are becoming more involved in their creation. There are also changes in the implementation of twentieth -century arts event forms in the twenty-first century. For instance, fringe arts festivals may be curated or semi-curated rather than for all-comers and the proceeds of popular performances not always shared fairly (Swain 2013). The nature of curation of such events seems to be changing where large arts fairs might be organized with works displayed at a venue as usual and also online in a virtual fair (see Art Basel 2013, which has a secure URL especially for these transactions). Meanwhile, the funding for either may come from a range of sources not possible in the past, but with some links to it as in the case of crowdsourcing.

However, local authorities will always want to have hallmark arts events and successful festivals, as well as market- or community-arts-focused ones, to attract tourists. How global and local ambitions are balanced continues to create an interesting tension for organizers, as does the ratio of contemporary and heritage arts in events that try to feature both. Arts events could also be said to be part of the entertainment industry, which is also undergoing change worldwide. A current trend that affects the creation of new events and event forms is that those with any kind of international focus can be very capital intensive and the amount required to offset operational costs can be formidable for all but the largest organizations or companies (Vogel 2011). Hence, some arts event forms are attracting companies with related merchandise and global appeal (e.g. the Aardman/BBC exhibit). Meanwhile, there seems to be a counter element to this phenomenon, where initial organizers of the first edition of a new arts event form are actively seeking to make sure it is popular worldwide, because it goes against the over-commodification of the arts. For instance, the initial organizers of the first Affordable Art Fair and PechaKucha Night are happy to see these events replicated in other places without requiring fees in return for people copying their initial concept.

3   Understanding arts events

This chapter will look more closely at definitions and propose a typology and a grid as a framework for understanding what kinds of benefits and impacts different kinds of events can offer. It will deal with a broad range of modern (and postmodern) arts events including festivals, fairs and expos, temporary and travelling exhibitions, studio- and gallery-related events, community arts events and specifically tourism-inspired arts events. Case studies of best practice examples from diverse locations representing different *types* of art events will be interspersed through the chapter (e.g. Hong Kong, Australia, USA, Canada, Croatia, United Arab Emirates, France, UK, Senegal, Israel, Russia and Macau) along with case studies working with a set of local arts events in the process of becoming global arts events for example Carnival (Trinidad) and Tango (Argentina). It is also instructive to visit some examples of compromised events that have had problems and overcome them, are overcoming them, or have failed entirely to overcome them.

A large number of popular and free arts events in recent times can be termed 'public art'. As this chapter deals in part with access and orientation issues, a definition and brief history of public art will be outlined here. Cartiere and Willis (2008:7) characterize public art as 'a complex, multifaceted discipline and it is this diversity and multiplicity that lies at the heart of its struggle for critical recognition'. They state that the definition of public art is also problematic. They note that:

> this is partially due to the relationship between public art, architecture, and urban design. Much of contemporary public art history is linked to Percent-for-Art initiatives that have combined the requirement for public art to be part of new building projects in many cities around the world.
>
> (Cartiere and Willis 2008:8)

However, although various artworks and performances may have been available for public appreciation over the years, public art was not an ongoing recognized practice until 1967, when the US National Endowment for the Arts created its Art in Public Places program (NEA 2013; Goldbard 2006). Meanwhile, some art historians place the beginning of public art as 1935, when the Works

Progress Administration (WPA) was created to help provide economic relief to the citizens of the United States who were suffering through the Great Depression. The Federal Art Project (FAP) was one of the divisions of the WPA created under Federal Project One as part of the New Deal. One of the earliest of these projects was a publicly supported mural programme that commissioned wall murals for public buildings to provide employment for artists, and formed part of the Public Works of Art Project (PWAP), which operated from 1933 to 1934 prior to FAP and 'Federal One'. The latter covered a greater diversity of art-forms from visual arts to music, theatre, and creative writing (Goldbard 2006).

In Canada the 1967 centennial (100th anniversary) of the formation of the country stimulated public art through the funding of commemorative projects. As Mackey (2002:60) indicates the centennial policy focus of biculturalism favoured the creation and funding (as centennial celebrations) of folk festivals reflecting Canada's cultural mosaic, in particular the music, costume and food of ethnic minorities, appropriating ethnic aspects as Canadian culture. This policy explains in part the choice of Montreal, Quebec as the setting for Expo 67. The theme of cultural pluralism delivered through arts events was continued with the 125th celebrations of the founding of Canada, for example with the federally funded play commissioned and delivered for the festivities, *Spirit of a Nation* organized by the Canadian Heritage Arts Society (Mackey 2002:74).

Needless to say, not all current public art relies heavily on public-sector programmes, policies and funding. The advent of many new community arts not-for-profit and non-government organizations in US, Canada, UK, Australia and other countries in the twentieth century provided a strong basis for arts events that could be independent of government funding and policy, when required. Many community artists funded by such organizations have been most successful when allowed to work closely with a community in a way that will help advance that community's agenda that has real world relevance and not one developed by a public-sector organization or even an international body which may not (Goldbard 2006). Community-based arts events grew out of this context and were as essential as other arts initiatives to achieving healthy arts and cultural ecologies in many locations. The section below outlines with a number of case studies how community, commercial, industry and artist/performer orientations can shape events and their quality, success and impacts.

Typology and orientation of arts events

To recap, this book initially defines event categories for successful and sustainable events as comprising *inspirational events* for building creative (social, cultural and human) capital; *affirming events* for encouraging links to cultural identity or heritage; *pleasurable events* that offer enjoyable recreational, leisure and touristic experiences; *enriching events* that create opportunities for personal growth and/ or to sell products or experiences, and finally, *celebratory events* that celebrate cultural diversity. As well as these general categories of successful events, it is worth looking more closely at the focus of arts events and where the key benefits/

Table 3.1 Four main orientations of arts events

Commercial		Industry
Investment, promotion, sponsorship, tourism opportunities, merchandising	International art fairs, award ceremonies	Networking, benchmarking/criticism, promotion, branding
Community arts events, international travelling exhibitions, many city arts festivals, gallery hops, affordable arts fairs, pop-ups, charity events	Events with broad appeal that successfully balance all four focuses	Some international film festivals, biennales, graduating exhibitions/performances for contemporary and heritage arts
Appreciation, awareness, cultural exchange, education, cultural identity, community affirmation	Most fringe festivals, arts seminars/conferences, studio openings, PechaKucha evenings	Knowledge transfer, acknowledgement, networking, inspiration, artistic affirmation
Public/tourists		*Artist*

impacts occur. Table 3.1 positions certain types of arts events in a grid in relation to four types of foci that are commonly found in marketing and planning or most events. The table allows for some overlap between those orientations that allow insiders as well as the public to participate, and who have to pay and who can attend for free depending of the key orientation of the event, namely, commercial, industry, public or artist/performer. Finally, understanding more about focus will help with identifying where the event is seeking its highest impact in terms of: attracting the private sector, networking, artistic or community affirmation or building public awareness.

Four foci or orientations (in no particular order) from Table 3.1 can be explained as:

1 *Commercial*: collectors, corporations, tourism- and destination-marketing organizations, owners/managers of commercial arts facilities operators such as galleries, theatres and performance spaces.
2 *Industry:* creative industry players such as film studios, producers, professional critics, professional arts/artists associations.
3 *Artist:* individuals creatively active and/or practising certain types of arts (e.g. heritage arts).
4 *Public:* general public through to creatives/informed public (locals and tourists), who are not creatively active, but who will participate in or appreciate the arts as a result of attending an event.

Trying to discover the particular orientation of an event can be quite challenging, particularly as some present too much promotional information and others not enough to discern the orientation. Questions that assist with understanding an event's key focus or orientation, which may be put to organizers or their public relations personnel include:

- What are the aims and activities for participants (percentage of attention paid to each of the four above)?
- Free, paid, professional/industry access only? And how much of each are available?
- Not-for-profit versus profit-generating?
- What is the selection process for artists/works? Who decides?
- Who goes to what?
- What is the event's reputation/brand/key association?
- Does it maintain its creative sustainable advantage (SCA) in some way over other events by the nature of its current focus? Have any problems arisen that indicate that it should change it?

The latter is one to ask as a result of conducting some research into the event or one which organizers should ask themselves if there are reasons to be dissatisfied with the event's planning and implementation. This chapter includes a few case studies of compromised events that have or possibly should consider conducting an in-depth analysis of their orientation. Reviews of an event's success are more often carried out by marketers in relation to developing strategies for audience building, however, revisiting the event's orientation is an important first step to discovering how to resolve any problems. A broader assessment framework that includes this aspect also will be outlined in more detail in discussions on maintaining SCA later in the book.

Key benefits and impacts

As observed earlier the social and cultural benefits of arts events are still poorly understood and their impacts have only been broadly measured in terms of enhancing economic goals. Yet arts events come in forms that meet a vast array of differing goals depending on their guiding principles and main orientation. When the organizers or the participants are not clear about how the goals are being implemented then conflicts may arise or opportunities will be lost to allow the event to reach its full potential. Mostly, these principles are clearly and sincerely presented in a way that allows the events to appeal to the right audience or market in order to prosper. Leading the charge are those events, which are considered inspirational in a way that allows for critical debate and deeper appreciation of arts and the context of their creation.

Inspirational events

There are two key areas that it would be worth exploring in relation to this category, namely: heritage, ideology and arts commerce in one corner and new arts forms that grow in popularity in tandem with certain kinds of arts events in another corner. There has been an increasing tension in the area of art fairs and biennales in relation to how far towards the orientation of the art market tastes and needs they should lean without abandoning their role as curatorial and ideological meeting places. This will be explored in relation to some case studies from emerging regions for visual arts appreciation, such as the Middle East and Asia. As these areas attract curators and art critics from established traditions as well as developing their own, they are also under tension as regional artists and art collectors develop expectations of how such events should work to their advantage. Mixed in amongst all this is how the unique heritage of each locale in terms of arts and the cultural context of their creation should be integrated within the exhibition and discussion of the works (Muller 2009; Smith 2012). One example is the Sharjah Art Biennal.

Box 3.1 Sharjah Biennial case study

Background

This event is evolving against a constant flux of ideas about how contemporary arts should develop and institutionalize in the Middle East. Visual arts over the last 20 years have been attracting interest from outside the region steadily as well as picking up pace developing within it. In terms of performance and gaze, artists have to contend with neo-Orientalist perspectives and a plethora of stereotypes about religious, ethnic, and cultural differences. When catering to a regional or local audience, there are obviously subjects and media that are off limits, sensitive or prone to censorship. The converse of this appears to be that, when outside the region, artists are expected to 'personify the historical and national(ist) as if their practice were only valid with a country code attached to it' (Muller 2009:13). Also, the mission of artists and event curators/organizers to bring more awareness about the nature of Middle Eastern art is tested when many cities still rely heavily on the larger and more internationally proclaimed arts events as platforms. That is not to say that there have not been national efforts to host exhibitions at major galleries and art fairs outside the region, such as at the Venice Biennale. It is just that to provide a more contextual presentation of Middle Eastern art requires appropriate events, large and small, to be held within the region, which will allow audiences a deeper appreciation of its complexity.

Developmental context

The first Sharjah Biennale was held in 1993 and since then it has been patronized by the ruling Sheikh Sultan Al-Qassimi and funded through the Emirate of Sharjah's Ministry of Culture (Sharjah is one of the United Arab Emirates). Its mission has always been to create 'a cultural bridge between artists, arts institutions and organizations locally, regionally and internationally' (Sharjah Biennial 2013). The event continued without controversy, until it suffered a setback six months before the seventh edition in 2004. All the first curatorial team was fired and a new one installed. Nevertheless, the new curator/director, Jack Persekian and his curatorial team, still managed to organize an accomplished event that received mostly positive reviews internationally (Wilson-Goldie 2005).

The Sharjah Art Foundation (SAF) was founded in 2009, while Persekian was still the Biennal's artistic director (and possibly at his instigation) to direct the Biennial and enhance the arts and cultural ecologies within the Emirate. The Sheikh's strong leadership in the arts in establishing both the Biennial and SAF also has been considered in some quarters to be almost visionary (Muller 2009). However, another setback occurred when Persekian might have come into conflict with the Sheikh, or other local authorities, and was also sacked in 2010 just before the 10th edition of the Biennal. A guest curatorial team was engaged on a one-off basis and this practice continued for the most recent 11th version as well (Saadawi 2011). Sheikha Hoor Al-Qasimi took on the role of both president of the Sharjah Art Foundation (SAF) and the artistic director of the Sharjah Biennial after Persekian's departure. The eleventh edition has received favourable reviews (e.g. Dhar 2013; Bodick 2013), hence reinventing the formula with local management of SAF and guest curation may work better for advancing its popularity with the region's slowly increasing art collecting/appreciating public. Accordingly, the Sharjah Biennial Prize, established by the Sharjah Biennial in 1993, is now awarded by Sharjah Art Foundation.

The event and artists

The event's orientation leans strongly towards the artist and interested public with an emphasis on 'process rather than product thus maintaining its reputation for encouraging artistic experimentation and supporting regional practice' (Dhar 2009:4). The event continues to provide a useful platform for discussion on ideologies, aesthetics and intellectual frameworks within Middle Eastern art. For instance, the 2013 Biennial theme was *Re:emerge, Towards a New Cultural Cartography* in order to address neo-orientalist concerns about the Western-centrism of arts related knowledge and the cultural relationship between the Middle East and other emerging regions. Guest curator Yuko Hasegawa stated that she was inspired by:

> the courtyard in Islamic architecture, in particular the historical courtyards of Sharjah, where elements of both public and private life intertwine, and where the objective political world and the introspective subjective space intersect and cross-over … Within the network of

intensifying international and globalizing links, the courtyard as an experiential and experimental space comes to mirror something of Sharjah as a vital zone of creativity, transmission, and transformation.

(Sharjah Biennial 2013)

This conceit was reflected in one way or another in the choice by the curator of 37 new commissions for exhibition and the work of over 100 artists, architects, filmmakers and performers. It was also contextualized and critically examined in the opening week that comprised a full schedule of performances, films, lectures, annual March Meeting, which is a symposium featuring thematic presentations and moderated panel sessions. The latter event, which also occurs in conjunction with the Biennal, is an annual gathering hosted by the Sharjah Art Foundation. It also has an experimental focus and attracts artists, art professionals and institutions concerned with the production and dissemination of art in the region and internationally (Sharjah Biennial 2013; Sharjah Art Foundation 2013). It is likely that because of the latter, the event sits closer to artists' end of the public art continuum than the general public end, as a few of the panels and sessions were only open to artists and critics. One review of the latest event noted that when some of the discussion about art and locality in the March Meeting debate was in danger of veering off into meaninglessness, a local young woman brought it back on track with an insightful comment indicating that regional understanding of the arts is not to be underestimated (Bodick 2013). Overall, the event is deeply concerned with creating the right conditions for artistic knowledge transfer, acknowledgement, networking, affirmation and inspiration. It was described in 2005 as having the potential to become an independent laboratory for artistic and intellectual inquiry, due to the absence of much of a public presence at that time (Wilson-Goldie 2005). While international authorities and artists are invited to speak (some after making an application first for funding to attend), the focus is on how their experience and expertise relates to the theme and its relevance to the majority of the participants, who (it is hoped) will be from the region. Even so, this arrangement aims for balance between local concerns and international trends in the discussion forums and presentations.

From one desert arts event to another – Burning Man (or Black Rock Arts Festival) has a very different essence to Sharjah, as it was created to run counter to the established public arts culture of the United States. The event began in 1986 as a loosely run summer solstice arts beach party organized by artists, Larry Harvey and Jerry James, before moving to a desert location. It was centred around the Burning Man ritual (similar to wicker man burning rituals of the prehistoric Celts), where a wooden statue is constructed communally over a fixed period and then set on fire at the end as an artistic statement and to mark the solstice. The organizers moved the event from Bakers Beach, San Francisco and reshaped it after local authorities in the city made it difficult to continue in the original spot, particularly as the effigy that started as eight feet high originally was by then 40 feet high when constructed and burnt in 1990.

Since 1991, it has been held in the Black Rock Desert in Nevada on an ancient lakebed known as the Playa. Over the years, it has grown in popularity to an event that now attracts over 48,000 ticketholders. The current organizers are a San Francisco registered company Black Rock City LLC, which does not always see eye-to-eye with some of the artists (Jones 2011). Its strongest principle is that all participants must truly participate – no spectators. Each year the settlement or 'city' that supports the event is built and operated almost entirely by volunteers and those who buy tickets provide artworks and experiences. Also, money from the tickets assists with funding an honorarium to help artists create or design the larger installations. A large part of this construction comprises art installations that are collaborative and often community-orientated and interactive. Numerous other activities are undertaken under the counterculture banner of the event, which make it better experienced than written about (see Jones 2011; Myecopaloosa 2012; Burning Man 2013).

By 2012, the Burning Man event had sold out for a second year in a row and had been the subject of a Bureau of Land Management environmental assessment (EA) as once again local authorities were concerned about its impact. The organizers worked with authorities on this to raise awareness with participants about what measures were being put in place to protect the playa and surrounding communities. The event has also developed a new non-profit organization to administer the functional infrastructure needed to promote the concept internationally and back in San Francisco. Its organizers hope for more in future in terms of having an artistic impact on urbanism movements in the United States and in being able to inspire new ways of experimenting with community and sustainability. They hope to tour some events based on the temporary city in Black Rock using their new organizational structure that will showcase how greater community and artistic collaboration can make a difference to the everyday experience of civic space and urban environments (Jones 2011; Burning Man 2013; Zaremba 2012).

Accordingly, inspirational events should be playing a key role in promoting new art-forms and activities. It could be argued that some events have had more impact than others in this role. A classic example from the history of arts development in Wales is how the Welsh National Eisteddfod and the associated *gorsedd* ceremony eventually led to the establishment of the Welsh National Theatre (for productions mainly in English), which in turn led to the National Theatre, Wales (Theatr Genedlaethol Cymru) in 2003 for productions in Welsh. Wales has maintained its nationalist ambitions, despite not having a natural frontier, and has managed to uphold its cultural ethnicity. It has also gone through a number of periods of cultural regeneration in response to modernization, industrialization and de-industrialization in addition to other factors since the Eisteddfod was first held in the twelfth century. These stalwarts of the Welsh arts scene not only managed to continue and grow in influence, but also to help initiate the establishment of Theatr Genedlaethol Cymru (Jones 2007).

The developmental history of the Eisteddfod has it being put most securely at the heart of Welsh culture from 1792 onwards, as a result of the prior influence of Edward Williams, also known as Iolo Morganwg, a charismatic figure associated with the arts. His vision of the event was that it should be focus point for music and poetry for the whole of Wales, not just at a local or regional level. He also invented an imaginative and mostly imaginary set of rituals based on mythology associated ancient British bards (Druidic poet/singers). This part of the event was titled the *gorsedd* ceremony and lent a certain mystique to the event with its central theme of metamorphasis. Participants in the event traded their real life identities for one almost like that in a virtual reality and enjoyed the pageant of dressing up in robes. From the 1870s, the event offered prizes for contemporary theatre works, often concerned with the life of coal miners (Shade 2004; Jones 2007). The involvement of English royalty in the 1894 Caernarfon Eisteddfod and its *gorsedd* ceremony brought the event acceptance and also that of its mission to affirm Welsh culture, both contemporary and traditional. It also helped in the debate regarding how far Wales could advance in its own national interest by setting up a new national theatre (Jones 2007). Accordingly, all three examples of inspiring events have moved either artists and/or their supporters in ways that were not originally envisaged by their initial organizers.

Affirming Events

Community development and arts events seem to be natural partners. Increasingly, the arts are being valued by communities in ways that help them affirm their collective cultural identity or assist with safeguarding related heritage, such as the street culture or storytelling, from which much of the inspiration might have sprung. If some financial benefit can also come to the community from sharing its artistic practices with a wider audience, then this might be considered an added benefit, but far from the only one. The case of Australia's Zest Festival considered in Chapter 4 is an example of an affirming event that has been primarily organized to benefit a remote community with limited financial resources, so any outside interest would certainly be welcomed.

Africa appears to be a latecomer in holding arts events in many of the forms described in Chapter 2. There are many music and arts festivals in South Africa and more developed areas elsewhere, however, it unusual to find a small one with both a local and international focus in the West and a strong arts affirmation message. Since 2002, the Festival International de Folklore et de Percussion de Louga (FESFOP) has been held in Louga, Senegal (Région de Saint-Louis), West Africa. It is organized by the non-profit organization, FESFOP, that guides its cultural content and by the Association for the Development of Keur Serigne Louga (ADKSL), which manages accommodation and artisanship. The festival usually runs from the end of December to mid-January. The FESFOP Tourist Village, which provides the infrastructure for tourists, has received funding and support from various local and international sources. The latter includes the United Nations World Tourism Organization (UNWTO) and the Italian chapter of the non-government organization CISV International (formerly Children's International Summer Villages), which has a strong educational mission (CISV 2013; FESFOP 2013).

The event attracts only around 150–200 international tourists per year, who stay either at the FESFOP encampment or are welcomed in host families (of ADKSL), where they can partake in the daily activities (e.g. cooking traditional culinary specialties), as well as attend the arts activities. The various arts and cultural activities are offered (e.g. stories by local storytellers, and workshops in percussion, and the local language) to allow tourists to discover the (tangible and intangible) cultural values in the environment they are visiting. Workshop classes on percussion, in particular, feature the premier musicians from a range of cultural traditions, from Africa primarily, but also a few other countries. Occasionally, international acts are also featured, such as Compagnia Artistica la Paranza del Geco from Torino, Italy in 2007 facilitated by CISV. However, the goal is to reinforce responsible tourism as a generator of wealth for local communities, safeguarding and valorizing the cultural and musical heritage of Senegal. Since, 2009 more Internet resources have been put into publicizing the event, however, it is likely that the majority of tourism is domestic (UNWTO 2012; FESFOP 2013). The FESFOP project illustrates the challenge of making the arts an engine of economic and social development in a region and a city that are a melting pot of cultural values of different ethnic groups.

The Hong Kong ArtWalk has been an important event in the arts and charity scene in Hong Kong since 2001. It has raised HK$5.4 million over that time for its designated charity partner, the Society for Community Organization (SOCO). The ArtWalk is held only once a year in March for one midweek night and the galleries use it to enhance their promotional needs, which are mostly satisfied with exhibition openings the rest of the time. Food and wine are provided for consumption at the galleries by a number of local restaurants and bars, only part of which is covered by the cost of the ticket as this is a charity event (ArtWalk 2010, 2013). Only people entering a gallery with a badge and map are seen as having a ticket to the event and will be served food and drinks at any participating gallery. People walk in small groups between galleries often carrying plastic cups of alcohol in their hands, turning the event into one continuous street party with different types of artworks to appreciate in the street, and the galleries. It is much more dynamic than a formal sit-down charity gala dinner, which is the key it retaining its SCA, because no event uses the streetscape of Hong Kong and its heritage so effectively.

SOCO is non-profit community organization devoted to improving the lives of over million people in the lowest income bracket of Hong Kong. Every year, the organization exhibits photos to event participants of the people it has helped. It is given a free space and the photography is undertaken for free by a local artist. Donations can also be made through the ArtWalk website. As well as helping SOCO, the ArtWalk has tried to raise awareness about the urban heritage precinct around the former Central Police Station, where most of the galleries are located. This area has many narrow alleys, courtyards and sitting out areas with their own special histories that can be used as cultural spaces for art happenings and installations on the night by local artists. The ArtWalk is the only time these spaces as utilized in this way. Descriptions of these activities appear on the ArtWalk map along with locations and descriptions of the art galleries and their exhibitions (ArtWalk 2013). In 2008, the event was linked to the Graham Street Markets conservation effort when its walking map appeared alongside promotional materials for the ArtWalk 2008. The Central and Western District Concern Group, a local heritage conservation resident action group, had just run the Graham Street Market Festival for which a walking map had been printed. It was also featured that year as part of ArtWalk to raise awareness about the future destruction of the nearby local street market area by urban redevelopment by the Urban Renewal Authority (du Cros and Jolliffe 2011).

There are also events that embody the sustainable development maxim that 'small is beautiful' (Schumacher 1989), because they are good examples of small locally managed arts events that affirm cultural identity, for instance the Summer in the Bight Festival. This festival has been an annual event since 2002 and held by the Rising Tide Theatre Company in the town of Trinity, Newfoundland, Canada. It has been working to affirming cultural identity by providing a range of theatrical fare at the festival that relates to local contemporary and historical themes. The company is committed to staging works about Newfoundland and written by Newfoundlanders. Since 1993, the annual festival programme includes the Trinity Pageant, a dramatic walking tour and theatre performance with actors portraying the past of the historic village of Trinity that provides the setting for the performance. The pageant has a strong educational function, because it can be linked to studies of Newfoundland heritage and is an enjoyable way for children to learn about the past through its animation of historic activities in actual geographical locations where they took place. Hence, the audience can follow the actors around the small town of Trinity for the outdoor part of the performance, in a similar way to the Kabosh Theatre Company's site-based events discussed in the next chapter. Established in 1974 before it was linked to the festival, the pageant is now the anchor product in the annual festival schedule. A more contemporary revue that satirizes politicians and popular figures is also another way the local community and others can collectively laugh at current affairs as a result of a professionally run local arts event (Newfoundland and Labrador Heritage 2013; Rising Tide Theatre 2013).

Another type of event with a broader reach and mission are the Caribbean (Trinidad and other locations) Carnival Festivals that deeply involve the diaspora from that region and allow participants to affirm their cultural identity far from home. Caribbean (Trinidad) Festivals at Home and in UK and North America diaspora case study.

Box 3.2 Caribbean (Trinidad) festivals at home and in the UK and North America diaspora case study

Background

Trinidad's Carnival has influenced similar celebrations around the world, however, how much of this emulation is to create a spectacular arts/leisure event and how much is based in a deep desire by the Caribbean diaspora to experience their own arts in another country has been an important issue for academic research. Wherever these festivals occur, they are certainly popular with steel bands, lavish costumes, pulsating music that encourage street parties and dancing. Trinidad's Carnival is usually held in early March and is supported by soca and calypso musicians, who play a key role in the Carnival's celebrations. Most of these musicians come from Trinidad and Tobago, however, sometimes members of the diaspora return and join in too (Nurse 2004; Green and Scher 2007).

Historically, the carnival has had many influences introduced to the mix over the years, since the initial colonization by Europeans. The Spanish and English colonial powers, French planters, African slaves, Indian indentured labourers, and the many other ethnic groups that settled there have all left an indelible mark on the festival. In 1783, the French brought their culture, customs and carnival, in the form of elaborate masquerade balls (now known as the Mas part of the Carnival), to Trinidad along with African slaves. The period stretching between Christmas and the start of Lent was a time for feasting, fancy dress balls and celebration for both the French and British. Banned from the festivities, slaves in the barrack yards would hold their own parties mimicking their masters' behaviour, while incorporating rituals and folklore originally derived from Africa. Once slavery was abolished in 1838, the freed Africans took their version of the carnival to the streets and, as each new immigrant population entered Trinidad, a new flavour was added to the festivities. However, the role of the visiting diaspora members and the advent carnival events in other countries cannot be underestimated in reviving local interest in soca and calypso music in the late twentieth century after the mass out-migrations of 1980s and early 1990s, when the local oil industry collapsed (Green and Scher, 2007).

Local to global – glocal?

The Carnival (Trinidad) described above is also an example of globalization of an arts event form from developing to developed world. Many countries in Africa and Asia struggle to adopt event forms from the developed world in order to satisfy public cultural policies or ambitions to be seen as leaders in their region by offering local versions of such forms. Carnival in the

Caribbean sense is also strongly associated with steel bands, soca and calypso music, which make its origins hard to mistake, where it is featured heavily at events, such as, the Notting Hill Carnival in London, UK and the Caribana in Toronto, Canada. Nurse (2004) estimates that there are now over 60 diasporic carnivals in Europe and North America, describing them as 'globalization in reverse' and that no other carnival can claim so many offspring.

In regard to the local benefits from the event, Nurse (2001:xiii) makes an observation:

> the carnival type festivals (for example, Trinidad Carnival and Barbados Cropover) have spawned entertainment industries that generate employment for artists and cultural entrepreneurs during the season and year round.

The Trinidad and Tobago Coalition of Service Industries have reported that three weeks of revenue from Trinidad and Tobago's Carnival exceeds US$100 million. The industry also generates significant economic activity in a range of sectors in the local economy, such as, entertainment, media, hospitality and retail sectors. Additionally, overseas diaspora carnivals generate hundreds of millions dollars in revenue (TTCSI 2013). However, one local authority has warned that opportunities have been missed locally for those hoping to benefit from Trinidad Carnival, where the local tourism industry still focuses more on the non-diaspora tourists. There needs to be more awareness about how the diaspora's contribution works to strengthen the market for the event and the destination (Nurse 2011). Other problems have occurred with overseas carnivals, such as at the Notting Hill Carnival in terms of security, police presence, with policing reportedly costing more than the production of the festival (Green and Scher 2007). The restraint that having a heavy police presence at a festival can play on party atmosphere may mean these festivals will start to diverge from the tradition started in Trinidad and Tobago and become less satisfying events for cultural affirmation for the associated diaspora.

Pleasurable events

Cultural policy and arts management authorities are increasingly trying to encourage the creation of arts events that address the needs of a public that perceive arts and leisure as linked and a vital part of their lives. Originally, this section of the public comprised mainly youth and retirees with enough free time and motivation to seek such experiences out (Vogel 2011), however, now there are indications that in contemporary society that there are people of any age, will seek out and pay to have richer experiences in a wide variety of arts. Carpenter

(2008a) observes that cultural and arts programming needs to take more of a leisure perspective to attract this group to events during their free time. Leisure behaviour is often typified as pleasurable and necessary to human development and a sense of social civility. Often leisure is undertaken for a reason and various authorities have had to acknowledge the influence of socio-psychological factors such as family and peer preferences, time constraints, previous experiences and how actively individuals wish to participate.

When applying leisure concept to understanding arts events, it would be useful to look at the concept of serious leisure, which sometimes also guides certain kinds of mindful cultural tourism (Moscardo 1996; Carpenter 2008a and b). In serious leisure, there are amateurs, hobbyists and even some volunteers who work very hard at their leisure pursuits and also achieve a deeper experience of an art-form through attending or participating in a related arts event (Vogel 2011). While not employed as professionals, serious leisure seekers often attend public talks and any insider sessions they can at events such as art fairs and film festivals. The type of events, which attract this kind of segment, and orientate themselves to continue to attract it, can be seen in Table 3.1 earlier.

Museums are increasingly considering the leisure element of their remit. Art museums in most developed countries are increasingly managing visitor experience in a more leisure-focused way to attract higher volumes of visitors. As discussed earlier, blockbuster temporary art exhibitions can draw record-breaking audiences by showing the work of high-profile artists or their most iconic works. Also, bringing the art to the public has been the subject of many smaller exhibitions held in shopping malls and other public spaces (Dicks 2003). Consequently, a range of contemporary events that have successfully and inventively attracted attention of leisurely types are outlined below as examples of how leisure, tourism and other pleasurable activities have become important to event organizers, specifically: Sculpture(s) by the Sea, Sydney and Perth; New Orleans Jazz and Heritage Jazz Festival; Saint John Gallery Hop, Canada; American Institute of Architects (AIA) Memphis Chapter Awards Night and the Cannes Film Festival, France. Sculpture(s) by the Sea is an event that has its greatest foothold in Australia, though it has set off a number of events that emulate it overseas in the same way as the Carnival (Trinidad and Tobago). Although it started as an unsubsidized event with only private sponsors initially, it received a temporary boost during the Sydney Cultural Olympiad that allowed it to develop more pleasurable activities and professionalism (see Box 3.3 for details).

Saint John Gallery Hop, New Brunswick, Canada, is an example of a small bundled arts event that is more linked to attracting locals and occasional tourists than the charity dollars focus of the Hong Kong ArtWalk. The former is held three times a year (spring, summer and fall) and provides the opportunity for participants to access a group of public galleries and small private galleries in much the same way as the ArtWalk. Sponsored by Uptown Saint John (the local business improvement association) and the city of Saint John, these arts spaces stay open for a Friday evening gallery hop, which is promoted by Destination Saint John, as a signature arts product for this historic city. Initially organized

Box 3.3 Sculpture by the Sea/Sculptures by the Sea, Aarhus case study

Background

The Sculpture by the Sea event was first held in Sydney in 1997 and has since been held in four other locations on the coast of Australia and also that of Denmark at various times. The concept for the event resulted from founding director David Handley's wish to create an iconic and free to the public arts event for Sydney linked to its landscape in some way. Inspired by other outdoor large community arts events such as 'Opera in the Park' and 'Symphony Under the Stars', he wanted to create a happening that would provide a sense of community that would result from partaking in enjoyable cultural activities that are free and not necessarily fringe. While living in Prague in the early 1990s, he was taken to an outdoor sculpture park set amongst thirteenth century ruins near the town of Klatovy in northern Bohemia. Handley observes that the kind of experience he was seeking for his event would be similar he hoped to one he felt whilst 'playing amongst the ruins and sculptures one night with my Czech art school friends (where) I had my first experience of the power, if not majesty, of sculpture' (Handley in Sculpture by the Sea 2013).

Handley returned to Sydney and in 1996 his friends (who knew about his idea) suggested he undertake the Bondi to Tamarama coastal walk. His second breakthrough came on the walk, 'all around me I saw natural plinth after natural plinth where sculptures of all descriptions could be installed' (Handley in Sculpture by the Sea 2013). Fortunately, a number of key people approved of the idea and helped to make the first exhibition a reality. Key protagonists in establishing the event were Anita Johnston at Waverley Council, which is responsible for managing the coastal walk, and Ron Robertson-Swann, a well-known Australian sculptor. From the first phone call Johnston was enthusiastic and guided the exhibition through the council's environmental, safety and crowd management requirements, while Robertson-Swann advised Handley on matters relating to installing and siting sculpture along the coastal cliffs and beaches. Robertson-Swann's reputation and endorsement of the event helped attract other substantial artists to Sculpture by the Sea and thereby ensuring from the beginning it presented work of a high standard to the public.

From being run from Handley's living room and staffed entirely by volunteers, the first exhibition started with only a hundred Australian dollars in the account. Through word-of-mouth through the artistic community over 100 artist submissions were made for the show, while media interest, council approval and a principal sponsor in Sydney Water (which sponsored the first sculpture prize), also assisted with advertising costs. The first exhibition had to be limited to daytime and therefore to one day only, because of a lack of a security budget, however, this had the advantage of allowing Waverley Council to see how the show would work, before authorizing a multi-day exhibition in 1998. Handley estimates that 25,000 people visited the 1997 exhibition (Sculpture by the Sea 2013). For the 1998 event, the Sydney Organizing Committee for the Olympic Games (SOCOG) through the artistic director, Andrea Stretton, commissioned five Sculpture by the Sea exhibitions around Australia for the 1998 Sydney Olympic Cultural Olympiad. This boosted the event even more in the arts community, such that artists responded with over 260 sculptures being installed among five locations around Australia (Darwin, Noosa, Albany, Bondi and the Tasman Peninsula) during the Olympiad. However, it was not to be able to maintain each of these interstate exhibitions without the SOCOG funding, though Handley tried to keep Tasmania running with an exhibition included in the 2001 Tasmania-wide arts fest '10 Days on the Island'. In 2005, Sculpture by the Sea, Cottesloe, was launched and is held annually at Cottesloe Beach, Perth on Australia's Indian Ocean coast. It has been successful because, as well as the art, event participants can enjoy its sunsets, sea views, teahouses and pleasant beach.

The event

The event at Bondi, Sydney, has since extended the exhibition over three weeks; significantly increasing the support provided to the artists in the form of awards and in some cases subsidies; developed ties with overseas sculpture organizations that see two dozen overseas artists exhibiting every year; developed the exhibition's sales were over one million dollars for the first time in 2007 (40 per cent of the budget to stage the whole exhibition comes from the commission on the sales); encouraged artists who incorporate the sun, sea, wind and rain to continue working in this area by developing an environmental sculpture prize; and developed a schools education program in which over 1,600 students participated in 2007. The event is juried and for 2013 had over 200 submissions from more than 20 countries. The proposals are reviewed by a curatorial panel, which changes from year to year and includes mostly leading authorities from public and private galleries. Once selected the artists have six months to make their works. To the deal with the event's growth in recent years, the organizers have professionalized its management taking the pressure off Handley and is now run by Sculpture by the Sea Incorporated (SXSINC), as a not-for-profit incorporated association. In this regard the company that previously produced the shows has given the rights to the exhibitions to SXSINC. Another recent change is the addition of Tactile Tours for the Bondi Site. Guided by a trained Sculpture by the Sea staff member, Tactile Tours provide an informed and interactive experience for visitors with disabilities and their assistants, facilitating discovery through dialogue and touch (Sculpture by the Sea 2013). Participants are encouraged to interact and engage with a selection of sculptures located in accessible areas that have been nominated by both the artist and site manager as being safe to touch (Sculpture by the Sea 2013). It is possibly one of the few events to provide such a useful activity for visitors with disabilities and others who would benefit from a more tactile experience of the artworks.

Finally, the event has spawned an imitator in Denmark with which it is on good terms. In June 2009 Sculptures by the Sea Aarhus, Denmark was launched, in association with the City of Aarhus and ARoS Aarhus Artmuseum, under the patronage of the Crown Prince and Crown Princess of Denmark. The royal couple is the initiator of the event due to their familiarity with, and enthusiasm for, the Bondi exhibition, which they visited as part of Sculpture by the Sea's fifteenth anniversary celebrations. Organizers state that,

> Sculptures by the Sea Aarhus – Denmark is financially and legally independent of Sculpture by the Sea Incorporated and is being produced by the city of Aarhus in collaboration with ARoS Aarhus Artmuseum at neither cost nor profit to the Australian organization.
>
> (Sculpture by the Sea Aarhus, 2013)

Nevertheless, the websites are linked and there is a flow of artists and artworks between them. With an estimated half a million visitors in both 2009 and 2011 Sculptures by the Sea Aarhus, Denmark is considered successful, and is embraced by both Danes and international tourists. Figures were not available at the time of writing (2013), however, it was notable that 27,000 catalogues had been sold. With its 64 sculptures from 22 nations along the shore and in the forest of southern Aarhus, supplemented by the Sculpture Inside exhibition, the event has developed a few variations on the original concept to suit the local environment and climate (Sculptures by the Sea Aarhus 2013).

informally, the popularity of the event led to the formation of the Saint John Gallery Association, which established criteria for gallery membership. The event is promoted by a poster and through the city's main tourist destination marketing website Saint John on the Bay of Fundy. The description from the Discover Saint John Web site above plays up the leisure experience of gallery hopping in this environment:

> 228 years of history provide a vibrant backdrop to the visual arts in Saint John. Art lovers will love the close proximity of Saint John's art galleries which makes for fantastic gallery hopping ... The art works of John Hooper,

Herzl Kashetsky, Fred Ross, Suzanne Hill and the fine crafts of Crimmons Pottery and Aitkens Pewter – among others – can be seen in the galleries that line our historic streets.

(Discover Saint John 2013)

Overall, this is a low-budget, mostly local event, but helps the city to promote its 'artistic' side in the historic urban core, and for galleries to informally partner with local restaurants, which offer specials on the nights of the gallery hop.

The New Orleans Jazz and Heritage Festival has over the years successfully combined both visual and performing arts along with a wide range of participatory activities. In 2011, there was even a Cajun cooking demonstration and voodoo rituals performed and explained, as it fulfils its mission to showcase Louisiana culture (see Plates 3.1 and 3.2). As a ticketed festival, it has been running since 1970 when its founder, George Wein, based it in New Orleans in order to highlight the city's role in the development of jazz. The event has showcased most of the great artists of New Orleans and Louisiana of the last half century: Professor Longhair, Fats Domino, The Neville Brothers, Wynton Marsalis, Dr. John, Branford Marsalis, Harry Connick Jr., Ellis Marsalis, The Radiators, Irma Thomas, The Preservation Hall Jazz Band, Allen Toussaint, Buckwheat Zydeco, The Dirty Dozen Brass Band, Better Than Ezra, Ernie K-Doe, Vernel Bagneris, The Zion Harmonizers, Beausoleil and many others. The festival has continued to promote local jazz musicians, while attracting performers from other places and genres of music (NOJHF 2013).

Industry arts events, which are mostly pleasurable for attendees, are a growing part of the arts world (Mazzer and Pedersen 2008). Most art-related professional organizations have an awards night, for instance. The Oscars awards night for the (for the Academy of Motion Picture Arts and Sciences) is an obvious example that receives a lot of attention, but smaller events where public scrutiny is much lower are usually the most pleasurable for the participants. One such example is the American Institute of Architects Memphis Branch Awards Night, which engages most participants and rewards a few for their efforts. Hopefully, losers are not too disappointed, although an effort is made by event organizers to make the event's atmosphere more sociable than competitive. Memphis AIA has been active for over 60 years and works as an advocate for its members and promotes responsible architectural design for a more sustainable built environment. The awards night is therefore an important event in the calendar of activities the branch organizes that also allows members and partners from outreach programmes and other projects to appreciate the best of their efforts towards this goal (AIA Memphis 2013). The attendees might include representatives of partner organizations such as arts and cultural organizations (e.g. museums, public art galleries, historic preservation groups), government arts and heritage agencies, civic organizations, construction and planning industry contacts, sponsors and members of the interested general public (Carpenter 2008b). An awards night event can be a pleasurable experience that allows the host organization to build or consolidate linkages with these partners and enhance its place in its arts/cultural ecology.

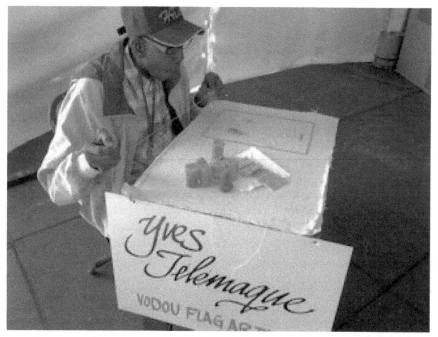

Plate 3.1 Yves Telemaque, Vodou flag artist, who is part of a local pavilion on *vodou* (*voodoo*) at New Orleans Heritage and Jazz Festival (du Cros 2011)

Plate 3.2 Vodou drumming ritual performance in the same pavilion at New Orleans Heritage and Jazz Festival (du Cros 2011)

By contrast, the Cannes Film Festival is usually much less inclusive and far more competitive. Perhaps, the pleasure is the eye of the beholder, that is, the inevitable tourists who line the streets and hang around outside theatres and hotels hoping for a glimpse of the glamorous. The film festival is an icon arts event that has raised the international profile of the French film industry, although it is just one of over 170 film festivals in France (Mazdon 2006). Accordingly, its start was more political than industry or tourism orientated. After several attempts at international film festivals before World War II that were not as successful as hoped due to pre-war tensions, Cannes was selected as a location in 1939. However, the event was cancelled due to the German invasion of Poland. The event was not held again until 1947 after the war and occupation (Mazza and Pedersen 2008). The Festival held currently has evolved from this beginning to be meant more for industry than the general public, but of interest of tourists, and tourism destination marketing certainly benefit from the stargazing.

Enriching events

Community, creativity and educational arts events are burgeoning in many countries, sometimes as a result of public sector programmes, but also as a private enterprise activity. One example of the latter is Edventures in Fredericton (New Brunswick, Canada) that provides enriching experiences to tourists in range of areas including the arts. This event promotes itself as educational tourism, however, there is definitely an overlap with creative tourism when these activities are examined closely and when activities associated with 'vacation learning in craft and culture' are offered within the areas of visual art, mixed media and design, fashion and sewing, jewellery and metalwork, photography and digital media, pottery and glass, textiles, heritage offerings (such as Canadian Aboriginal paddle making) and writing. In 2013, the operator (Fredericton Tourism) also offered master classes, as well as workshop offerings, with well-known artists, such as international and locally based photographer Freeman Patterson, bookbinder Don Taylor, and sculptor and metalsmith Mary McIntyre (Fredericton Tourism 2013). The event is held over the summer months of July and August. It has the capacity to attract in total around 900 participants, who are over 16 years old and are not in family groups. Workshops suitable for youth and children are offered by its partner, University of New Brunswick Arts Centre and Science East. Edventures' vision reflects the creative tourism philosophy:

> to provide an exceptional learning experience from top-quality, experienced instructors in a refreshing, easy-going atmosphere. We'll weave that first-rate learning opportunity in a rich tapestry of exciting cultural offerings and connections to our friendly people. It's like no other vacation you've ever taken.
>
> (Edventures, 2013)

Creative tourism has become popular in Europe and Australasia since a recent series of conferences and other activities have boosted its profile within the tourism industry and creatives have become more aware of the role they can play in providing more interactive, mindful and diverse cultural tourism products for a destination. One definition of creative tourism offered by UNESCO Creative Cities Network is that it is:

> travel directed toward an engaged and authentic experience, with participative learning in the arts, heritage, or special character of a place, and it provides a connection with those who reside in this place and create this living culture.
> (UNESCO Creative Cities Network 2006:3)

This definition follows from the original one offered by Richards and Raymond (2000:18), who defined it as a form of

> tourism, which offers visitors the opportunity to develop their creative potential through active participation in courses and learning experiences which are characteristic of the holiday destination where they are undertaken.

Gordin and Matetskaya's (2012) study for St Petersburg, Russia, looked at the potential for making arts festivals more interactive in this way by integrating creative tourism activities. They reviewed 334 art festivals, festivities and contests of different genres organized by a range of organizations in the city in 2010. The authors proposed five factors that were vital for increasing the level of interactivity in an arts festival, especially for tourists:

1   making interactive events in the festival programme;
2   contest events (preferably ones that entry requirements favour tourists and locals equally);
3   educational events (master classes, public lectures, workshops and so on);
4   sub-events oriented toward promoting professional communication (seminars, conferences, panel debates);
5   sub-events oriented towards non-professional communication (meeting actors, visiting backstage spaces, artist studios and participating in activities there).

Gordin and Matetskaya (2012) concluded that most of the festivals they studied had only very low levels of interactivity based on these criteria and that much more could be done by all stakeholders, particularly for theatre festivals, to remedy the situation. Meanwhile, the more developed examples for Europe include creative tourism activities that are provided by creative networks in Barcelona, Paris and Austria offering a range of creative experiences for visitors including visual, performing and culinary arts, fashion and design, writing and philosophy and gardening. In Austria, leisure pursuits are being brought together with a range of creative experiences at various 'creative hotspots' around the country. Creative Tourism Austria has devised a model to accomplish this collaboration by developing close relationships with commercial partners, including hotels and spas, drawing these new partners into the arts/cultural ecology within which the activities are based to provide more holistic arts/education/leisure experiences (Richards and Marques 2012).

Box 3.4 Arts Bus: On the Move! case study

The purpose of the Arts Bus is to promote education and public awareness of arts and culture, with emphasis on participation, for the betterment of the general public in Hong Kong. This is an innovative, energetic and creative community arts project where each year 22 buses become mobile arts venues, and two of them carry unique themes and artistic activities for the public to partake in. The remaining 20 buses are decorated with winning designs from a design competition for schools to enter, and the winning artworks go on public display in Hong Kong. The aim of the first competition in 2011 was for every bus journey to carry artistic vision and message of road safety into the community, thus matching the theme of the whole project, that is, to involve Hong Kong society in various artistic activities, and get arts 'On the Move!' in their daily lives. The 2013 edition of the event's theme for the competition was 'Green City' (HKIEd 2013; Do and Leong 2012). Each year, the design-bearing buses circulate for around six to eight months with periods of concentrated activities on the two venue buses, usually twice a year.

Through a series of artistic events, such as photography, sketching workshops, mini concerts, arts parade, mobile exhibitions and artists' information sharing seminars, the project continues to promote arts to the public, raise public interest and awareness in arts and create a platform for them to participate in different arts activities (see Plates 3.3 and 3.4). The organizers have stated that certain principles apply in the project regarding arts equity of access, similar to those in the Seoul Agenda, 2010 (UNESCO Bangkok 2013). Their vision that embodies these principles can be seen in the extract below:

> We feel that arts do not belong to artists only or any particular groups of people, if given the opportunity, everyone can appreciate and create arts. We believe that arts can improve the quality of many aspects of life such as mental health and parent–child relationship. At the same time, we also hope to display to the public the 'creative education' tradition of the HKIEd, as well as the creative combination of arts and education.
> (Do and Leong 2012:4)

Support for the event comes from a public/private partnership between the Hong Kong Institute of Education (HKIEd) and New World First Bus (NWFB)/ Citybus (for supply of appropriate buses) with growing support from schools, local arts organizations, Hong Kong government's Leisure and Cultural Services Department, K11 Art Mall, Hong Kong Art Galleries Association, Hong Kong PechaKucha, local artists and performers (PechaKucha 20 × 20 2013b; NWFB 2013). K11 hosted the school design awards for the second year's buses and intends to be a long-term partner and sponsor of the event.

New activities offered in 2013 were the performances at the Hong Kong ArtWalk, Free Music Festival and more activities, which became part of K11 Art Mall's winter and summer programmes for shoppers.[1]

The impact is mostly local with no international linkages at this point, except through the Hong Kong UNESCO Observatory for Research in Local Culture and Creativity in Education (RLCCE). The concept seems to generate immediate enthusiasm amongst most partners, particularly given the buses visibility in the community. It is a possibility that K11 may join NWFB/Citybus in supporting the project over the long term, as it gives the concept art mall's management a set of ready-made activities on a seasonal basis that attract families to the mall.

Plate 3.3 The decorated front of one of the Arts Buses. These circulating buses maintained high visibility in public for the Arts Bus activities (du Cros 2011)

Plate 3.4 An African drummer was one of the locally based artists who assisted with bringing arts activities to the public through the Arts Bus: On the Move! (du Cros 2011)

Celebratory events

Even before the UNESCO Universal Declaration on Cultural Diversity (2002) and the UNESCO Convention on the Protection and Promotion of the Diversity of Cultural Expressions (2005), many arts and heritage organizations have been using arts events as a way to raise awareness regarding the rich fabric of the World's culture and to promote cultural exchange. Some of these events started out as a way to connect with overseas artists and others have a strong mission to promote an art-form internationally, whilst yet others have a strong tourism and leisure focus. For instance, the International Tango Festival (including the World Championship of Tango Dance) is held in Buenos Aires, Argentina, annually in August, and works hard to safeguard and promote the art-form internationally. Tango was inscribed in 2009 on UNESCO's Representative List of the Intangible Cultural Heritage of Humanity and is also valorized under the UNESCO Convention on the Protection and Promotion of the Diversity of Cultural Expressions (2005).

Argentina's Tango Festival, which is the largest of its kind in the world, began in 1997, and the World Championship was later added in 2002. The international festival includes free musical entertainment, exclusive performances (not repeated outside the event during the festival period), new productions, classes, seminars, and presentations by established and emerging dancers. The festival is free of charge and has a strong educational message as well an entertainment one. The Ministry of Culture of the City of Buenos Aires is responsible for the festival, supported by various local organizations and private sponsors from the tourism sector. The Office of Cultural Tourism was recently created in order to commercialize this and other cultural festivals (e.g. by including them in tourism packages). The 2009 edition of the festival was attended by over 300,000 people, of which 85 per cent came from abroad (34 per cent from neighbouring countries, 31 per cent from Europe, 22 per cent from other Latin American countries, 8 per cent from the USA and Canada, and 5 per cent from the rest of the world). The festival has a very positive impact on the city's economy as the influx of tourists contributes to consumption of a variety of tourism products and services. While tango has become popular across the globe, the challenge for Buenos Aires (where it originated) is to retain its authenticity (City of Buenos Aires, 2013; UNWTO, 2012). The marketing of tango is still in its infancy and it requires a sustained approach to ensure that tango is firstly seen as an Argentinian art-form and secondly, those from regions new to the art-form, such as Asia and the Middle East, have the opportunity to experience it fully at the festival.

Croatia has developed a strong focus on arts events as both tourist attractions and opportunities for cultural exchange. Even its one world music festival in the city of Varaždin is as much about the acts invited to perform as about the heritage and arts evident locally allowing participants the opportunity to absorb both at the same time. A strong cultural and economic platform supports such events in Croatia, which is backed by local city authorities, the Croatian Chamber of Economy (an independent professional and business organization of all legal entities engaged in business) and the Council of Croatian Affiliation for Cultural Tourism (a multi-disciplinary body including museologists, archaeologists, travel agents, hoteliers and so on) (UNWTO 2012).

Box 3.5 Špancirfest World Music Festival, Croatia, case study

Background

Since 1998, Špancirfest has welcomed over 10,000 performers from all over the world, and has attracted over 1.8 million visitors to city of Varaždin, Croatia over one week near the end of August. It is considered to be a unique event amongst the country's array of arts festivals, because of how it utilizes its surroundings and local culture, whilst also having a strong international focus. Hence, the festival is an event that has built part of its identity upon the recent production of *world music,* with some well-known exponents of that genre attending, while the public can also be entertained by anonymous street musicians, who assist in providing the experience of visiting a 'global musical kingdom' (Varaždin City Tourist

Association 2013). There is the opportunity to experience contemporary music from many countries, as well as local singing poets and other artists (*chansonniers,* as well as rappers). Nevertheless, what makes the festival special, according to its organizers, is the street programme. This is mainly a fringe effort and somewhere between theatre and circus, with a diverse range of street performers (acrobats, puppeteers, stilt-walkers, clowns and illusionists) (City of Varaždin 2013).

A dynamic event

The festival almost runs 24 hours a day with the majority of the street performances during the day and the majority of indoor performances at night. Arts and crafts products – traditional handicraft and contemporary products – for everyday use from Varaždin and from all over Croatia can be seen and bought at the festival. Artisans were a vital part of the economic and cultural tradition of Varaždin in the past. However, Varaždin has long ceased to be the city of arts and crafts. Still, some of the most active artisans can be found at the Square of Traditional Trades, where they continue to make items by hand for daily use as well as souvenirs. The availability of these locally made items that can be purchased as mementos of place by visitors adds both depth and authenticity to the festival that reflects the sense of place for this community (Kelemen 2011).

Funding and support

Local sponsors, exhibitors and caterers support the event financially. It is also funded and organized by the Varaždin City Tourist Association and partly subsidized by local government (the city of Varaždin and the Varaždin county), the Croatian National Tourist Board and the Ministry of Tourism of the Republic of Croatia. Efforts have been made by both the festival organizers and the local authorities to disperse various activities throughout the year in order to maintain a livelihood for local artists and continuation of heritage arts' traditions, thus countering the seasonality that is inherent in festival-based craft markets. The best example of the activities associated with the Traditional Crafts Square that was created especially for Špancirfest and that has become a special tourist attraction throughout the year[2].

Heritage arts festivals come in many forms and are often a way for more unusual art-forms to promote themselves to new and different audiences, as well as affirm their popularity with those that have supported them for many years. One music form that underwent a revival in Europe and North America in the 1970s and 1980s is Klezmer music (Ray 2010). One of the more striking events connected with this music is the Klezmer Festival in the small Israeli town of Safed. It is a three-day open-air evening event that has been running for over 26 years. The performances of the music are held on a number of outdoor stages against a backdrop of small town vernacular architecture. It is held in the evenings between 9pm and midnight, when it cooler, as this is a summer event. The festival is also a non-ticketed event with families and children encouraged to attend the activities and walk around the historic town and artisan's quarter, where activities are held. The town closes off its roads early to allow visitors to walk freely. One stage is set up for 'Klezmerim for Kids', which allows children to try Klezmer instruments. This stage also presents storytelling and a magic show, demonstrations of unusual instruments, and plays. Organizers also offer musical themed tours of Safed, where Klezmer musicians act as guides. There are also tours and workshops that include sections on the Kabbalah, also meetings with or information on the 'Safed Personalities' (who number certain famous rabbis). Klezmer jam sessions are offered and tend to go on into the early hours well after the families have retired to bed. During the week preceding the festival, five days of master classes are held on the art-form. Students from all over the world come to study with the Klezmer musicians and each evening a performance is held featuring the students and the teachers (Safed Israel 2013).

Finally, postcolonialism and soft power can find their way into the celebration of the arts in certain situations. This trend was probably more evident in some festivals and events in the twentieth century as various empires broke up and colonies became independent. However, a more recent example was observed in Macau by one of the authors, which developed a unique twenty-first century twist as the People's Republic of China is emerging as a more active diplomatic (Kurlantzick 2007). Macau's Lusofonia Festival has evolved from being an event to showcase the living culture and arts of the city's residents (and few visiting acts) from countries that were previously Portuguese colonies to one that now includes a series of artists and performers from China. The event was originally established by a few Portuguese residents immediately after the return of Macau to Chinese sovereignty in 1999 and is now run by the government's cultural and tourism agencies. Its original objective was to celebrate the culture of the lusophone (Portuguese-speaking) community, and that of residents from former colonies in order to maintain Macau's cosmopolitan society post-handover. However, sinification was inevitable as Macau moves closer to China culturally and the Portuguese influence wanes (see Plates 3.5 and 3.6). What was somewhat unexpected was the use of the event as another example of China's deployment of its cultural soft-power approach. China has for some years tried to build cultural linkages with other countries in order to set up trade linkages and have better access to commodities such as oil. In particular, China has used this strategy to offset the influence of the US with former Portuguese colonies, particularly in Africa (Hartig 2011; GIGA 2012). By establishing cultural institutes there and by using Macau as a mediator or place of mediation in this process (Leung and du Cros forthcoming), China is slowly flexing its muscles in the diplomatic arena.

Hence, the Festival is now linked and promoted heavily alongside the 'Cultural Week of China and Portuguese-Speaking Countries' that occurs concurrently.

Plate 3.5 Dancers from Goa India take part in Macau's Lusofonia Festival to emphasize links between the ex-Portuguese colonies and Macau (du Cros 2012)

Plate 3.6 Chinese acrobats from the People's Republic of China are featured at the festival to remind everyone of Macau's Chinese heritage and the change of sovereignty from Portugal to China in 1999 (du Cros 2012)

Together, they include a variety of performances by artists from Portuguese-speaking countries, Macau and China at the Taipa House Museum site and a traditional handicraft and art fair in Taipa Old Town, along with gourmet food stalls, parades, exhibitions, a seven-a-side football tournament and traditional games from Portuguese-speaking countries held at various locations around Macau (Delta 2012; *Macau Daily Times* 2011). Despite increasing Chinesification of Macau, the festival still aims to present the active Portuguese cultural elements in the city and promote cultural exchange, as it did in its first years. Whilst, it would not qualify as being a 'compromised event' in the same way as some of the examples below, it has certainly undergone a significant postcolonial change of direction to fit in with the aspirations of its current public-sector organizers.

Compromised events

Arts events often take more risks to stand out and be more popular than other kinds of events. This bold mission can either enhance or detract from their SCA. It may even compromise their operation briefly or prevent them from being ongoing. Such actions can also be as much a source of contention amongst stakeholders (or be turned around and used as) an opportunity to collaborate positively. The following discussion includes a number of examples, popular and not so well known, that have had problems due to lack of, or too much, creativity, too much competition, political conflict, bad conceptualization, loss of funding from changing circumstances, lack of practicality or some fatal flaw in their planning or implementation. How they are or were orientated or focused is also one key concern in this analysis.

A sign that not all is well can be when, for instance, an annual event is cancelled for a year to tweak management or other problems. Glastonbury Festival of the Contemporary Performing Arts (colloquially referred to as Glastonbury) closed for a year after a particularly problematic event in 2000 to solve the problem of overcrowding due to gatecrashers, and to work on tightening security and ticket management. After this closure, the Festival was finally able to leave behind some aspects of its looser organization that originated during the Woodstock era of counterculture and alternative lifestyles. While some participants were nostalgic for elements of the older festival, its growing popularity over the years meant that some kind of professionalization of the management regime was necessary to avert disaster. The year it was absent from the music scene was used to undertake work to establish new measures to overcome the 'growing culture of illegal entry to the festival as well as ensuring a secure and safe environment for legitimate festival goers' (Glastonbury Festival 2013). Overcrowding was problematic because it meant that the event was in breach of licensed attendance numbers made by the local community living in close proximity to the venue. Both of these offenses resulted in the organizer being fined £5,000 and £1,000, respectively. However, this is probably nothing compared with having the main stage – the iconic pyramid stage – burn down in 1994. The current stage from 2007 is much more state-of-the-art and more costly than the first effort of wood covered with metal sheets that was erected during Glastonbury's more alternative phase on a leyline that supposedly runs through Worthy Farm, Pilton, in the direction of the pyramids. The 2013 Festival was licensed to attract 130,000 legitimate ticket holders, as against estimates of as many 250,000 participants in 2000 – of which only 100,000 had bought tickets (Glastonbury Festival 2013; BBC Entertainment Asia 2013). Where Glastonbury and numerous other open-air rock festivals have set up certain expectations for this form of arts event, it can be very difficult for a new event to establish itself, as can be seen from the Stone Music Festival example provided (see Box 3.6).

Box 3.6 Stone Music Festival case study

Background

The Stone Music Festival, Sydney, was originally aimed at Australian baby boomers and some of their progeny (the over 35-year-old market), who would appreciate the opportunity to see a number of so-called 'classic rock' bands together in one place over a weekend. The original promoter, Andrew Cartwright, who obviously likes this kind of music, brushed off initial criticism of it being another 'old farts festival' by trying to have it develop its own special personality, one harking back to the early days of rock music and the counter revolution in America and Australia. The problem with its conceptualization probably started with the name being already very close to another annual outdoor rock music event in the nearby city of Canberra, namely Stonefest, and continued from there.

The name was originally explained on the event's website as being inspired by 1974 Ozploitation film, *Stone*, about motor bike gangs. In addition, there were plans for screenings of a director's cut of the film during the festival and new production was underway that was somehow linked to event. Talk of an ancillary event to attract thousands of bikers started to worry financiers, especially as one of the local bands, Baby Animals, withdrew from the event, because they did not feel comfortable with this direction. Consequently, all talk of the film and latter event were dropped from the festival's promotion and the official website. Meanwhile, the management company, Ardline Media, had secured more headlining acts for the event (Newstead 2013). Billy Joel and Van Halen were contracted to appear exclusively at the event and not tour Australia before or afterwards. This was seen as rather unusual for festival acts and may have caused some chagrin amongst other promoters, who could not afford to do the same in such a tight event promotion market (with so many other events vying for the same or similar audience). Halfway through the ticket sales period, the event received mixed press and public reports of industry spats over the source of its financing (Jones 2013). This negative publicity and the peculiar behaviour of the original promoter may have affected how some potential attendees viewed the event.

An ambitious project

Another issue was that the choice of venue was also ambitious. The Sydney Olympic Park's ANZ Stadium is a venue that has struggled to attract events and reach capacity after the Olympics were held in 2000, due to its size and operational requirements. Another risk was situating the festival at the end of the summer festival season for Australia, but before most bands started touring the northern hemisphere for summer rock festivals there. Possibly, this strategy was adopted, because it made it easier to catch certain bands before they were heavily committed to staying up north. However, it meant that there was the problem that some Australian fans may have already suffered 'festival fatigue' and would not want to attend. Finally, that the weather would be more unpredictable or unpleasant.

However, it has been reported the event was conceived to follow a three-to five-year business plan with some room to deal with teething problems within that time frame. Organizer Stephen Duval (director of corporate event organizer SEQ) observed after the first edition in April 2013, 'it was quite a fatigued market at the moment and we knew that the economy wasn't great … but sales weren't so low that it wouldn't be back' (Mann 2013). Exact figures are not available at time of writing, but estimates were that tickets for somewhere over half the 25,000 capacity of the stadium were sold. SEQ are a company that facilitate finance for a range of special events (mostly sports-related) and took over the promotion of the festival from Richard Cartwright and his company halfway through the process of setting up, which led to a reconciliation with its main competitor and critic, rival promoter Andrew McManus, who then moved his headline show with Aerosmith into the event only two weeks before it was held (Fitzsimons 2013). Afterwards, the event seem to run fairly smoothly although a few unfortunate decisions were made, such as selling half-price tickets on the day of the event to the chagrin of full-price ticket holders. These decisions may be the result of the key organizer SEQ being orientated more towards sports and the profit side of event management in order to retain the event's backers, rather than providing a completely satisfying rock music festival experience for attendees.

The event experience

Reviews were mostly positive for the event, despite its stormy inception. For instance, *Sydney Morning Herald* music critic Kate Hennessy commented:

> Happily, Stone Music Festival doesn't commit the two great sins of big outdoor musical banquets: muddy sound and too-short headline sets. The weather is dubious, the stadium soulless and the food bland but every plastic poncho-clad punter here knows Aerosmith will play for 90 minutes and Van Halen for longer.
>
> (Hennessy, 2013)

Facebook comments on the official page for the event also lauded the performances of the headline acts and were generally satisfied with the way they were scheduled and presented. For instance, one commented, 'Had a great time! For all the critics let's keep in mind the spirit of the festival – Music, Freedom, Life, Mateship. Yes, there are glitches associated with putting on something so massive but i [sic] think most people had a great time'. While another commented wryly, 'Low attendance had advantages for crowd: no queues for food/beer/toilets and the people that did go being the friendliest rock crowd I've come across' (see Stone Music Festival Facebook 2013).

Some reviewers and attendees did notice operational problems that might hark back to the turmoil of the event's inception and some other factors. These can be summarized as concerns about last-minute cancellations; complicated nature of the ticketing, seating and entrance/exit to the venue related to that; sudden appearance of a second stage for acts; variable quality of sound engineering/mixing and the weather. Also, anxiety about the appearance of the headliners were fuelled by the loss of one act early in the event's development and the possibility that one or more headline acts would follow, especially as Van Halen had cancelled shows the year before and many thought they might again. All festivals have problems of this nature from time to time. Even Glastonbury Festival of Contemporary Performing Arts discussed briefly in this section, has been known to lose an act at a critical moment. However, the only cancellation on that weekend was a less famous band and most attendees were not too disappointed. Headliners are vital to any event of this kind and organizers had taken the risk to sign Van Halen exclusively to the festival (expensive!) and it would have meant a huge loss for them as well.

The price of the tickets was probably set too high initially, given the slow take up. Possibly there was an underlying assumption that an older market for this event would include corporate and more high-flying types, who would expect the equivalent of a premium seating at a sporting event. Hence, tickets were divided into platinum (for assigned seating and corporate areas) and general access with one day and full day options for each. Then all tickets were cut to half price on the day due to slow sales beforehand. There were many complaints on Facebook about this move and some people even asked for refunds on their platinum tickets. Other issues included: freedom of access in and out of the stadium (pass-outs), last minute inclusion of a second stage blocked views, sound across the venue was variable and should have been checked earlier. The weather was not good on the first day but areas under cover were available to those during the rain. However, an opportunity was missed when merchandise stalls did not open quickly enough to take advantage of the situation (Stone Music Festival Facebook 2013).

Afterward

Organizers response to this criticism has not been strong on the Facebook page, although note has been made elsewhere to tighten the management on the next edition. While demand for live music is often difficult to model (Earl 2001), it is hoped there will be a stronger effort made in future to understand the market for this kind of event, before initiating changes. However, the biggest change may be to include more 80s, 90s bands and 2000s acts and even a few current bands with the view of attracting a broader audience than just over-35-year-olds. What will make it different from similar events that showcase such bands will be the promise that financiers will bankroll deals to make the headlining acts exclusive to the festival, instead of the first stop on an Australia-wide tour as is the case elsewhere, as promoters of such bands often demand that of organizers (Fitzsimons 2013). Whether this approach is sustainable and can prosper in the current rock industry climate is an interesting question given how competitive and cramped the market has become.

The inaugural Stone Music Festival 2013 in Sydney is an example of an organizer trying to break into this tight market with a new annual event and meeting a host of problems from the start. From the case study, it is noticeable that some are related to the inexperience of the organizers and some are associated with the saturation of the market for these events – a type of 'festival fatigue'. For instance, in the same week that the Stone Music Festival was held, two outdoor hip-hop festivals were cancelled. So, even though there were many positive comments about the April weekend festival from attendees, the sheer weight of bad publicity and operational problems may eventually discourage sponsors and future fans. Another similar event in Hong Kong also suffered negative press before it was held, however, this time for a set of reasons unique to the city's current socio-political climate (see Box 3.7 Hong Kong Dome Festival).

Orientation and key aspects of inspirational, affirming, pleasurable, enriching and celebratory events

This chapter has presented a new framework for analysis to assist with understanding an event's key focus or orientation and how this expectations of and activities for participants. In Table 3.2, there are some striking examples of events that have activities aiming squarely at one orientation, such as the Cannes Film Festival's strong industry focus, PechaKucha evenings, or Sharjah Biennial/March Meeting events' key benefits being for artists. However, most events have at least two orientations and could be plotted on a continuum somewhere between the two. For instance, any one of the Affordable Art Fairs are still more of a commercial event (artworks are there to be sold) than an educational one, although there are

Box 3.7 Hong Kong Dome Festival 1 July 2013

Background

A first-time summer pop music festival suffered a major backlash on Facebook and in the press prior to the event, as it was alleged to be a government tool to reduce youth political activism on a Hong Kong public holiday afternoon that has been the occasion of the annual pro-democracy protest march for the last ten years. The event was organized by the Hong Kong Performing Industry Association (PIA, a music industry lobbyist organization incorporated in Hong Kong) (Hong Kong Companies Registration 2013). The only other previous event organized by the association was the Summer Pop Live in Hong Kong concert in 2009, which was principally aimed at attracting youth tourists to the city with reasonably priced tickets (HK Clubbing 2009). The Hong Kong Tourism Board supported this one-off event, whilst the Dome festival was expected to be ongoing summer pop festival (similar to the Tokyo Dome Festival) with primarily private sponsors, such as local land developers, hotels and other corporate sponsors. The concert headliners for the 2013 event were the K-pop artists Shinee, f(x0, EXO, Super Junior-M's Henry and BoA. When these bands visit Hong Kong, their tickets can cost as much as HKD 1,000 each due to the high demand and their immense popularity in the region (locals and tourists attend these concerts). Local bands, such as, Mr and Rubberband, were also included with the popular Korean bands in order for PIA to fulfil its stated mission of promoting local bands and the need for better concert venues for them. PIA was particularly keen to publicize the idea that there be a new facility built by the government with a 30,000 seat capacity. The nature of the sponsorship deal brokered by PIA meant that a large number of tickets were available for a fifth of the normal price in order for the event demonstrate that there was the demand for such a stadium. As it was, the event sold out within two hours, mainly due to the popularity of the K-pop (Korean pop music) artists. Some fans even obtained free tickets through their schools, possibly thanks to some of the sponsors wanting the event to be successful (Nip 2013; Chow and Lo 2013).

Politicization of the event

The event was held by PIA on 1 July 2013 outdoors at the old Kai Tak airport which is in the process of slowly being developed by the Hong Kong government into a leisure, retail and transport hub with some private home ownership scheme flats. The organizers, PIA, had both the political allegations and a number three typhoon signal (public warning that a typhoon is approaching) to contend with on this day, and so this event has had a difficult birth and may not continue into the future. Even so, most of the 18,000 ticketholders turned up and many K-pop fans waited for hours or days in advance to get the best position near the stage. One of the concert staff commented to the media, 'if this show is cancelled now (because of the typhoon), those teenage girls will probably jump into the sea. They are hardcore K-pop fans. Some have been camped here for five days' (Chow and Lo 2013:A4). In comparison, the protest march attracted 93,000 participants of all ages, despite the weather (*South China Morning Post* Staff Reporters 2013).

Meanwhile, the backlash against the local bands participating at the same time as the annual march was intense (see Boycott HK Dome Festival 2013). Consequently, rather than drop out, the bands used the occasion to give their sets a distinctly political theme. Rubberband appeared all in black t-shirts with the letters "NO" in white on the front. Their frontman, Mau Hou-cheong, introduced their cover of *I Have Nothing,* a famous mainland Chinese Tiananmen Square protest anthem by Cui Jian, with 'It is [Hong Kong's partial democracy] an unhealthy election system that creates all the problems ... we need to fight for 2017 universal suffrage and freedom of speech' (Chow and Lo 2013:A4). No doubt many agreed with him, whilst a number near the stage were probably just hoping his band's 30-minute set would finish soon, so they could see their K-pop idols. Other comments in the media were more about the overly tight restriction on traffic flows and refreshments by the organizers than about whether participants felt conflicted about attending the event instead of the protest (Chan 2013).

The PIA may well have had good intentions in organizing an event with the view to providing young local residents with free and discounted tickets, however, the unfortunate timing of the event and the addition of very popular K-pop headliners made it look to many like some form of government intervention (cloaked by its private-sector supporters) along the lines of 'give them bread and circuses' to head off a possibly larger than normal 1 July protest. Both this event and the protest march went ahead, despite the typhoon, and neither seemed to suffer overly from competition from the other. Whether the allegation is true or not, it is likely that the PIA will still have to work hard to change this mindset against the event in some quarters and whether changing the date for the next festival will resolve the problem is an interesting issue. Instead, if repetition of the event in the same form occurs it could be seen by some social media commentators as a confirmation of government influence, rather than the opposite.

Table 3.2 Orientations of key case studies from Chapters 2 and 3

Commercial		*Industry*
Investment, promotion, sponsorship, Stone Music Festival	International art fairs, most award ceremonies, Hong Kong Dome Festival, Basel Art Fairs, Asia Hotel Art Fairs, AIA Memphis Award Ceremony	Networking, benchmarking/criticism, promotion, Cannes Film Festival (and tourism a little)
Community arts events, international travelling exhibitions, many city arts festivals, gallery hops, affordable arts fairs, pop-ups, Hong Kong ArtWalk, Arts Bus: on the Move, Summer in the Bight Festival, WOMAdelaide, St John Gallery Hop	Events with broad appeal that successfully balance all four focuses, Sculptures by the Sea, Carnivals, International Tango Festival/Awards, Glastonbury, New Orleans Jazz and Heritage Festival, Singapore Arts Festival (new version), Edinburgh Arts Festival, Edinburgh Fringe Festival (current)	Some film festivals, graduating exhibitions/performances for contemporary and heritage arts, Edinburgh Film Festival, Venice Biennale
Appreciation, awareness, cultural exchange, education, Edventures in Canada, FESFOP Senegal, Špancirfest World Music Festival, Cultural Olympiad, Klezmer Music Festival	Most fringe festivals, arts seminars/conferences, studio openings, Burning Man/Black Rock Arts Festival, Welsh Eisteddfod and Gorsedd Pageant, Edinburgh Fringe Festival (old)	Knowledge transfer, acknowledgement, networking, inspiration PechaKucha evenings, Sharjah Biennial/March meeting, self-curated exhibitions (for Young British Artists movement)
Public/Tourists		*Artist*

far more opportunities for new or potential collectors to receive information about and purchase more affordable works than at a traditional international arts fair. Alternatively, though Arts Bus: On the Move! is a public–private partnership with some attention to the requirements of City Bus, its private sector partner in terms of promotion, it is clearly aimed at raising public awareness about the arts in Hong Kong not about City Bus. Hence, the Cannes Film Festival would be closer to the commercial end of a continuum than the public end and the latter is much nearer to a public orientation in its spirit, activities and benefits. Finally, there are events that succeed in having a very broad focus, though there is always tension as different players compete for benefits from them, even when – and probably particularly – when they are highly popular. The Edinburgh Fringe Festival appears to be one of these events that are under constant scrutiny and tension about how well it delivers its promise of affordable performances from all-comers that will fulfil the varying needs of each of the key orientations. And as the festival form expands globally the tension between competing orientations continues.

The next most important issue for understanding where key benefits are occurring after the question of 'who' for the orientation is the issue of 'what', in terms of the types of events that fit with a particular orientation or set of orientations. This leads event organizers to unconsciously aim for one or more of the five arts event categories outlined earlier: inspirational, affirming, pleasurable, enriching and celebratory. Table 3.3 shows how the examples in this chapter in particular range in relation to the types discussed and a brief summary of why they have been classified this way. Hopefully, this will be helpful to event organizers (of events not outlined here) and others in terms of thinking about where other events might be classified.

Table 3.3 Summary of arts events typology for Chapter 3 examples

Event(s)	Orientation	Type	Comments
Sharjah Art Biennal, UAE	Artist	Inspirational	Most of the activities are heavily orientated to artists/arts criticism
Burning Man (or Black Rock Arts Festival), USA	Artist/public	Inspirational	Both artists and non-artist participants inspired by activities and experiences of the event
Welsh National Eisteddfod/gorsedd ceremony, Wales	Artist/public	Inspirational	An event that has inspired the creation of other art activities in Wales, (national theatre company and performances) and similar events around the world
Festival International de Folklore et de Percussion de Louga (FESFOP), Senegal	Public/tourist	Affirming	Arts and folklore of the region is affirmed in activities that are also on opportunity for cultural exchange with tourists and performers from outside Senegal
Hong Kong ArtWalk	Public/commercial	Affirming	Art from all over the world is still sold, as a result, as well as heritage conservation, local artists and charities supported as people walk between galleries
Summer in the Bight Festival, Canada	Public/tourist	Affirming	Creativity and heritage of the town is affirmed and presented to the local community and tourists
Caribbean (Trinidad and other locations) Carnival Festivals	All	Affirming	The heritage and music of the region is affirmed, not just amongst the local community and tourists, but also in other locations by the Caribbean diaspora
Sculpture(s) by the Sea, Australia and Denmark	All	Pleasurable	An opportunity is provided for leisure activities, such as, walking and enjoying scenery to intersect with the appreciation of sculpture. Ancillary activities are offered that make it accessible to school children and the disabled as well. It is well regarded and supported by the arts world
Saint John Gallery Hop, Canada	Public/commercial	Pleasurable	Bundling the galleries together allows a pleasurable experience of them and their surrounding environment
New Orleans Jazz and Heritage Festival	All	Pleasurable	Ticket holders are offered a broad range of arts experiences in the home of jazz, which offers a pleasurable sense of history
American Institute of Architects Memphis Branch Awards Night	Industry/commercial	Pleasurable	A small event that allows architects to showcase the best of their work to key partners in a pleasurable atmosphere

Event	Industry/tourist	Pleasurable	Description
Cannes Film Festival	Industry/tourist	Pleasurable	An iconic event that has a strong insider and outsider division. While much is going on behind closed doors that has consequences for creative and commercial development of film, tourists can view the public spectacle for some superficial pleasure
Edventures in Fredericton, Canada	Public/tourist	Enriching	A rich offering of summer courses for the local community and tourists alike that assist in building their creative capacity
Creative tourism examples (Europe)	Public/tourist	Enriching	Events that vary in orientation as to whether they serve the public more than tourists and their leisure needs
Arts Bus: On the Move! Hong Kong	Public	Enriching	An emerging event that is trying to establish a new and more flexible way to engage the public and schools in arts education and appreciation
International Tango Festival/World Championship of Tango Dance, Argentina	All	Celebratory	The iconic event that celebrates all aspects of tango dancing for a variety of orientations in order to ensure its survival into the future
Špancirfest World Music Festival, Croatia	Public/tourist	Celebratory	A festival with a strong emphasis on attracting tourists to assist in keeping contemporary and traditional arts alive
Klezmer Music Festival, Safed, Israel	Public/tourist	Celebratory	An event that celebrates all aspects of Klezmer music and associated traditions to ensure its survival into the future
Lusofonia Festival, Macau	Public/tourist	Celebratory	A pluralistic offering of arts and culture from former Portuguese colonies (performers and participants from which have moved to Macau), and China all set in a curious postcolonial context
Singapore Arts Festival	Public/tourist attempting to change to All	Inspirational or Pleasurable?	A city arts festival undergoing a face-lift, which may completely change its direction (or only appear to). Until the next festival, it is hard to say whether it will be more for artists or more for the public and tourists
Glastonbury Festival of the Contemporary Performing Arts, UK	Public/tourist	Celebratory	An iconic event that has slowly become more professionally run and less alternative in management style in order to deal with its immense popularity
Stone Music Festival, Australia	Commercial	Supposed to be pleasurable	Developmental problems inevitably influenced ticket sales and led to a mixed reception from the media for this new event. It is possible that the event will be repeated, but in a different format
Hong Kong Dome Festival	Commercial/industry	Supposed to be celebratory	Political problems led to mixed support from social media and local artists for this new event. It is possible that the event will be repeated, but a different date would be better

4 Key issues in planning and developing arts events

This chapter examines the principles of planning arts events by combining the viewpoints of both arts and event management. The issues most common to the success of developing arts events at the initial planning stages will be identified here. Relevant case studies from Australia, Europe and Canada are interspersed throughout the chapter as examples of the creation of both creative and sustainable arts events.

The planning of arts events should be systematic with ongoing evaluation being a part of the system. Key components of planning discussed in detail below are concept development; selecting venues; partnerships and sponsorship; and community involvement. Issues related to human resources; marketing and promoting; risk management and evaluation will be discussed in Chapter 5.

The motives for developing arts events will differ especially in profit versus not-for-profit situations. In profit making situations the goal of making money will influence the development of the event. In not-for-profit settings, where events would aim for a break-even financial situation there may be other dominant goals such as encouraging the development of the arts and fostering community economic development through the arts.

Arts events concepts

Arts events are acknowledged as the most common type of festivals (Allen *et al.* 2002). An arts event may be staged as a one-time special event or may occur regularly, such as on an annual basis. Concepts may thus be developed creatively for new events or be more traditional and amended for those held annually, as changes may be made over time based on actual experience and evaluation. New event strategies will obviously require more intensive planning while existing events will begin planning based on previous experience and evaluation of past events.

An important part of planning at the conceptual stage is the understanding of the market for an arts event. An essential aspect of strategic market research will be identifying the market segment or segments for the event, consisting of those whose needs will be met by the event. Different types of segmentation may be utilized, including geographic segmentation (relies on location) demographic segmentation (characteristics such as age, gender, occupation, income, education and cultural group) and psychographic segmentation (lifestyle and values) (Allen *et al*. 2002:245–6).

At the stage of developing a concept, the public policy environment within which the event is situated should be clearly acknowledged, as this will contribute to determining the types of events that are encouraged by public arts policies, as well as the availability of funding for the events (Henderson 2003). In developing an arts event concept, it is also important to engage communities, such that broad-based community consultation is now noted as a prerequisite for the successful planning of events (Page and Connell 2012).

The case of Australia's Zest Festival demonstrates a number of aspects of developing a viable concept for an arts event, including understanding the market and the public policy context and employing a broad based community consultation and participation in the planning of the event.

Box 4.1 Zest Festival case study

The Zest Festival is a five-year planned cycle of annual festivities in Kalbarri, Australia. This small town is located in mid-western Australia, about 600 km north of Perth, bordered by the Kalbarri National Park on three sides and the ocean and rivers on the other. The town and area has both aboriginal origins and European influences. 'The local Aboriginal Nanda people inhabited the area for thousands of years and have a dreaming story about the Rainbow serpent forming the Murchison River as she came from inland to the coast' (Zest Festival n.d.). It is believed Kalbarri was named after an Aboriginal man from the Murchison tribe, and it is also the name of an edible seed.

The Zest Festival is a contemporary creation, initiated in response to the then upcoming 300-year anniversary of the *Zuytdorp* shipwreck and leading up to the 400-year anniversary of the initial landing of people from the *Batavia* (both ships of the former Dutch East India Company). While the initial impetus for the festival was the anniversary of the shipwreck, rather than create a commemorative event, the community took a creative approach towards this opportunity to create an arts festival that would connect their world with others, involving a broad segment of actors, participants, supporters, partners and sponsors from within the community and beyond. The festival adopted a cross-cultural approach in particular reaching out to countries linked to the former Dutch East India Company: South Africa, India, Indonesia and the Netherlands.

Concept development

This case profiles the planning for this event that has included a thoughtful and practical plan for partnerships, offering lessons for the implementation of events in a planned, phased and sustainable manner. A highlight of the case is that the event has been conceived and implemented within the community through a solid base of local support, but also partnered with external agencies that had an interest in or connection to the heritage of the Zuytdorp shipwreck, for example with the Dutch government who had initially approached local government with regard to possible anniversary celebrations. A particular focus is on the aspects of partnership that have been built upon to ensure both the sustainability and longevity of the festival as an enduring arts event.

The festival is planned by a committee made up of ten community members, working as part of the Kalbarri Development Association (KDA). The KDA has recognized the importance of not only economic but also of social and cultural development. The president of the committee is also the coordinator of the event, initially working on a part-time basis once funding was secured some of her work is salaried (three days a week) but she still works full time on the planning and implementation of the event. There is a strong level of community participation with community members across a broad spectrum being involved[1]. In the period leading up to the first festival drama groups, writers and locals were invited to write and create pieces that would be performed. The naming of the festival not only reflects the vibrancy of the arts included in the event, but also connects to the promotion of the *kalabari* spice available in the local area, as it is traditional in Australia for bush plants to be used as spices and there is increasing interest in their contemporary use. The festival thus also included a Trade Winds Tasting Tent.

View from the event coordinator

The event coordinator Bec (Rebecca) Millar sees the Zest Festival as 'a community art(s) practice between the public and private spheres in response to heritage in multiple cultures' (personal correspondence). Generated by the community the event was triggered by an international event (the anniversary of the Zuytdorp shipwreck) yet the local response, using performance and related arts (including storytelling) is able to cross both indigenous and European cultures in a contemporary response to a historic event. The event coordinator speaks of using participatory processes in a creative manner, for example to include all 783 students in the local school in the event by incorporating aspects into the curriculum.[2] In the same way a local arts and crafts group was involved in the festival, in an evolving and synergistic manner. A key focus of the initial event was thus the Chamber of Rhetoric Storytelling Event.

Partnering at the concept stage

Arts festivals depend on a variety of partnerships, which are acknowledged to be important for themed events (Long 2000). Partnerships can be key at the conceptual stage, as partners may be able to contribute to the development of festival concepts and to offer the hope of practical support. The KDA event committee has partnered with local, national and international organizations, from the local school to the national museum to an international museum in the Netherlands; through these partnerships this small community has connected itself with the world.

In addition once the arts event has been conceived sponsorships, both financial and in-kind, will contribute to the realization of the event. The KDA event committee deliberately did not seek financial or in-kind contributions from local businesses, this may happen in the later years of the festival, but by attracting outside sponsorships (the Shire of Northampton, the Australian Research Council Centre of Excellence, Centre for the History of Emotions, and the Western Australian Museum) the festival organizers believe that they are creating a viable foundation for the future.

This arts festival was conceived as an annual event to be offered on a five-year cycle. This time frame significant as it facilitates continuous event improvement. This case the festival has been held once (2012) and at the time of writing implementation plans for the second one (2013) are well underway. While some in the community initially thought that the plans were ambitious, the committee was able to implement a range of activities that resulted in 4,000 people participating in the event in 2012, the first year. This participation is expected to double in the second year (2013). The event is held over a weekend and includes storytelling, art exhibitions, a parade and other arts activities. The Zest Festival was also able to build upon an existing event, Kalbarri's annual Canoe and Cray Carnival, positioning this preexisting event as the inaugural activity for the new event.

Conclusion

This arts festival has been very successful at developing a sound and sustainable community base of support from which to engage in external partnerships and sponsorships. Partnering has created opportunities for the community; in the case of the receipt of artefacts from both national and international museums for example in 2012 artefacts from the Western Australia Museum's Shipwreck Collection were exhibited. In addition as an arts event the festival employs a variety of media that affords the opportunity to engage a broad range of actors from the local community, and a diverse group of sponsors outside of the community. It is also notable that such a small and geographically remote community can mount a sustainable and creative event, not on a one-time basis, but on a planned cycle of five years. This provides an important lesson for other arts events operators, of the benefits of taking a long-term perspective when planning their events.

Arts events venues

Venues or physical settings for arts events will vary immensely, in terms of size, location and function. Arts events may in some cases be held in traditional meeting facilities such as hotels, convention and conference centres, theatres, amphitheatres, stadiums and sports facilities. Hassanien and Crispin (2011) propose a typology of event venues under the themes of strategic, market, physical and activities – demonstrating the diversity in the nature of the event venue industry.

The infrastructure needed to stage an event can be determined by the choice of venue. A purpose-built venue such as an exhibition centre will already have much of the needed infrastructure in place. Non-traditional venues, such as outdoor parks and large industrial warehouses will be lacking in the usual facilities, which will need to be brought in for the purpose. Arts events will also be held within the physical plant and facilities of arts organizations, such as art galleries and museums; or on occasion within the workspaces of the artists themselves, in studios and workshops. In the case of artist's studios an event may be held at one studio or the studios may be linked or bundled together in a studio tour or art walk (du Cros and Jolliffe 2011). These linked venue events typically happen in both urban and rural contexts, on a district, city, town or regional basis in a defined geographical area.

Arts events have the ability to adapt to unusual venues, such as streetscapes, vacant warehouses and other unusual venues. Pop-up art galleries may also be incorporated into spontaneous art events. Arts events may thus be held in facilities not designed for events, such as shopping malls, industrial warehouses and airplane hangars. This mass utilization of unique venues is a trend in particular in contemporary event management. Some venues have also developed as a form of urban renewal, giving new life to old and defunct facilities. An example is the Spinnerei in Leipzig, Germany, an old cotton factory site turned into an arts facility housing over one hundred artists, a community gallery, galleries and supporting businesses hosts an annual Autumn gallery tour event (Spinnerei 2009). Outdoor public spaces such as parks can also be ideal locations for arts events, especially if the events are free to the public. In addition some arts events, in particular arts festivals may be held in a number of venues at a specific geographic location. An example is London Mela, Europe's largest arts festival of South Asian Culture, which is held in eight zones (Goodwin 2010).

The venue for some arts events will be predetermined by the nature of the event and its affiliation, for example in the case of events associated with arts institutions. However, in other situations where a venue needs to be found for an arts event there are a number of considerations including: audience, logistics, scale, ambience and security (Shone and Parry 2004) and in this case an event requirement check list will be useful. It may in fact be necessary to compare a few potential venues to determine the optimum facility for the event in question. This process will involve identifying potential sites and then making a site visit. Important factors to note at this stage will include access to the site by public or private transport, availability of services such as power, washrooms and catering facilities. According to Fenich (2011) the key in dealing with any venue is a fourfold approach consisting of researching, understanding, communicating and verifying.

There are also practical considerations in choosing either an indoor or an outdoor venue, as the outdoor venue will be subject to weather, so in case of rain some enclosures (tents and so on) will have to be organized and in case of severe weather (such as hurricanes) then there will have to be a contingency plan for the postponing and rescheduling of the event. For example in the summer of 2013 The Artist Alley of Uptown Waterloo (Canada) event, scheduled for every other Friday in June and July and the first Friday of the month in August and September, after being rained out several times adopted a 'Rain or Shine!' policy in case of rain using the facilities of the adjoining Waterloo Community Art Centre (Shellenberger 2013).

In fact, weather is acknowledged as a major risk factor for events, as it can affect both turnout and on-site sales (Getz 2012). Timing of arts events is also significant and as many of these events are typically held in summer they are also dependent on good weather. The following case of Kabosh Theatre Company delves into the challenges of using outdoor venues for arts events.

Box 4.2 Kabosh Theatre Company case study

Founded in 1994, Kabosh is a not-for-profit professional theatre company committed to 'challenging the notion of what theatre is and where it takes place' (Kabosh Theatre Company n.d.). It is the only theatre company in the north of Ireland designing and implementing site-specific theatrical events. (In the Republic of Ireland, the Performance Corporation founded in 2004 is taking a similar approach to site-specific theatrical arts events.) The purpose of Kabosh is to tell stories using local histories and a number of media to animate space. The company takes an innovative approach to the creation of arts events that incorporate locals and professionals in delivering a rich experience for participants.

This case focuses on the challenges of planning arts events in outdoor site-specific venues. In particular, the case study will review how Kabosh has used the various neighbourhoods of the city of Belfast as a stage, and employed both local inhabitants and professional actors to tell a story, reflecting trends in using urban settings for heritage tourism (Chang *et al.* 1996). Case studies are useful in the study of tourism products (Xiao and Smith 2006) and the information for this one was developed through participant observation on-site in Belfast, discussions with Kabosh staff members and the use of secondary information and related literature.

Kabosh has delivered a number of theatrical events that have drawn the attention of both audiences and the media (Gray 2010). Kabosh has commissioned site-specific products that reflect, challenge and re-imagine local histories and stories. As of 2013, Kabosh's annual audience is approximately 11,000; with over 600 participants and 200 artists involved in a diverse programme of professional production, cultural tourism and community engagement.

Belfast Bred

The culinary/historical promenade production Belfast Bred traces both the cuisines and history of central Belfast, commissioned from a local playwright Seth Linder, using an actor in character as a former chef's assistant on the Titanic, engaging with the proprietors of food establishments and sampling their food products (see Plate 4.1). The tour was developed initially at the request of the local council, who wanted to achieve a celebratory interpretation of the culinary history of the city for visitors and citizens. The three-hour tour with a ticket price of 25 GBP has been offered annually on Fridays and Saturdays from June to September since 2010. Audience capacity is determined by the number of participants who can comfortably be accommodated in some of the indoor food establishments that are included in the tour, with a typical average of 20 per show. Since the tour ends at Saint George's Market where participants can experience more of Belfast cuisine, open Fridays, Saturdays and Sundays, this in some ways has determined the scheduling. Performances for special events and groups are also scheduled at other times of the year.

The West Awakes

The West Awakes is a political walking tour of the Falls Road area of west Belfast, a major conflict sites during 'The Troubles' (the common term for the ethno-nationalist conflicts in Northern Ireland dated from the late 1960s to the 'Good Friday' agreement of 1998) guided by a representative of either Coiste (walking tours delivered by Republican ex-prisoners), or Taxi Trax (Belfast taxi tours) interspersed with dramatic scenes at five locations, beginning at St. Comgall's School, proceeding to Conway Mill, Cultúrlann (Irish Cultural Centre), the City Cemetery and Milltown Cemetery (see Plate 4.2). The West Awakes involved the commissioning of five separate scenes from four playwrights (Seth Linder, Jimmy McAleavey, Laurence McKeown and Rosaleen Walsh). Delivered by an actress and an actor each small play or scene in the tour, all set pre-1969 the start of the conflict, brings alive the past social and political history of this contested area of west Belfast providing a context for the contemporary post-1969 personal reflections of the tour guide. This product builds on the existing success of the political murals tourism in Belfast (Simone-Charteris and Boyd 2010) employing a tour guide from one of the local political/cultural organizations who is able to convey a direct and authentic experience of 'The Troubles', while adding the theatrical element of interpretation through drama.

Plate 4.1 Belfast Bred beginning of tour (Jolliffe, 2013)

Plate 4.2 The West Awakes actors at the Conway Mill (Jolliffe, 2013)

Impact of Kabosh productions

The deep-rooted history and traditions, of the neighbourhoods chosen as event locations as contested sites of both industry and conflict (Wiedenhoft Murphy 2010), is reflected in the productions themselves. Site-specific theatrical events such as those delivered by Kabosh have logistical issues that must be addressed by both the director and the stage manager who accompanies each tour. Logistical considerations include, weather, keeping the actors warm, notifying actors of the timing of tours and arrival time for the next scene, and possible interference by citizens. Local agreements and permissions also have to be sought out where the outdoor tours briefly enter into indoor spaces and even for some of the external locations – particularly contested, protected or niche user spaces. Delivering a site-specific product mainly in an outdoors venue therefore does have challenges and for the most part necessitates the products being delivered seasonally in better weather.

From a practical perspective, one of the benefits of the type of arts events created by Kabosh is that they do not have to carry the overhead costs of operating a traditional theatre space. The company is also able to develop meaningful experiences with a level of authenticity not possible in traditional theatre, by involving community members alongside professional actors performing locally commissioned pieces in telling the stories. In the post-conflict setting of Belfast (McDowell 2008), Kabosh is not afraid to tackle controversial subjects, such as the root of 'The Troubles' in the north of Ireland – as in the case of *The West Awakes*. The theatre company is acknowledged as contributing to the peace process here through its productions (Maguire 2008).

As arts events, the tours/performances offered by Kabosh are developed, promoted, ticketed, stage managed and evaluated. In addition the company is using new technologies to extend the reach of their performances, having produced two smartphone apps for *Belfast Bred*. International downloads of these apps enable Kabosh to develop new audiences for their work in new media and diversify income streams through app purchases. At the time of the writing of this case (early 2013) a smartphone app for *The West Awakes* tour is in production in cooperation with Coiste, Failte Feirste Thair and the digital media company Design Zoo (Audiences NI 2013). This will be entitled 'Fall's Road' and is the first in a series of apps under the banner 'Streets of Belfast'.

Kabosh also shares with other groups and organizations in both Northern Ireland and the Republic of Ireland who are delivering similar products, as reflected by the Cultural Tourism Showcase day held in March 2013 with funding assistance by the Arts Council of Northern Ireland and the Department for Culture, Arts and Leisure, Northern Ireland, in which Kabosh delivered both *Belfast Bred* and *The West Awakes*. At the event artistic director Paula McFetridge noted that the work of Kabosh in cultural tourism is the result of continued demand from local authorities as well as business and special interest groups and arts organizations looking for ways to increase visitors to their site, building or space. After the event Kabosh invited the participants, who included representatives of local and regional tourist boards and other theatrical and tour groups, to provide feedback on the events, evaluation, which will feed into a continuing export programme of activity for the company.

Summary

In summary, the choice of a venue is very important and critical to the work of Kabosh, as the location inspires the commissioning, scripting and staging, and determines the participation of locals. In addition, the company believes that opening contested space with original drama will assist communities imagine new possibilities for the future – essential for the development of a healthy post-conflict society. Delivering an experience that is mostly in an outdoor setting allows this innovative theatre company to operate sustainably without the burden of the costs of a traditional theatre space, and to deliver experiences with a creative spark that are more authentic, incorporating as they do elements of stories delivered by real people told in their own environments, augmented by short theatrical performances written by local playwrights but yet inspired by local histories, contexts and locales. The case of Kabosh thus provides an excellent example of the use of a sustainable creative advantage in the creation of arts events in Belfast, Northern Ireland.

Partners and sponsors

The funding of arts events is often made possible through partnerships and sponsorships. Despite the historical lack of cooperation between the arts and tourism, due to the differing objectives of the two sectors, partnering is on the increase (Smith 2003). The result of such partnerships, exploiting culture for touristic purposes is noted as a social process linked to identity construction (Page and Connell 2012) that handily includes a consumable commercial product. It is therefore typical for arts events to involve partnerships between different groups. Long (2000) analysed the inter-organizational partnership that developed the concept, organized and managed the arts event, 'Year of Visual Arts', held during 1996 in the north of England. The year aimed to heighten awareness of the arts in the region. Tighe (1986) probed the arts and tourism relationship suggesting that there is opportunity for increased interagency cooperation between arts and tourism entities. In recent times local arts agencies are increasingly being involved in destination management through events that include arts events (Hager and Sung 2012).

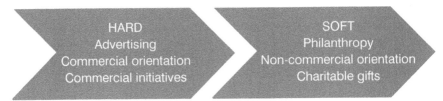

Figure 4.1 Continuum of business support for arts events (adapted from Godfrey, 2006)

Funding for the arts comes from both public and private sources and is in some cases self-generated by arts institutions. Arts events benefit from both the core funding of the agencies that offer events as well as dedicated event-based sponsorship that can come from public and private sources. Public sponsorship ties directly into government policies for the arts (Henderson 2003). Corporate sponsorship can further the objectives of corporations and/or contribute to their social responsibility agendas. O'Hagan and Harvey (2000) studied corporate sponsorship of the arts determining that promotion of company image or name was the main motivation of sponsors. While studying business support for arts in festivals in Britain, Godfrey (2006) identified a range of objectives for business support lying on a continuum with hard commercial marketing objectives at one end and at the other end softer, more community-relevant objectives. This continuum can be applied to the broader field of arts events (Figure 4.1). Godfrey (2006) also noted the hard approach as being high profile and related to short-term objectives whereas the soft approach was low profile and linked to long-term objectives. Research finding such as those discussed here can inform arts events managers who are seeking support for their events.

For arts events sponsorship partnership (with financial or in-kind support) therefore offers a number of benefits, both in terms of branding, attracting audiences and funding. The association with known sponsors can add value to arts events, as the sponsor may bring valuable advice and moral support, in addition to contributing to the cost of staging the event. The following case from New Brunswick, Canada demonstrates how partnership is critical to the creation of arts events.

Box 4.3 Sculpture Saint John, Saint John, New Brunswick, Canada

The first international sculpture symposium to be held in eastern Canada, Sculpture Saint John (SSJ), was held 2 August to 15 September 2012 in Saint John, New Brunswick. In particular this case highlights the support strategies adopted for this arts event in terms of community partners and sponsors. The model for this event, offered under the overall direction of the New Brunswick International Sculpture Symposium Inc., is that of the international sculpture symposiums and dates from the first in Austria in 1959. At that event international and local sculptors were invited to a location to work together for a period of time, to create sculptures that remain as public art in host communities once the artists departed, permanently becoming an integral part of the landscape. The legacy of that first event is that of an international sculpture symposium movement that assists in improving the quality of life for residents and visitors. Sculpture is acknowledged as being important to experiencing urban environment (Smith 1973). The SSJ event therefore very much reflects the ethos of the initial 1959 event in Austria founded by the sculptor Karl Pranti, who, breaking new ground in the arts, invited colleagues, who in turn invited their international sculpture friends to create sculptures in the open air, drawing upon the location for their inspiration (Kley 2011).

Organization

The Saint John event was also influenced by a similar arts event, the Schoodic International Sculpture Symposium (SISS) held biennially since 2007 in Prospect Harbor, Maine, USA (Schoodic International Sculpture Symposium n.d.) (see Plate 4.3). Both the Maine and the New Brunswick symposiums build on the local traditions and history of commercial granite production in this border region of the two countries. In Maine, this production dates back to the 1800s. In New Brunswick, commercial granite quarries date back to the 1840s. These symposiums in Maine and New Brunswick are thus different from some other international sculpture symposiums where stone can be quarried to artists' specifications, in that they highlight historic stonework cultures, and act as agents for regenerating the use of granite from historic local quarries.

Plate 4.3 Sculpture Saint John entrance (Jolliffe, 2012)

These international symposiums are typically organized by local planning committees, in the SSJ case, the New Brunswick International Sculpture Symposium Inc., a not-for-profit incorporated company was set up to take care of the policy directions for the initial sculpture symposium (SSJ) and any subsequent events that might develop in New Brunswick. Planning needs to be done on a long-term basis, with policies adopted for the application by artists to participate, as well as the details of their remuneration and the ownership of the works. Sculpture Saint John is the operating committee that implements the local symposium.

Partnership

Community involvement was a hallmark of the inaugural SSJ symposium held in 2012. Committees were set up in each of the local communities (City of Saint John, Rothesay, Grand Bay, Quispamsis and St. George, and the University of New Brunswick Saint John) where the sculptures would be hosted after the symposium. These committees were also able to assist with in-kind fundraising, recruiting volunteers and hosting the artists and interns as well as the logistics of placing the finished sculptures in each community.

During the inaugural SSJ six international artists carved 120 tons of New Brunswick granite into six sculptures that are now located in the surrounding partner communities who had participated in the planning and implementation of the event. This was an interactive arts event held on the waterfront (former Coast Guard site). The public was encouraged to visit often during the process of creating the impressive pieces of art, interacting with the artists, and with local interns (arts students) assisting the artists. The event is acknowledged by organizers to have been the largest arts event in New Brunswick during 2012 with over 35,000 visitors (Sculpture Saint John n.d.). Following this success a second symposium is now planned for 2014, with the expanded participation of sculptors, from six in 2012 to eight in 2014. This event will assist with the goal of working towards an international sculpture trail between New Brunswick and Maine. This is planned as a cultural tourism product, which will ultimately be supported by an International Sculpture Trail map and smartphone app. In other areas of the world, for example in China at Changchun, international sculpture symposiums have directly contributed to the development of international sculpture parks, which remain as arts attractions long after the symposiums are completed (Fusco 2003). The SISS has created a Maine sculpture tour has already been created based on the sculptures in place, and working in cooperation SSJ is thus actively participating in creating an International Sculpture Trail between New Brunswick and Maine linking the sculptures produced by the two symposia. These international sculpture symposia as arts events are therefore contributing to the development of arts experiences and arts tourism products, long after the events are over.

Sponsorship

For SSJ, a unique approach was taken to sponsorship, with over half of the CDN$400,000 budget having been derived from in-kind contributions from local individuals, companies and organizations (Plate 4.4). The event organizer acknowledges that this approach was possible because of the small size of Saint John and the network of the members of the committees implementing the symposium.[3] At the municipal level, local sponsoring communities provided a direct contribution of CDN$15,000 each. Categories of funding recognition were established, including major sponsor, Rodin sponsor, Donatello sponsor, Moore sponsor, apprentice sponsor and friend. In addition donations of time and talent were recognized. A key contribution of CDN$40,000 from the Province of New Brunswick was announced just days before the launch of the symposium. The provincial minister of Culture, Tourism and Healthy Living, Trevor Holder indicated:

> Sculpture Saint John contributes significantly to our cultural landscape, it also provides an opportunity for worldwide artists and a group of young local sculptors to work together, offering these budding artists the chance to learn more about their craft. Together, they create timeless works of art that are made accessible to the public. Opportunities to enjoy art through sculptures contribute to a better quality of life, and our province is committed to helping this symposium thrive.
>
> (Sculpture Saint John, n.d.)

Plate 4.4 Sponsored van, Sculpture Saint John (Jolliffe, 2012)

Plate 4.5 Last day, Sculpture Saint John (Jolliffe, 2012)

A high level of community involvement was certainly essential to the success of SSJ, both official and at an informal level. Due to the costs of running the symposium, securing and servicing a site for the creation of the sculptures, funding the artists (honorarium, travel, accommodation and meals) and the local interns/apprentices (honorarium, accommodation and meals), as well as the cost of securing and transporting the granite and providing tools for working with it, it was necessary to achieve a solid financial basis for the symposium. The symposium organizers were able to accomplish this due to their creative approach to fundraising through in-kind contributions. The time contribution of volunteers was also necessary to the efficient operation of the symposium, at the same time facilitating a high level of community involvement (see Plate 4.5).

Lessons

Challenges in organizing SSJ included the level of funding required and the scale of the infrastructure and equipment needed for the creation of the sculptures. In addition, detailed planning was needed in order to select both the artists and the interns and to create opportunities for community involvement during the process of creation. As Diana Alexander, Chair of SSJ indicated after the initial symposium:

This symposium was a beginning but not an end. Look for us in 2014 as we continue to build on what we have begun toward the creation of an International Sculpture Trail between New Brunswick and Maine. When we encourage public art, we also encourage creativity and thoughtfulness and build a richer future for all of our citizens.

(Sculpture Saint John, n.d.)

Establishing an overall legal entity and building a solid financial plan are particular lessons this case can offer for the planning of other arts events. By involving artists, sponsors and the public, creating opportunities for arts education and improving the urban landscapes of the participating communities the organizers of SSJ have thus laid a sustainable and creative foundation for the future of this arts event.

Community involvement

Communities and their members are key stakeholders, partners and sponsors in the development of arts events; in many cases community members form the majority of the audience for such events. These events can in fact contribute to nurturing a sense of place and identity for communities. Arts festivals and events that evolve to represent the interests of community members and organizations are thus those that endure, as in the following case of the OK.Quoi! Contemporary Arts Festival. Museums and arts galleries have traditionally played a role in community education (Chadwick 1980) and arts festivals provide a vehicle for fulfilling this mandate, as reflected in this case by the participation of Sackville's Struts Gallery and the Faucet Arts Centre in bringing new aspects of the contemporary arts to public notice.

Box 4.4 OK.Quoi?! Contemporary Arts Festival, Sackville, New Brunswick, Canada

The small university town (Mount Allison University) of Sackville, New Brunswick promotes itself as the cultural crossroads of the Maritimes, as reflected by being awarded Cultural Capital of Canada in 2008 and Municipality of the Arts, 2003. Here, OK. Quoi?!, a contemporary arts festival encompasses a concept that engages a diversity of media (both new and traditional), numbers of artists (over 40), a substantial list of sponsors (over 20) and a large group of volunteers. It has been held for a number of years (2012 was the eighth year) not within a traditional gallery setting, but spread out over the downtown core of the town during a five-week period. The concept for the event has evolved over the years reflecting a strong sense of place and home, with artists converging on Sackville for the festival, is characteristic of cultural movements in the town (McCabe 1998).

The individual events within the 2012 festival included exhibitions, performances and workshops. For example, a key exhibition, organized by Sackville artist Peter Manchester, was the Struts Puts exhibition, an indoor mini golf course with local artists invited to contribute various holes (see Plate 4.6). Speaking of the festival, Amanda Fauteaux, program manager at the Struts Gallery said 'it is really dedicated to contemporary art. It has a strong base. It's a festival where you can see not only artists from the region, but also artists from much farther away' (Smith 2012a). In concept the festival thus strongly aligns itself with the contemporary arts movement (see Plate 4.7).

Local involvement

Several not-for-profit arts organizations act as core organizers, specifically The Struts Gallery and Faucet Arts Centre with other groups partnering and participating, such as the music festival, Sappyfest, that occurs downtown concurrently on a week-end within the timeframe of the OK.Quoi?! festival. Another parallel event running within the festival is the Tête-à-Tête Media Talks, a series of media arts talks geared to artists and the public that includes roundtable discussions, screenings, artist's talks, installations, performances and workshops. This level of partnering and cooperation between different groups in a small-town setting is a key characteristic of the festival, creating a strong sense of place that draws in both artists and visitors, as well as being somewhat of a homecoming for artists trained here at Mount Allison University.

Conclusion

There are a number of local supporters of the festival (individuals, businesses, local organizations and volunteers), but it is significant that governments and cultural agencies at all levels also provide funding including the town of Sackville, artsnb (New Brunswick Arts Board), the New Brunswick Department of Wellness, Culture and Sport, the Canada Council for the Arts, and Canadian Heritage (the latter two being federal agencies). This case therefore demonstrates the value of partnerships and sponsorships at various levels, ensuring the successful implementation of an event concept for a small-town contemporary arts event.

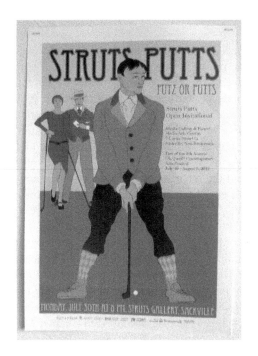

Plate 4.6 Struts Putts' poster, OK.Quoi?! Festival (Jolliffe, 2012)

Plate 4.7 City Mail Art Project, OK.Quoi?! Festival (Jolliffe, 2012)

Conclusion

To be creative and sustainable arts events need to be systematically planned, both in relation to public policy contexts and to constituent communities and with consideration for event logistics. Planning will include concept development; choosing venues; budgets, partners and sponsors whereas implementation will take into account human resources; marketing and promotion; risk management and evaluation. For events to gain the sustainable creative advantage (SCA) outlined earlier in Chapter 1, they will need to be planned by representative arts agencies and groups, with close attention to the needs of both target markets and communities and the interests of both governments and potential corporate sponsors. In order to engage audiences for arts events, concepts will need to be innovative and adaptable with a realistic assessment of success in delivery. A venue can contribute directly to the success of an arts event and the choice of facilities, from a broad range of possibilities (indoor or outdoor, purpose-built or adaptive, traditional or non-traditional) should reflect the event concept and theme as well as its objectives for partners and sponsors. Achieving a solid financial grounding in terms of securing partners and sponsors and involving the community at the planning stages will also lay the foundation for an arts event before it moves to the implementation stage, to be discussed next in Chapter 5.

5 Lessons learned from implementing arts events

Implementing an arts event is a complex endeavour. It is important that such events are executed within a systematic framework (Figure 5.1). Operational aspects are considered here in terms of the carrying out of events while maximizing their benefits and impacts to a broad range of interests. While events differ greatly in terms of their size, complexity and frequency, this chapter includes an illustrative variety of arts event cases (literary to visual arts to general arts to music) from a number of jurisdictions in relation to specific implementation issues, providing readers with a best practice resource and ideas for implementing creative and sustainable events in the arts.

Getz (2008) defines the festival as a public themed celebration. In particular arts festivals are noted to be celebratory in relation to a theme, using human creative skill in areas such as poetry, painting and music, and may in addition involve celebrating an artist, artists or an historical art event (Williams and Bowdin 2007). Cases of festivals are thus highlighted here from Europe, Asia and North America,

Figure 5.1 Framework for implementing an arts event

as they are a typical type of arts event likely to include a multiplicity of activities within them, thus leading to complexity in implementation. In addition several cases of exhibitions from both Europe and Asia are profiled, illustrating a range of issues including access and merchandising

Chapter 4 dealt with the structural and foundational aspect of planning for events that includes the development of the event concept and the identification of activities, resources and stakeholder participants. This chapter deals with the processes of implementing an event, in terms of analysing (financials, risks and evaluations) and mobilizing (leadership and human resources) and coordinating (scheduling, marketing and promotion, and merchandising).

Financial/risk management and evaluation

Risk management is the process of assessing, analysing, mitigating and controlling risk (Fenich 2011). According to the Arts Council of England (n.d.) risk management can be part of a self-evaluation process for arts entities, with key assessment questions being: (1) how do we identify, monitor and mitigate potential risks; and (2) how do we minimize the impact of risks when they do occur? The four stages of risk management are: (1) preparedness, (2) mitigation, (3) response and (4) recovery (Fenich 2011). Early in the planning process arts events planners should thus first conduct a risk assessment and analysis to assist in identifying mitigation measures. For events, risk management is essentially ensuring a safe environment (Goldblatt 1998). It will also be essential to managing risks for the not-for-profit boards and organizations and their members who are running arts events.

For every art event there will be both legal and ethical considerations. Arts events organizers will need to know how to read and design contracts, also referred to as agreements, memorandums of understanding, or letters of intent or proposal. For larger arts events insurance against event cancellation or postponement can be taken out and for all events public liability insurance is necessary. Other insurance considerations will include coverage for borrowed equipment and personal liability for staff, committee members and volunteers. The cost of insurance will need to be included when budgeting. Advice is often given by cultural agencies for insuring 'public art' a category under which arts events could fall. It will be important to have the relevant local permits and licenses. Overall managing risk will be an important part of implementing the event, taking into consideration preparedness, mitigation, response and recovery (Fenich 2011). Having conducted a risk assessment as part to the event planning process will assist in identifying mitigation procedures embedded into contracts, insurance, and security arrangements.

Once a site for an arts event is chosen, the event organizer will need to deal with appropriate permits, licenses and insurance (Page and Connell 2012). If an arts event is to be held in a public space there may be local (municipal) regulations for permits or licenses. For instance, a permit will be required if the catering for the event is to include liquor in certain jurisdictions. The individuals, agencies and organizations putting on the event will need to ensure that they have public liability insurance. Contracts will also need to be signed with the artists and performers participating in the arts event. There will also need to be documents signed between the arts events organizers and sponsors. All of these arrangements will be encapsulated in a contract, a document that may also be referred to a letter of agreement, memorandum of understanding, letter of intent, or proposal. When signed by two cooperating parties this becomes a contract. According to Fenich (2011:211) the essential aspects of a contract are: an offer by one party, acceptance of the offer as presented, and consideration, for example of price or other benefits. Contract offers can be terminated prior to acceptance, for example if not signed within a reasonable and stated time period. Contracts are typically binding upon being signed by both parties. There also need to be a process for resolving disputes regarding the contract should they arise.

As identified earlier in Chapter 4, weather is a major risk to outdoor arts events. However, arts events managers who arrange alternate indoor settings to be used, for example in case of rain, are employing risk management. The case cited in Chapter 4 of The Artist Alley of Uptown Waterloo (Canada) event demonstrates that arts organizations do not always have a contingent weather plan in place for their arts events, as the event was rained out on several occasions, before an alternate location was put into place to mitigate the impact of adverse weather (Shellenberger 2013).

Arts events, especially large events, are typically expensive to run, an example being the Edinburgh Festival, one of the leading events in the arts in the UK. For events of this nature, besides fixed expenses related to the venue, there are operational costs, artists must be paid, staff must be paid and there may be associated vendors. Marketing and promotion costs must likewise be taken into account. Catherwood and Van Kirk (1992) divide the costs of an event into the four main categories of (1) operation or production costs, (2) venue/site rental (3) promotion and (4) talent. It is common, especially for larger events, to undertake feasibility studies that will include a conceptual estimate (ballpark figure) of the costs for planning purposes. A quote or definitive estimates is vital, some larger events will put out a tender for services required (Catherwood and Van Kirk1992:334).

Sponsorships, both in-kind and in cash, previously discussed in Chapter 4, will be an important factor in achieving a balanced budget for the arts event. Arts event organizers must therefore be able to show the benefits that sponsorship will bring to potential sponsors. Managing obligations to and benefits for sponsors will be an important aspect of implementing the event. Frost *et al.* (2009) note that the corporatist model of events focuses on operational planning in order to satisfy the objectives of formal stakeholders, for example sponsors.

Budgeting is an essential aspect of planning for an arts event and ensuring that there is a financial platform for creating an event with a sustainable creative advantage. Once the event concept has been developed and the venue chosen then budgets will need to be prepared and related funding strategies adopted. The budget will thus have been developed in line with the process of developing an event concept reviewed in Chapter 4. Getz (1997) indicates that event managers use the budget first, to forecast the financial future of the event, second, to help set priorities and plan and third, to manage spending within set limits. It is therefore important to have a financial timetable, a process that will contribute to assessing the financial feasibility of an event, as well as to effective management through the event implementation stage (Watt 1998). Financial operating structures need to be established, some arts event structures will include either a financial controller or a finance committee. Annual and recurring arts events can use past experience to prepare realistic budgets. In these cases Getz (1997) indicates that the previous year's financial statement will provide a starting point for the budgeting process.

Evaluation needs to be built in at the planning stage to be integral to the arts event and ongoing, before, during and after the event. Evaluating not only the operation of events but also the visitor experience will allow for arts events organizers to undertake a continual process of improvement, as adjustments in programming can be made based on the immediacy of results from a continual process of evaluation. Establishing key measures of success to be evaluated, beyond the traditional technique of assessing attendance statistics, will be valuable in the forward planning of events in the arts. This will also be useful in reporting to stakeholders, partners and sponsors who may be assessing the impact of their role in the events, a process that will influence further participation.

Evaluation of arts events, in particular of arts festivals is now commonly required by funders and sponsors and is an important tool for event management (Williams and Bowdin 2007). Bowdin (2010) identifies three key periods when it is necessary to undertake evaluation of an event. This includes pre-event assessment (formative) and post-event evaluation (summative) stages; in addition evaluation will be on going during the event. Goldblatt (2002) indicates the event management process is a spiral, with the first phase relating to the last (evaluation) as evaluation is an integral part of the process of managing events. Watt (1998) indicates that end evaluation is vital and must be carried out, using both hard (objectives – tangible and quantitative) and soft (processes – intangible and qualitative) indicators.

While events have traditionally been evaluated for both their economic and social impacts evaluation is now also including participant experience and service quality (Laws and Beaven 2006). This trend addresses in part a concern expressed by Getz (2008) that research is needed on customer satisfaction of events. Evaluating the customer experience can provide valuable information that will be useful to arts planners undertaking future events.

Admissions to an arts event may be either on a fee-paying/revenue-generating basis or free of charge, or alternately a combination of both approaches may be undertaken. Admission fees are commonly charged for cultural attractions, including events, although where events are local in nature there can be some dissonance on the part of locals about paying fees and in some cases dual fee structures are implemented, one for locals and the other for visitors (Timothy 2011).

The following case of the Bookworm Literary Festival illustrates an approach to administering admissions, in the case of a gated (entrance fee payment) English language literary arts festival in China (PRC).

Box 5.1 Bookworm International Literary Festival case study

Background

This festival, based in Chengdu has been held annually six times over the since 2005. In 2013 the Bookworm (International) Literary Festival (BLF) was also held in Beijing and Suzhou. This independently funded arts event has been created by the owners of the Chengdu-based Bookworm Café and curated by Catherine Pratt (Kidd 2013). The café offers food in a literary setting, complemented by a small English-language bookshop, a lending library and an event space hosting regular live music performances and readings. This is a private business that also operates now in Beijing and Suzhou. In the case of Chengdu, in a city with a population of over ten million (*China Today* 2013) and an expatriate population of around 20,000, the Bookworm Café contributes to the quality of life of the expatriates in the city by offering cross-cultural programming while also acting as a destination attraction though listings in English language magazines and tourist literature. Visiting the Bookworm Café, it is evident that the patrons include both expatriates and locals. In addition the BLF, featuring for the most part authors who write and publish in English about China, contributes to the active arts scene in the city of Chengdu.

Implementation

This case examines the implementation of the festival in particular as a gated arts event, that is an event with an entrance fee. Charging a fee offers a number of advantages, the organizers of this event are guaranteed a dedicated audience, the issuing of tickets provides a way to manage and estimate attendance, and in an establishment where food is served, numbers can contribute to menu planning and attendees can boost restaurant sales. The BLF also demonstrates flexibility in pricing, offering both tickets to individual events at 50 RMB and a complete festival pass at 400 RMB. Selling tickets also makes it possible to forecast attendance (Putler and Lele 2003) and to track participation as a form of evaluating the success and financial sustainability of the event. Entrance to each event also includes a glass of beer, wine or a soft drink; this complimentary beverage serves to offer hospitality to the event participants and to stimulate food sales for the café. In addition when authors read copies of their books are for sale, some publishers are thus involved in the BLF as sponsors and the Bookworm Café makes a small profit on sales.

The owners of the Bookworm Café have developed their event over time, and since it is offered annually they have time in between events to scout for authors to participate in each upcoming festival. The line-up for the sixth annual BLF in 2013 consisted of nineteen event segments offered over several weeks in March, including panel discussions, author talks, performances, workshops and demonstrations. Author involvement and enthusiasm is essential to the success of this literary arts event, as evidenced by the interviews with two of the authors (Derek Sandhaus and Jen Lin-Liu) (*Chengdoo CityLife Magazine* 2013). Some of the segments were participatory, for example the event from author Derek Sandhaus reading from his book *China Drinks* included tasting of the alcoholic beverage *baijiu*, and author Alison Lester used her book *Write on Kids* as the basis of a workshop to help children from four to eight years old to write and draw about their own lives. Overall, the festival organizers see their event as contributing to the arts scene in Chengdu:

> BLF is a forum for literature, thought and debate. Every year the authors who visit Chengdu comment on the warm welcome and keen engagement with their work that they experience from the Chengdu audience and festival volunteers.
>
> (Bookworm International Literary Festival 2013)

Sponsorship

The BLF benefited from the contribution of main sponsors, associate sponsors, local Chengdu sponsors and media sponsors. This broad level of support ensures a wide-ranging participation in the event and communication of event specifics through media channels, as well as contributing financially to putting the event into place. The delivery of the festival is also made possible by the involvement of a group of enthusiastic volunteers and the support of the regular expatriate clientele of the café. This arts event will also be of interest to the growing number of tourists visiting Chengdu, particularly those cultural tourists interested in the arts and literature, as arts festivals are recognized as an essential part of urban tourism (Quinn 2010).

Conclusion

As an arts event the BLF offers lessons about the progression of a themed festival over time, with a loyal following predominately made up of Chengdu Chinese and local expats as well as volunteers the event organizers have been able to develop a rich, creative and yet sustainable programme that is supported by sponsors, authors, participants and volunteers. As a gated event, the ticketing serves multiple functions, including creating a revenue stream for the complementary businesses of restaurant/café, bookshop and event venue operated by the Bookworm Café. The ticketing approach also offers insight into the use of ticketing at events with admission or entrance fees to manage demand for arts events. This case also demonstrates the value of developing ancillary streams of support from a broad-based range of stakeholders in order to ensure the sustainability of an arts event.

The Bookworm Literary Festival has likewise built on the network created by the festival hosted at the three Bookworm Cafés in Beijing, Suzhou and Chengdu with an outreach in the form of the *New York Times* BLF Literary Caravan (Bookworm Literary Festival n.d.). This project reaching many other cities in China, is increasing the total number of event venues to over 200, spreading the word of the paid festival through this parallel program.

Timeline and production scheduling

On-site management of arts events will depend on a timeline-production schedule, described by Goldblatt (2002:190) consisting of the timeline, a sequential list of tasks that take part before and after the event, and the production schedule, a detailed list of tasks with specific start up and stop times from event setup to delivery. Since events consist of many elements that must be coordinated, the use of a timeline-production schedule is acknowledged by Goldblatt (2002) to contribute to improving event performance, and financial effectiveness. Scheduling will in addition need to take account of catering management and audio-visual effects management (including video), as well as the direction of artists and performers.

As noted earlier, some arts events will be ticketed or fee-paying, others will be free or 'ungated' with revenue having come from sponsors and partners. In the case of ticketed arts events, a model for the forecasting of ticket prices and sales has been proposed by Putler and Lele (2003) and customer loyalty to ticket distribution channels has been investigated (Laws and Beaven 2006). Timed ticketing can be used as a means of controlling the visitor flow to an arts event, such as an exhibition, for example in the case of the blockbuster Leonardo da Vinci exhibition at the National Gallery in London, England in 2011 (Holloway and Humphries 2002) discussed in more detail in the case below. Timed tickets can be beneficial in preventing crowding, particularly at large art exhibitions, by spreading out demand, in the case of arts institutions such ticketing to special exhibitions may encourage the greater use of other facilities such as shops, restaurants, and regular exhibitions.

Monitoring event progress, dealing with contingencies and shut down logistics are all part of scheduling an event. A pre-event briefing of staff and volunteers can review any changes in scheduling, as well as outlining measures for dealing with any possible changes during the event. Daily briefings can contribute to the efficient implementation of event activities, while contributing to solving operational issues as they develop. A post event briefing will contribute to the process of evaluating an arts event.

The following case of a blockbuster exhibition profiles an arts event that is complex in terms of planning, design and scheduling, while also highlighting a number of aspects of ticketing, managing the visitor flows and improving the experience.

Box 5.2 Leonardo da Vinci Exhibition case study

As museums have become popularized, large thematic exhibitions (referred to as blockbusters) have been developed to create a new audience base, and to attract both visitor numbers and funders, as museums sought to strengthen their fiscal foundations (Karp *et al.* 2006). A characteristic of these contemporary blockbuster exhibitions is their inauguration and design by large museums and a touring circuit for the most part to the cultural centres of developed countries such as New York, London and Paris, rarely reaching the centres of less developed countries (Karp *et al.* 2006). One of the themes tried as a focus of these blockbusters was of treasures never or rarely seen, a focus reflected in this case of the Leonardo da Vinci Exhibition put together by London's National Gallery. The exhibition, entitled 'Leonardo da Vinci: Painter at the Court of Milan', was designed to be circulated as well to other locations.

Visitor management

As mentioned earlier in this chapter it is typical for visiting these blockbuster exhibitions to be managed through timed ticketing, as this is a measure to prevent crowding, while allowing as many people as possible to view the exhibition. In the case of the Leonardo da Vinci inaugural exhibition showing at London's National Gallery (November 2011 to February 2012), while there were timed tickets to this exhibit (as is the normal practice with blockbuster exhibitions), the gallery decided to drastically limit the numbers admitted to improve the visitor experience and prevent crowding. The number of visitors was thus set at 180 every thirty minutes versus the usual 230 (Selka 2012). However, in an effort to increase access and fulfil demand they also decided to lengthen the gallery hours to give more people a chance to visit, increasing capacity by twenty per cent. These developments were fully reported in the media, documenting somewhat of a repositioning of goals in managing a blockbuster for the gallery, from wanting to develop and increase audiences and achieve financial support, to improving the visitor experience for those attending the exhibition.

Arts education

For large and long-established art galleries who have a mandate in arts education, these blockbuster exhibitions also provide a valuable tool for stimulating an interest in art in students through related educational programs and suggestions for school-based activities that can be scheduled alongside of the exhibitions. Galleries are now able to provide online resources such as guides to exhibitions that teachers can use with students, either in preparation for gallery visits or independently. As large institutions that are self-funded (such as the Royal Academy in London) continue to mount blockbuster exhibitions there are discussions in the arts community about the value of these exhibitions to their institutions and their publics (Selka 2012).

Conclusion

Blockbusters such as the one profiled in this case demonstrate forms of inclusiveness (increasing access to art to new and larger audiences) and at the same time, by their very location in large cultural centres with hefty ticket prices, are still reflective of the exclusive remit of the traditional art galleries and museums.

Human resources

An increasing understanding of the importance of human resources in both the arts and events fields is directly applicable to arts events. For example, in Canada the Ontario Council of the Arts has developed an *HR Handbook for the Arts* (Ontario Council of the Arts n.d.). In the area of events management, human resources are recognized to be pivotal to success. Arts events organizers will need to determine what kind of event coordination arrangement is needed. Will the event be coordinated in-house for example by a committee or alternately will external consultants be employed? Those planning arts events will need to assess their internal capacity for event planning and implementation and it will be useful to identify elements of event staging, where external assistance may be required.

It therefore takes human resources, either on a paid or volunteer basis – or most often a combination of both, to implement an arts event such as a performance, exhibition of a festival. A core group of either paid staff or a volunteer committee will need to be in place in the long term to plan for and then implement and follow up after the event. In many cases arts festivals are professionally managed, of over 500 arts festivals identified in the UK over 60 per cent are professionally managed (Williams and Bowdin 2007). Event management is the process of being professionalized, however identity as a profession has not yet solidified, at least as reflected by a recent study of event organizations in the UK, that included the British Arts Festival Organization (Thomas and Thomas 2013).

Arts management is being developed as a modern field of management (Bendixen 2000). Postulating that arts management has a focus on skills required to construct, develop and stabilize cultural environments in the arts. Dewey (2004) identifies a paradigm shift from arts policy and management to a broader based concept of cultural administration. Applying this concept to the management of arts events, administrators will need to be sensitive to the arts, with the skills necessary to develop events with the sustainable creative advantage (SCA) that we postulated earlier in the book. Dewey's (2004) paradigm shift towards cultural administration is reflected by an increase in training opportunities in administering the arts, including relevant event management programs.

In smaller communities with limited resources, the contributions of volunteers are especially important in making an arts event a reality, for annual events this is especially important in contributing to the viability of an event year after year. In some cases, therefore, volunteers may be both managing and staffing the events. Derrett (2009) posits that festivals represent a human ecosystem that nurtures resilience in smaller regional communities. Hede and Rentschler (2007) profiled mentoring of festival managers in rural Australia examining a pilot scheme put forward by a regional arts agency and concluding that mentoring is beneficial to both enhance the management and focus the artistic directions of the festivals.

Since much activity will be concentrated during the time period immediately leading up to, during and immediately following an arts event, this is where increased levels of staffing are needed and groups of volunteers are often enlisted to provide assistance with information, directions, security and the various services that surround an event. Involving and keeping event volunteers is acknowledged as a key challenge for the organizers of cultural festivals (Smith and Lockstone 2009). Recruitment, selection and retention of volunteers are thus key issues for the organizers of arts events.

Turning to the case study of the Reykjavik Arts Festival (Iceland), a large, diverse, and professionally managed festival is profiled. This long-running festival has been held annually over the last three decades. This is reflected in the stability of the festival organization and management that ensures consistency from year to year. Alongside a core of professional staff volunteers are beginning to play a role in the festival.

Box 5.3 Reykjavik Arts Festival case study

The Reykjavik Arts Festival (RAF) is one of a number of arts festivals organized annually in Iceland (Sigurðardóttir and Young 2011) and is referred to as the country's premier cultural festival. Established in 1969, the event was held biennially from 1970 until 2004, and annually since then. The festival is scheduled every May for two weeks with the programme including a number of exhibitions as well as concert, dance, theatre and opera performances. While a primary focus is on the past and contemporary culture of Iceland, the festival is also noted to host many international artists and performers. The theme of the 2013 festival was 'on the creative space where the arts intersect; on new works and reinterpretations of older works; on innovation; and on history as a source of inspiration' (Reykjavik Arts Festival, 2013).

Operations

The RAF is operated by a not-for-profit organization, whose main purpose is to organize an annual arts festival. It is governed by a board of directors of three members and led by a professional team headed by an artistic director who has been appointed by the board, consisting of the Minister of Culture, the mayor of Reykjavik and a member from the Council of Representatives. Presiding over the festival in alternating years is the Minister of Culture and the mayor. From a human resources perspective, this stable governing model and professional team contribute to the successful operation of the event. In addition volunteers have begun to play a role in the festival, for example, through allied projects organized by SEEDS, an Icelandic non-governmental volunteer organization set up to promote intercultural understanding.

The principal source of financing is from the government and city council. This is supplemented by revenues from admissions and by sponsorships, although levels of sponsorship have declined in the period following the financial crisis of 2008. However, with public funding the event, nonetheless, has a stable financial base and is able to operate on a sustainable basis from year to year. The tourism policy of the city (2011–2020) supports the importance of the development of festivals and events for tourism to the city, especially in terms of developing a four-season destination (City of Reykjavik 2011). The city is actively involved in producing many of the festivals, including the RAF.

Impact

As a sustainable event, the RAF plays an important role in supporting development of the creative arts sector in Iceland. It supports the development of a national culture and identity, however, at the same time it allows for cross-fertilization, through exposing Icelandic artists and audiences to international artists. The event is noted for its diversity in terms of coverage of the arts and participating artists and for the commissioning of new works. For example:

> Opening with a newly commissioned work in the central area of Reykjavik harbor, the RAF will feature nearly 600 artists from more than 30 countries taking part or having their works presented in museums, libraries and concert halls across the city.
>
> (Iceland Naturally n.d.)

The RAF thus demonstrates the sustainable creative advantage postulated for the development of arts events (Chapter 1).

Conclusion

This long-running arts festival consequently contributes to Iceland's vibrant arts scene for the benefit of both locals and visitors. In an island nation that is geographically isolated, the festival has also served well in connecting Icelandic artists with those from other parts of the world and in introducing Icelandic artists to international visitors.

Leadership

Event leadership is an important aspect of the arts event, for staff and volunteers will need to be trained and to have clear directions as to their responsibilities (Goldblatt 1998). Event leaders can be professionals or volunteers, and in the latter case it is important that these leaders have access to professional development opportunities within local arts and events communities. A leadership model for events is outlined by Smith and Peterson (1988). The event manager is in effect the producer of the arts event, sometimes referred to as the artistic director, as in the following case of the Belfast Festival at Queen's, this level of direction ensures that a creative remit of these festivals is fulfilled.

This case profiles an annual arts festival that was initially established by a student in 1962, and now has professional staff directing it, highlighting various aspects of the professionalization of the festival, including the hiring of consultants to rebrand their website, the introduction of online sales and actions to deal with a funding crisis in 2007.

Box 5.4 Belfast Festival at Queen's case study

This annual festival was first held at Queen's University, Belfast, Northern Ireland, initiated by a student, Michael Emmerson, in 1962. From its earliest beginnings as a small festival, it grew through the 1960s and 1970s to a two-week-long arts event, now held at several venues across the city of Belfast, including; the Queen's Film Theatre, the Mandela Hall, the Grand Opera House and the Waterfront Hall. The festival has evolved to cover a wide variety of aspects of the arts, including visual arts, political debates/discourse, theatre, dance, literature, comedy, classical, jazz, folk and popular music. The festival is routinely covered on an exclusive basis by BBC Northern Ireland (BBC Northern Ireland 2013).

Moving towards professional management

So how did a festival established by one student develop to one that now has professional staff directing it? Over the years, from its base at Queen's University Belfast, the festival has grown and various aspects have drawn on professional expertise to improve both the functioning and viability of the festival. For example, in 2004, the festival hired a consultant to help with the rebranding of its website and the functioning of e-commerce online. Funding from the Arts Council of Northern Ireland allowed for the introduction of online box office software, in an effort to encourage online sales. In 2007, the festival had a funding crisis, and the university introduced a 'Save Belfast Festival' campaign. The results were temporary government funding for the 2007 festival and subsequently a grant over

---

three years (Quinn 2007). Early in 2008 the Ulster Bank Group followed with a three-year sponsorship deal. These funding packages were noted as a new beginning for the festival that had previously been underfunded (McReary 2008). As a result the festival is now named the Ulster Bank Festival at Queen's. By 2012, the annual attendance was reported as being around 60,000 (Belfast Festival at Queen's n.d.).

The context for the transition of the Belfast Queen's Festival from a small student-initiated event to a full-scale professionally administered event now billed as the largest arts event in Northern Ireland are found in part in its location within a university that to a certain extent has provided the infrastructure and the continuity for the festival to flourish and grow. This is reflected in the Acting University President's welcome to the festival in 2013:

> Last year we delivered Festival 50, our most successful to date and one, which served as a showcase for the best of Queen's and Northern Ireland. This year, we welcome our new Festival Director, Richard Wakely. His creativity, extensive knowledge and significant experience with international arts, will bring a further rich dimension to one of Northern Ireland's premier Festivals. In this 51st edition, Richard offers us a glimpse of how the Festival will evolve and grow with a diverse and rich programme of contemporary events featuring international and local artists and an emphasis on taking work right across the city in partnership with a range of like-minded community organizations.
>
> (Belfast Festival at Queen's n.d.)

The quote demonstrates the pivotal role of the university in the continued operation of the festival, but also the import of having a professional and creative director on board. Director Shan McAena took over the job of director of the festival early in 2012 followed by Richard Wakely in 2013.

Conclusion

Healthy funding for the arts in both Northern Ireland in general and Belfast in particular has also contributed to festival scene in the city and the Belfast Festival at Queen's has been able to draw from government arts funding to improve its product and at times to sustain its operation.

Marketing and promotion

Planning for marketing is integral to the implementation of the arts event. As mentioned in Chapter 4, marketing will be informed by the market research that has been undertaken for the arts event, as any subsequent advertising and promotion will be aimed to reach the target market for the event. According to

Watt (1998) market research can help to plan an effective marketing strategy and to analyse how effective it may be.

Another essential aspect of developing an arts event at the planning stage is adopting strategies for both marketing and promotion. The activity of marketing links the individual arts events with its audience, while promotion can help to expand the potential audience. The foundation of these activities is market research so that the organizers understand the audience for the event. An audience profile will guide the tone and nature of both the marketing activities, creating a profile and demand for the event, and outlining possible marketing and promotion activities.

However as indicated by Colbert (2003), the marketing process in the arts is different in that it starts with the creative product, that cannot be altered to fulfil the needs of the consumer, thus most arts products try to attract appropriate audiences to the art form, that in the case of the arts event can be nurtured and retained for future events. In some jurisdictions, public agencies have been set up to develop and expand audiences for the arts, such as in Northern Ireland (Audiences NI 2013).

Marketing research should clearly identify the target groups relevant to a specific arts event. This information will support the event-planning process and will influence the marketing strategy. Since the target groups may vary immensely – for example, including sponsors, funding agencies, media, staff and participants – more than one strategy may be used to target the groups identified (Watt 1998). A recent trend in the arts that is significant for arts events is towards audience development (Barlow and Shibli 2007). In a number of jurisdictions public audience development agencies have been launched to assist arts organizations with such audience development – for example in the UK twelve such agencies have been established in England, Scotland, Wales and Northern Ireland with the purpose of providing support to arts and cultural organizations to grow their audiences including developing best practice in cultural marketing and encouraging the use of digital research. In addition research on understanding the motivations of both arts audiences (Keaney 2008) and individual arts consumers (Hand 2011) will be relevant to those planning arts events.

Each arts event must have the right balance of the marketing mix, consisting of the four primary factors of place, product, price and promotion (Andreasean and Kotler 2003). Promotion brings the arts event to the attention of the public. This is the communication part of marketing, dealing with the image and presentation of the arts event as a product. Considerations here for the arts event include the development of a logo, the possible use of a mascot, and an advertising plan. In addition to paid advertisements promotion can include cross promotions, public relations and street promotions. Goldblatt (2002) indicates that cross promotions and tie-ins (such as tag lines on partner advertisements) are an effective means of reaching larger markets cost effectively. It is important to ensure that communications are distributed both internally and externally, keeping the event staff and committees up to date on the promotion and advertising efforts. Advertising and promotion agencies can be employed in the development and implementation of marketing and promotion strategies, or these functions can be undertaken in-house by the arts event organization.

The internet and social media is now contributing to the successful promotion of arts events as well as facilitating new methods of promotion and spawning new types of arts events such as pop-up festivals and events discussed in Chapter 4. Online marketing is now thus an important aspect of the marketing of events (Goldblatt 2002:281). Many events are now taking advantage of social media tools that have relatively low costs, while being flexible in messaging format (Nickerson *et al.* 2014). Social media is thus increasingly playing a role in the promotion mix for arts events, and is indeed making possible new forms of impromptu events in the arts, by creating a direct channel for sponsoring agencies to connect with their audiences. Advertising, however, still plays somewhat of a role in promoting arts events through the traditional media (radio, television, newspaper, magazine, direct mail, flyers, brochures, billboards). In the case of the not-for-profit arts organizations sponsoring events this form of promotion is often paid for by identifiable sponsors. As artists and arts agencies need to innovate and look for both new forms of advertising and sponsorship, a city tax on billboards – for example, in Toronto, Canada – is set to contribute to funding the arts (Knelman 2013).

Media relations are an important part of connecting with stakeholders and promoting an arts event, Watt (1998) notes that early contact with the media is essential, suggesting the use of a catch phrase or logo to easily identify the event. Press releases and where appropriate press conferences may be used to introduce the arts event to the media when announcing the event, or to launch the event. It will be key for arts event organizers to develop a good relationship with the media, and to create opportunities for the media to interact with the event, for example through the provision of free event passes for ticketed arts events.

The following case of the Celtic Colours International Festival demonstrates the creation of an arts event that while established for economic development goals related to tourism has effectively implemented marketing and promotion strategies that have resulted in not only a successful event but significant recognition in the form of a number of awards, but also nurture the maintenance

---

Box 5.5 Celtic Colours International Festival case study

This annual event, the Celtic Colours International Festival (CCIF), has been held on the island of Cape Breton, Nova Scotia, Canada since 1997. The mission of the festival is

> to promote, celebrate and develop Cape Breton's living Celtic culture and hospitality by producing an international festival during the fall colours (change of the leaves) that builds relationships across Cape Breton Island and beyond.
>
> (Celtic Colours International Festival n.d.)

The culturally focused event celebrating the island's Celtic heritage consists of concerts, educational workshops and community events. The islands Celtic heritage is due to the immigration of settlers from Scotland and Ireland, and the geographic isolation which until the mid-twentieth century, when a causeway to the mainland was built, protected this culture. In particular the Cape Breton fiddle music developed as a distinctive tradition in the area. A unique aspect of the festival is that its events are held in various venues across the island, and not in one central location. Another notable aspect is the inclusion of educational workshops, achieving a type of creative tourism (Richards 2011), whereby locals interact with visitors sharing local knowledge of Celtic music and related traditions.

Marketing and promotion

The not-for-profit Celtic Colours Festival Society established in 1997 administers the event. CCIF is held for nine days each October and has been acknowledged for its significant economic, social and cultural impact in this peripheral region of eastern Canada (Brown and Geddes 2007). In an economically depressed area, where traditional industries such as coal mining have closed, the festival has a particular significance in supporting the creative industries as an alternative industry and in stimulating tourism in the shoulder season (the period after the main summer tourism season). Brown (2009) indicated that the success of the CCIF indicated the market for Cape Breton Celtic music as well as the ability of this type of festival to extend the tourism season. Marketing and promotion is done in cooperation with agencies such as Destination Cape Breton and the tourism offices or officers of the municipalities in the region.

Achievements

The festival has garnered a number of awards, including:

> The Tourism Industry Association of Canada's Event of the Year (2007), has received four East Coast Music Awards for Event of the Year, (2005–2008), two Tourism Industry Association of Nova Scotia Crystal Awards (Events/Conferences 2002, the Golden Hospitality Award 2005), and was named American Bus Association's Top Event in Canada and Attractions Canada's Top Cultural Event in 2001.
>
> (Celtic Colours International Festival n.d.)

The CCIF has therefore had a level of success as a cultural tourism product and has certainly stimulated the creative music industry in the region as evidenced by receipt of a number of East Coast Music Awards. It has as well involved locals as volunteers and brought a new sense of meaning to community venues such as fire halls and schools, once accessible only to locals. However, to a certain extent the festival has contributed to shaping the culture and identity of both tourism to Cape Breton and of the residents, a point discussed with some contention by some academics (Ivakhiv 2005).

Conclusion

In conclusion, this well-established cultural event has overall made a sustainable and positive contribution to the communities of Cape Breton, extending the tourist season through promoting and marketing of a shoulder season event, bringing new life to rural communities and venues, encouraging creativity in the arts and allowing the young musicians and performers of the region a means of developing new creative industries for the future.

of Celtic traditions and the allied creation of related livelihoods and benefits for the residents of Cape Breton.

Merchandising

Merchandising can provide a major revenue stream for events (Salem *et al.* 2012) and retail sales are acknowledged as a common revenue source for cultural attractions that include events (Timothy 2011). This retail aspect can be an important aspect in the marketing and implementation of arts events. Through developing merchandise related to the arts event organizers are able to further extend the event impact on the participant, fulfilling visitor interest in acquiring a souvenir as a memory (Wilkins 2012), while at the same time developing revenue streams augmenting funds from sponsorships and admissions. Blockbuster arts exhibitions (such as that profiled earlier in this chapter) are normally accompanied by catalogues, which are available in either paperback or hardcover form. Now with the advent of the museum exhibition e-book (e.g. the Gugenheim became the first museum to provide this product with its catalogue of 'Maurizio Cattelan: All', in 2011), the institutions promoting blockbusters have another revenue source that will endure beyond the event (Guggenheim Museum 2011). Examples of other merchandise from arts related events include: posters, catalogues, mugs and clothing such as hats and t-shirts with event logos. Since many arts events are operated on a not-for-profit basis, these additional revenue sources can have a considerable impact on generating event revenues.

Merchandising is a key part of the fiscal operations of the following case of the circulating exhibition of Pulitzer Prize Photography. The existence here of a commercial element reflects influences of the commercialization of the American museum sector dating from the 1970s (Toepler 2006). In this case this exhibit

Box 5.6 Pulitzer Prize Photography Exhibition

The travelling exhibition 'Capture the Moment: The Pulitzer Prize Photographs', at the time of writing (2013) had appeared in more than thirty cities, both in the United States and abroad with more than three million people having seen it since opening in New York in 2000. This circulating exhibit is attributed to the Newseum, a Washington, DC based museum of news and visitor attraction. The exhibition was created by Cyma Rubin and is coordinated by the Business of Entertainment Inc. The exhibit content of the award-winning Pulitzer Prize (a US award in journalism) photographs is updated annually, with a three-month 2013 showing in Taipei, Taiwan reporting that the exhibit contains 151 prize-winning photographs dating between 1942 and 2012. Additional sponsors in Taiwan included the TPK Culture and Art Foundation and Palais de Chine Hotel with logistics being coordinated by Taiwan's Media Sphere Communications Ltd. Public programming for the Taipei exhibit included Pulitzer Prize-winning photographer Carolyn Cole visiting Taiwan to hold a photography workshop sharing her experience as a war photographer. The final attendance for the showing in Taipei was reported as 170,000 with long lines for entrance the final week of the show (Business of Entertainment Inc. n.d.). After this showing the exhibition was due to travel to Kaohsiung Museum of Fine Arts, Kaohsiung City, Taiwan, and the National Constitution Center, Philadelphia, ending up at the Frost Museum of Art, Miami, an exhibit concluding in mid April 2014.

Reach of exhibition

With regards to both its subject matter, location and attendance the show has truly had a global reach, in somewhat the same way as the MOMA 1955 'Family of Man' photographic exhibition, discussed in Chapter 2. The Pulitzer exhibition was organized along a very similar line with traditional labels and interpretation, although now an audio guide is available. Like the earlier MOMA exhibition some of the Pulitzer photography is quite disturbing, dealing with wars, famines, conflicts etc. For example, the collection includes a photograph of the World Trade Center in New York after it was struck on 11 September 2001 in a terrorist attack. The Taipei Times report on the exhibition was entitled 'Indelible Images' (Bartholomew 2013). Reports indicate record-breaking crowds for the showing in Taipei (Business of Entertainment Inc. n.d.), a fact collaborated by a field visit during this period. Notably, the audio guide was only available in Chinese, although there were captions in the English labelling beside each photograph.

Merchandising

There were not only crowds going through the exhibit but also through the well-stocked shop featuring Pulitzer Prize themed souvenirs, strategically located at the exit of the refurbished exhibition venue in Taipei's Huashan 1914 Creative Park. Merchandising is no doubt a revenue stream that parallels the collection of admissions (adult entrance TWD 220) for the exhibition. Local exhibit organizers will have paid a three-month licensing fee to Business of Entertainment Inc. in order to host the exhibition. One of the souvenirs available is an award-winning book with all of the photographs in it and another is a video documentary featuring the photographs. Individual photographs and merchandise featuring the photographs was also available. This variety of merchandise represents a trend on the part of both museums and exhibitions to increase their range of goods, not only for profit, but also as a means to extend the exhibition experience (Mottner and Ford 2005).

Conclusion

This case not only demonstrates the mass appeal of this internationally hosted photographic event, but also effective merchandising, venue adaptation and exhibition management techniques. The two-level venue was able to accommodate a large number of visitors at one time, capturing their interest in purchasing mementos of their visit by positioning the shop at the exhibition exit. Mementos created for the exhibition have a long shelf life and a large market as they accompany the exhibition on its touring schedule around the world. In addition, by creatively bundling copies of the award-winning Pulitzer Prize photographs into a travelling exhibit, transported in just eleven crates, the organizers have been able to literally take the exhibition that is adaptable to a variety of venues to new audiences around the world.

with a broad appeal to the public has a strong merchandising component with a shop located just before the exhibition exit, a retail formula also adopted by blockbuster exhibitions.

Conclusion

Implementing an arts event is a complex endeavour undertaken either by in-house teams, or by professional event managers or committees made up of members with various competencies. Here the role of paid and unpaid staff is equally important. The type and scale of the arts event will determine the organizational structure under which it is implemented. It is however essential that these events are implemented within a framework of responsible financial/

risk management and evaluation, timeline and production scheduling, adequate training of volunteers and staff, and promotion and marketing. Assessing risks, financial and otherwise and having a solid evaluation plan will contribute to both the quality of the arts event delivered and the justification required for sponsors. Having a detailed timeline and production scheduling will ensure the smooth delivery of the event for the benefits of stakeholders that will include artists, arts institutions, sponsors, partners, staff, volunteers and most importantly the public arts participants. The professionalization of both event management and cultural administration furthermore has the potential to contribute to the more effective implementation of arts events, informed by current research and thinking coming from these fields. With the advent of social media arts events are now able to more effectively put into place promotion and marketing endeavours that reflect the creativity of their events. Through merchandising arts events organizers are also able to extend the reach of their event branding while creating needed revenues to support these events.

6   Assessing arts events

Glocalism, arts ecologies and SCA

The rise in professionalism in event management and use of social media explored in the last chapter are providing a new foundation for greater experiments in glocalism (the process of combining the global and the local), where the international arts ecology has a closer relationship with local arts ecologies through repeatable arts events. The *more successful* the events are, the *healthier* the local arts ecology (AE) becomes (for all stakeholders public, private and NGOs) and *the better* that is for creating a positive impact and relationship between the inner rings and the outer ring of global AEs, sustainable development and tourism marketing and or city benchmarking (Figure 6.1). In terms of arts events the global/local nexus or glocalism allows for these events to be agents in responding to and interpreting global forces at the local level.

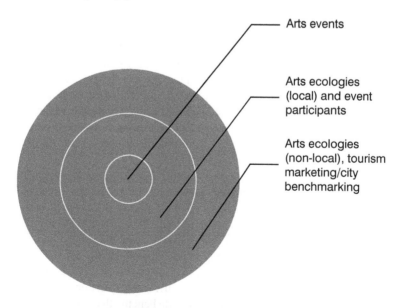

Arts events

Arts ecologies (local) and event participants

Arts ecologies (non-local), tourism marketing/city benchmarking

Figure 6.1 Inside-out nature of glocalism from the arts events' perspective

Assessing the performance, sustainability and the generation of creative capital of arts events is essential for both short-term and longitudinal research on these phenomena. Three case studies outlined briefly earlier in the book will be examined in depth using a special development assessment framework in this chapter. These comprise Hong Kong's ArtWalk, Art HK/Basel HK (art fair) and *Artsbus: On the Move!* Other examples also mentioned earlier in the volume will be featured in relation to the main criteria for the framework. For instance, Sculptures by the Sea Aarhus (Danish version of Sydney's Sculpture by the Sea), The BBC Proms (UK), Sharjah Biennial (UAE) and Stone Music Festival (Australia). This chapter will discuss key concepts and tools, such as maintaining sustainable creative advantage (SCA), which can be applied by both academics and practitioners to their own real-life examples. Points raised in the preceding chapters about the planning, marketing and management of arts events indicate that key areas where arts events need the most attention to create and maintain a SCA are: glocal orientation and support; image, orientation and position; conceptual uniqueness; and event experience, implementation and management.

Building glocality: orientation and support

Knowing more about the nature of a glocal orientation and support for an event is important for understanding the enabling conditions for achieving sustainability in relation to arts. Such conditions are also important for creating a sustainable advantage that is place-based and makes the most of available creative capital (creativity, creatives, creative processes and cultural/arts ecologies). That is why one of the first issues to investigate or review is the number and strength of arts community networks that might support the event and how the event could be considered a point of connection with these communities within an arts ecology. A successful event needs a critical mass of artists and art activities, and which only becomes available to arts event managers, if these connections are strong.

Not only should the benefits spread outwards to the participants, sponsors and community, if the events are well planned and implemented, but the connections should also ensure that a repeated event is viable for years to come. Support for an event from the local and international (if relevant) arts communities in terms of building on social connections that organizers may already have needs to be carefully scrutinized in any assessment of an event's success. Connectivity is crucial to the public and private goodwill that arts events need to develop and survive. As previously discussed, many events start off quite modestly in terms of where they can seek assistance and build partnerships. After a few successful editions of an event, a reputation is built that, along with carefully planned publicity and public relations, can expand to include more and better-known players in an arts sector or ecology (local and non-local).

Overall, SCA in this context is a two-way street: you have to be creative and consistent in helping others to help yourself. Asking questions about flow-on effect, such as, 'how does or will the event provide benefits that flow onto the community and other sectors?' is important in understanding where to build mutual goodwill and important social capital in terms of connectivity with arts/cultural ecologies. Mapping or identifying multiple pathways of potential connections stemming from the event is crucial to finding potential partners and participants, and ways to engage the latter, whilst offering something in return for them. Needless to say, this is more evident in community arts styled events that are free to the public than in events that are heavily orientated towards industry or commerce, or artists or performers only. However, event organizers trying to focus on all four orientations (commercial, industry, artist and public) must consciously examine these relationships and connections on a regular basis in order to ensure balance is maintained. Accordingly, in the age of the internet and social media, events in different places across the world that share an orientation and something more in common, such as the Bondi, Cottesloe (Australia) and Aarhus (Denmark) versions of Sculptures by the Sea event, have the option to link each other's websites and promote strong and synergistic ties between each countries' cultural/arts ecologies rather than to ignore each other and to try individually to compete for international attention. The Basel group of international art fairs with annual events in Basel (Switzerland), Miami (USA) and Hong Kong Special Administrative Region, China, use this kind of connectivity to a strong commercial advantage to reinforce its brand image as a market leader internationally (Art Basel 2013). The Bookworm Literary Festival (BLF) in China has likewise used the connectivity between the festival hosted at the three Bookworm Cafes in Beijing, Suzhou and Chengdu with an outreach in the form of the *New York Times* BLF Literary Caravan to reach other cities bringing the total number of event venues to over 200, reinforcing the BLF brand and image in China (Bookworm Literary Festival n.d.).

Marketing: brand, image and position

Audience building often requires studies of audience impact and many arts organizations, particularly for the performing arts, conduct these regularly without specific reference to particular events (du Preez and Bailey 2010). The issue then becomes whether market research for arts events should differ greatly from that conducted for other kinds of special events or not. Where the difference might lie is with how to integrate useful information from audience building/impact studies into the mix. How many extra sources of data beyond those associated with the basic demographic and psychographic questions need to be included in surveys for events depending on their orientation? One interesting example for an art fair in 2013 was an online survey conducted first in German and then translated into English for gathering market research regarding the success of the Art Basel Hong Kong. The German version was obviously created for the event when held in its point of origin in Switzerland. The Hong Kong version appears to be very interested in the views of collectors, critics and journalists and not so much those of the general public. For instance, out of a seven-page questionnaire only two pages were on the respondent's demographic details and experience of the event, two pages were concerned with their experience of arts institutions and events elsewhere, one page on favourite art movements and artists, one on the art market,

Table 6.1 Potential subjects for a marketing questionnaire for art fairs (based on Basel HK, 2013)

Topic area	Typical concerns
Demographic details	Gender, age, place of residence, level of education, nature of profession, income level
Experience of a specific event	Repeat visitor/first to this event/others, time spent, nature of pre-planning, ticket purchased, intentions, expectations, activities undertaken, orientation, nature of social interaction during visit, nature of trends exhibited, galleries representative of art market?
Visual arts appreciation generally	Art fairs/biennales/institutions, private galleries visited, favourite art movements/journals/information sources, purchasing habits, interest in virtual art fairs
Personal arts appreciation and preferences	Preferred art forms, nature of art appreciation, value of this event's activities in enhancing arts knowledge/ appreciation, this event's influence on appreciation/ purchase
Art market trends	Importance/influences on pricing, impact on contemporary arts, opinions on other factors, overall impression of art market and art fairs, capacity of event to provide networking opportunities for professionals

and the final page on arts and geo-politics. The latter pages were aimed at trying to identify the depth of knowledge and understanding of the art world and the orientation of the respondent towards collection, criticism or other aspects (Basel Hong Kong 2013) (see Table 6.1). Collecting more than basic demographic and psychographic information would assist the organizers in ensuring that the event is establishing its brand, image and position in the eyes of its key market in the Asia-Pacific region, where Basel is a new competitor.

Events with a different orientation, such as events with a strong local and educational purpose, would of course be seeking data about the arts awareness and educational needs of the local community. Dividing this up into specific surveys for different participants may be too labour-intensive for some organizations, whilst others who can draw on voluntary and student assistance may prefer this approach. However, overly long surveys rarely get completed to the end if they are not conducted face-to-face with some kind incentive offered. Hong Kong Institute of Education (HKIEd) took the approach of using student helpers to quickly survey different participant groups with relevant questionnaires that targeted key marketing concerns. For instance, school students were surveyed in relation to the *Arts Bus: On Move!* school-focused activities. On these occasions the Arts Bus was displayed in school playgrounds, transforming the school campuses into arts festivals that were open to the public. A series of activities including information sharing, performances by students and local artists and educational workshops involving different art forms were held. These activities extend beyond arts appreciation, as they were designed in such a way so that participants can be actively involved in experiencing visual and performing arts. After the activities and before leaving to go to the next school, student helpers collected information on impact of the event on awareness of the arts forms featured, enjoyment of the experience and disposition to repeat it, impact on interest in studying arts and the historical and cultural context within which various art forms can be found (HKIEd 2013). By focusing on the psychographic and educational aspects, the surveys collected useful information for shaping future instalments of the event for schools. Support of partners and sponsors are crucial to enable this event to continue beyond the current time frame of three more years. Accordingly, Australia's Zest Festival from Chapter 4 has been planned as a five-year project with a formula that is repeatable. Connections and funding will be important to any reiteration of the project.

As the BBC has slowly expanded its international network of TV and Internet resources the BBC Proms has gained greater recognition outside of the UK, especially in Asia. This long-time association between the BBC and the event since the late 1920s has brought exposure in line with its first conductor's original vision. The concerts are broadcast live on radio, TV and streamed online throughout the season. The incredible popularity of the last night concert means that there is huge demand for one of 5,500 audience members that can be safely allowed into the Royal Albert Hall. In addition to the internet and online broadcasts, the BBC runs parallel concerts in Hyde Park, Belfast, Glasgow and Swansea with giant screens to link live to the Albert Hall for the traditional finale. The Hall is still the primary concert venue over the period the event runs and is where the current Prom's director, Roger Wright, and his 25-person team are based over that time, while also coordinating arrangements for the other venues (Silverman 2013).

Conceptual uniqueness

Planning an arts event and re-inventing one have a certain amount in common in terms of ensuring conceptual uniqueness that will ensure its success and continuation as a repeatable event. As well as all the practical aspects covered in Chapter 4, there also needs to be some remarkable element that assists in marketing the event, so that it fits with its orientation and attracts the right partners, sponsors, participants or attendees. It also needs to be attractive to the artists or performers featured. From general to specific, the development of an event with conceptual uniqueness first requires a strong foundation or supportive environment with certain kinds of structural or institutional capital that makes things happen in that location. It is no accident that most event forms start in one place with this kind of capital and then variants appear in other places with a similar supportive environment. Hui's (2006) study of creative capital measured eight types of societal conditions that are contributors to the growth of place-based creativity, which are the presence of:

- a supportive legal system
- lack of corruption
- freedom of expression

- information and communication technologies infrastructure
- social and cultural infrastructure
- community facilities
- financial infrastructure.

In terms of assessing whether an environment is supportive for the kind of creativity to conceptualize and implement unique events, it would seem reasonable that places which welcome freedom of expression and respect the arts as an embodiment of that are likely to have more arts events. Where the rights of participants at an event to express themselves and those of another group have come into conflict, events have been restructured or moved elsewhere, as in the case of Burning Man, mentioned in Chapter 3. After becoming too exuberant for the community near the San Francisco beach, where it first started, it was moved to the desert. Even so, too much spontaneity can make event management run less smoothly and possibly affect security and safety of the participants, as in the case Glastonbury at times when too many people were able to access the venue, due to lax security still operating on a more relaxed counterculture model.

Many events run by or in partnership in some way with museums use these facilities as cultural infrastructure. The recent advent of museums being used for night activities, such as sleepovers for children, has only really become quite popular since the Hollywood film *A Night at the Museum* (2006) opened curators' eyes to the potential that afterhours activities could yield (see Kotler 2001). Seeking inspiration from outside museum studies and arts administration, and finding new ways to use existing community facilities are trends that event planners could follow in future. So, one aspect of conceptualizing uniqueness is thinking in new ways to turn some existing practices on their head to see if new activities or themes could be devised that will support an event's SCA.

Finally, using or setting an event in a particular context that catches the attention of audiences is another aspect of ensuring its conceptual uniqueness. This approach requires a deep knowledge of the art form(s) or associated intellectual property. It can draw on the people, history, successes, failures and its aspirations of a place or an arts tradition. It can explore new ways of constructing knowledge, new ideas, skills and pathways that can be generated by the event. Sharjah Biennial used this approach as a theme for its 2013 event to link local concerns about heritage conservation (tangible and intangible) to current international art debates about identity, form and content in the visual arts (Sharjah Biennial 2013). This approach was appropriate for an event orientated towards participants who also share a deep knowledge of that context, who would be excited by its exploration, or ones who would wish some kind of engagement with it for educational purposes or personal growth.

Event experience

When the orientation of the event is identified in terms of who are likely to gain the key benefits from it (public/public sector, commercial sector, arts industry, artists/performers), the nature of the experience offered by activities planned and implemented should indicate where it sits in relation to inspiring, affirming, pleasurable, enriching or celebratory experiences for participants. Each orientation should take a different approach to evaluating event experience by participants in order to focus on key objectives. For instance, events planned to have a strong public/public sector orientation need to assess social impacts of and contributions to community cultural development in terms of providing enriching experiences. Goldbard (2006) has observed that there are at least six criteria by which to judge whether arts projects, including arts events, have been successful in this respect, by providing enriching experiences that ensure:

- mutual and meaningful relationships are developed by practitioners and participants;
- opportunities are offered and taken to allow co-production of activities by participants;
- participants notice a difference in their arts knowledge and skills, self-awareness, and thirst for further personal growth as a result;
- satisfaction in the ability to communicate through arts media has grown for participants;
- aims and expectations of participants have been advanced in terms of improving their potential for impact after the event (e.g. sharing or distribution of arts media related products);
- boosting of participant's confidence in partaking more fully in the arts and cultural life of the community.

Measuring many of these mostly intangible benefits is likely to require a data collection process that continues long after the event has been held and allows for participants to express their opinions in an unstructured way, other than through a typical satisfaction survey. Developing a cyber-community based on the event may be one way to track participants, particularly if they are happy to provide links to their personal profiles and web pages where they discuss arts experiences and their successes or failures in regards to putting what they have learned into practice. More traditional methods such as focus groups, in-depth interviews and survey can also have a role where there are the resources to conduct these activities.

The Danish version in the seaside town of Aarhus of the earlier Sydney example of a pleasurable event from Chapter 3 namely, Sculpture by the Sea, ran in June 2013. Afterwards, organizers posted a report on the event on the Internet. The interesting thing about this report is that, as well as the usual facts and figures to support the organizers' appraisal of the event as a success, it also describes how artistic goals were being met by the event. Criteria for such goals are likely to be more subjective in nature than those for its economic impact, whilst who is qualified to undertake their assessment is an interesting question. One report states 'artistic goals were also met, especially due to all the site-specific artworks that made this year's exhibition even more unique' (Sculptures by the Sea Aarhus 2013b). It is highly likely that where arts events sometimes differ from other special events is that appraisal of their relative quality of aesthetic experience and artistic value is always going to have to use arts criticism traditions as a framework that may not be readily accessible or understandable to outsiders to the arts world. However, that is not say that such events ignore the opinions of the public who are not arts professionals, but who still gain pleasure from the aesthetic arrangement of the sculptures in the seaside landscape. The organizers of this event state that they used a local market research company to undertake a visitor satisfaction survey and analysis, which was made public in their exhibition report later in the year after each event (Sculptures by the Sea Aarhus 2013b).

The way that some events with a strong commercial-sector orientation use social media to access information on the pleasurable nature of the event experience can be completely different from the above, as its purpose is more closely aligned to evaluating the event's popularity in order to make a profit for the event promoters, after all other costs and expenses have been taken into account. What organizers need to avoid is appearing to be exploitative when gathering feedback on event experience. Responding to negative as well as positive comments needs care and timeliness to appear professional, whilst indicating that personal notice has been taken of participants' opinions. For instance, the Stone Music Festival organizers were keen to use Facebook and Twitter as key platforms for interacting with ticket-holders before, during and after the event. The only problem with this approach is that while it can offer some useful feedback to organizers, the sources themselves are in the public domain and can be accessed by music critics who may have a different interpretation of this feedback and use quotes in their reviews. Also, platforms such as Facebook and Twitter can be accessed by hostile users (colloquially known as 'trolls'). These users may offer disruptive or false comments online for fun or have been paid to do so by competitors. The problem is that this occurrence may enhance or inflame other genuine responders, who may have been ambivalent before at best. While 'trolling' is recognized by many social media users as a problem, and most can recognize it in action, there are still some people who can be influenced by it in its more subtle form. Therefore, organizers for this and similar new events (which may have suffered initial bad publicity) would have to sift carefully through this information to gather perspectives on the event experience of attendees beyond what they themselves observed on the day. Once again, responding to trolls requires similar skills to dealing with problem customers during a service encounter where a succinct response, politeness and professionalism is hopefully going to calm them down and win over any interested bystanders.

When undertaking studies of participant experience for any form of arts event, data should be collected before in relation to expectations, during and after in relation to whether these expectations have been met and in order to contribute to the continuous evaluation of the event. No arts event planner or manager can ignore this kind of research whether they file it with market research or studies of the efficacy of the event's management. It is hoped that most will recognize that it is an area that deserves to stand on its own. Understanding more about relevant experiences is important because events are increasingly part of the 'experience economy' and how an event is experienced could influence a participant's or attendee's choice for years to come. Finally, information about event experiences can be used to suggest changes to just about any area associated with holding an event, so it should not be glossed over or ignored lightly.

Another area of studying event experience is that of versions of events held specifically for industry insiders and cultural professionals working in the area of the event. For example, Kabosh (profiled in Chapter 4) held such an event in March of 2013 for their on-site performance pieces, *Belfast Bred* and *The West Awakes*, hosting a roundtable lunch and discussion with Kabosh staff and performers in between the two performances, and then surveying participants after the event. The short web survey distributed to participants contained only five questions. The first asked which section(s) of the event the participant attended. The second asked if the participant found the event interesting, engaging, educational and elicited further elaboration for the answer. The third asked for feedback on any elements of the day that were not particularly useful and or enjoyable, again eliciting further comments. The fourth presented a ratings scale and also elicited comments from participants about content, which performers and Kabosh staff used to assess how appropriate and useful a day's programme had been towards fulfilling the goals of the event. This question also asked about the broader themes of the tours. The fifth question also used a rating scale for participants to rate both events, as well as pre-event information, food and transportation logistics. Kabosh indicated to participants that the survey results would contribute to the preparation of resource packs for both events.

Event implementation and management

Arts events that are larger in scale are also increasingly becoming subject to professional management regimes, which work to ensure that fundamental implementation of management would fall within the expectations of the event planners. However, whether an event is professionally managed or not, there still needs to be an evaluation of how it has succeeded in being creative and sustainable, if the plan is for it to be ongoing. Based on previous discussion in the last few chapters, criteria for each of these areas should be developed by event organizers to mix and match to fit specific needs. Four key areas for all arts events are likely to be:

1   *Concept and content*: appropriateness of conceptualization and selection process for artists/works/performers/activities/facilities/nature of participation by attendees (if any).
2   *Timelines*: scheduling for timing of tasks associated with putting on the programme/exhibition/ancillary activities/competition with similar events.
3   *Connectivity*: quality of management of sponsors/partners/cross-cultural issues/media and communication/responsibility structures.
4   *Resourcing*: that staff levels (both paid and volunteer), training needs, insurance, safety and security are all adequate and within budget.

These aspects will require attention before, during and after the event in either implementation or review and revision (through ongoing evaluation) for the benefit of improving the event's impact within its cultural/arts ecology and build glocality. As discussed earlier in Chapters 4 and 5 this proposed scheme for event implementation and management reflects the need for continuous and integral planning of an event concept, establishment of timelines, while ensuring connectivity and resourcing.

The assessment process

The assesment process is basically to identify, document and analyse information relevant to the event to assess its overall SCA and find specific ways to improve or enhance the event and its benefits by addressing any problems through a series of strategies and actions (Table 6.2). This is proposed as a significant new tool for evaluating arts events. The stages in the process begin with identifying key information about glocal orientation/support, brand/image/position and conceptual uniqueness (first) as a background to documenting and analysing whether event experience, implementation and management (second). The object here is to assess whether the latter are actualizing the obligations and promises that underlie the former in ways that are likely to sustain the events' creative advantage for its key orientation. At the initial stages of planning and conceptualizing an event, this scheme (Table 6.2) could be the used to evaluate differing event concepts and forms in a planning workshop with the sponsoring arts organization, key stakeholders including community members and prospective partners and sponsors.

Applying the process

For the purposes of clarity and to explore how the assessment process might be implemented, it will be applied using a few examples with which the authors are most familiar in Hong Kong (Hong Kong ArtWalk, Arts Bus: On the Move! and Art HK/Basel Hong Kong). A full assessment of each example in reality would be more detailed than is possible for this book and include more sub-criteria were necessary to uncover issues (Table 6.3 and Figures 6.1 to 6.6).

Conclusion

The versatility of the assessment process used in this book is potentially quite high. Table 6.4 summarizes the results of the above applications from Table 6.3 in order to see how effective the process is improving and enhancing SCA for the three examples. Organizers, academics or other researchers can use this approach to assess not only their own event, but also others in comparison. They can either concentrate on one event or put it in context with others that are similar geographically, historically, or culturally. Alternatively, comparisons are also possible and can be made between similar art forms or between arts events of a similar orientation. In Table 6.4 is an example of a comparison of different arts event forms that is place-based, which is just one of the possible options.

Table 6.2 Key tasks, topic areas and issues for SCA analysis

Task	Area	Key issues
Identify	Glocal orientation/support	What support is there for holding the event? How is the event playing a role in cultural/arts ecologies (local/non-local) or in community cultural development (if relevant)?
	Brand image, orientation and position	Is there any evidence of the way the marketing has shaped and presented the event has been effective in attracting participants/partners/sponsors/media attention/goodwill from all sectors?
	Conceptual uniqueness	Is the event standing out from others in some way that is positive and creative?
Document/ analyse	Experience (for each market/orientation) in terms of inspiring, affirming, pleasurable, enriching or celebratory experiences	What are the positive and negative elements of participants and others experience of the event before/during/afterwards?
	Implementation and management	What minor changes were made during implementation?
		How effective were managers in ensuring the requirements of the four key areas of concept/content, timing, connectivity and resources were fulfilled?
Recommend	All	Strategies/actions
Review/Repeat	All	All (where required)

Table 6.3 SCA comparison of three Hong Kong arts events

Area	Key Issues	Hong Kong ArtWalk	Art Basel HK	Arts Bus: On the Move!
Glocal orientation/ support	What support is there for holding the event? How is the event playing a role in cultural/arts ecologies (local/non-local) or in community cultural development (if relevant)?	1. Support from most members of HK Gallery Association, Society for Community Organizations (SOCO), local university arts departments. Partners do drop out occasionally, but new ones join in. 2. Event has become part of the arts scene and increasingly involves local artists. Its Facebook site actively promotes relevant activities conducted by its partners all year round, particularly participating local artists, galleries and SOCO.	1. After 2012 sale of ART HK to Art Basel support has continued from Hong Kong Gallery Association, critics, auction houses, the media and sponsors. The Basel brand and the growing reputation of Hong Kong as an art sales hub has ensured that galleries, critics and curators have joined the event in greater numbers. 2. Still part of the Hong Kong arts scene, however, the organizers are increasingly involving overseas galleries featuring more international artists and their works with attention to quality and saleability.	1. Support from broad cross-section of HK arts world and Citybus. Limited international exposure. Event orientation is strongly towards the public sector to provide enriching educational arts experiences. 2. Event is becoming a leading arts education initiative for the city and increasingly involves local artists, students and their works. Its Facebook site actively promotes relevant activities conducted by its partners all year round, particularly participating local artists and students (of all ages).
Brand image, orientation and position	Is there any evidence the way the marketing that has shaped and presented the event has been effective in attracting participants/ partners/sponsors/media attention/goodwill from all sectors?	Event held since 2001. Gallery owners interviewed in 2013 opined that the brand is still very strong within Hong Kong. However, timing has become an issue for maintaining a prominent position, as events calendar is much fuller since HK seen as arts market hub. Still attracts positive publicity due to its role in local charity and due to greater interest in local visual arts since more progress with West Kowloon Cultural District.	Original event first held 2007 and in its last year in 2012 it had 630 applications for the 230 places offered for the event. Gallery owners interviewed in 2013 about the new Basel event said it attracted a lot of interest within Hong Kong and outside. More media interest in connection with the growth of the art market in China.	Event received an award from the HK Public Relations Professional Association in 2011. Organizer interviewed said that the brand is growing even stronger within Hong Kong. However, there is a new competitor to this mobile arts event in Savanah College of Art and Design (SCAD) that sometimes hires harbour ferries. Arts Bus attracts positive publicity, due to its role in enhancing local community cultural development

Conceptual uniqueness	Is the event standing out from others in some way that is positive and creative?	No other event with the same mix of overseas and local art galleries, street art and heritage and charity collection.	Currently no other event in Asia with the Basel brand, image and approach to running an international arts fair. However, it has retained the original event manager, Magnus Renfrew, whilst the event name owners for ART HK have moved on.	No other event with the same mix of visual and performing arts that uses buses as both a canvas for students' artwork and for visiting schools, community centres, K11 Art Mall and the Hong Kong ArtWalk. It has more potential to grow and develop.
Experience (for each market/orientation)	What are the positive and negative elements of participants and others experience of the event before/during/afterwards?	Before: Tickets can be hard to get for student concessions (limited number) and some residents (available through selected galleries). During: The pleasurable experience of being at a social evening with a casual, not raucous, street party is positive if the weather is good and there are not too many bottlenecks accessing popular galleries. New activities in 2013 were Arts Bus and City University Culture and Heritage Management students offering a free iPhone app based around local heritage After: Sometimes undertake satisfaction surveys. Not much use of Facebook page	Before: Ticketing practices and prices for the public remained unchanged. More VIP tickets and lounges were offered. A similar type and number of activities to ART HK were offered with the exception of one headlining talk, co-hosted by Intelligence Squared that was very popular During: The experience of participants from each sector differed (see Table 6.1). More tours were available than before After: In excess of 60,000 people attended. Reviews generally favourable, however, no results of the online survey are available publicly in order to judge the event in more detail for this analysis	Before: There is a lot of work with schools in preparation for the design competition each year for the best designs, which will be carried by the buses. The organizers are still struggling with resources to reach more schools. At present, 163schools are involved with the capacity for more During: The enriching experience of workshops and other activities give the participants a new perspective on the arts. After: Some analysis of survey information is only available for 2012. The Facebook page is very active, but not a formal part of the analysis of event experience

continued...

Table 6.3 continued

Area	Key Issues	Hong Kong ArtWalk	Art Basel HK	Arts Bus: On the Move!
Implementation and management	What minor changes were made during implementation?	Streamlining number of food and beverage sponsors so that any associated costs do not push up ticket prices. However, this has meant less diversity. Organizers have encouraged more local involvement by artists and others to balance the increase in overseas art being promoted by international galleries, so that the experience remains as affirming and about charity/cultural development	Event had a different layout in 2013 to that of past years. It approximately followed the Basel formula of dividing galleries into areas marked out into different colours on the map representing 'Discoveries', 'Insights', 'Encounters' and other exhibitors. The three named areas also included one that was individually curated by Yuko Hasegawa to include large-scale sculptures and installations from around the world	Event is still evolving and demand for activities is growing so more visits to schools have been made over 2013. Linkages to other events may be a continuing trend. Organizers have stated that public relations requires that something new needs to be added every year to maintain media interest and satisfy sponsors
	How effective were managers in ensuring the requirements of the four key areas of content, timing, connectivity and resources were fulfilled?	Content: Organizers encourage as many galleries as possible within easy reach of Central district, community arts and university partners to participate in providing art experiences for participants. Timing: The event's new position in the art world calendar of a month later is mostly well received. However, tickets were selling slower than in the previous years. Could a result of competing events around the same time? Connectivity: Still quite strong as the event has resolved various issues over the years, however there is more media exposure than in previous years	Content: Organizers for both the previous and current event practised a selection process. There was less information publicly available about Art Basel's process than that for ART HK's. Timing: The event took the same time slot for 2013 as before. That allowed it to continue its relationship with important auctions and other arts events that were likely to complement its activities and offerings. Connectivity: Quite strong as the event organizer did not change and there was new funding and enthusiasm to build new partnerships. However, there was	Content: Organizers encourage as many schools, community arts and service partners to participate in art experiences as possible. Select local artists/performers to participate. Timing: The timetabling is fundamentally dependent on the availability of buses, funding and school timetables. This means that activities can vary year to year. Connectivity: Quite strong, as the event has resolved various issues over the first few years and many partners like the concept, however there is more media exposure than in previous years and participants able to easily access galleries.

Resources: The event organizers have achieved a level of professionalism in managing resources after 12 years holding the event. This is only a problem if the current individuals want to drop out for some reason.

a lot more media exposure than for previous years (when the event was known as ART HK) in order to herald Basel's arrival in Asia and to attract more critics, curators and collectors.

Resources: The event organizers have achieved a level of professionalism in managing resources after six years holding the event. Basel seems content to maintain Renfrew, but equally could replace him at any stage with someone just as professional from its organization. His regional connections likely are what make the difference.

Resources: Event organizers have other responsibilities (e.g. teaching and other projects at HKIEd), so human resources for the event's management still need careful attention for it to be sustainable over the long term. Event's support by City Bus is guaranteed until 2016, when it will be next reviewed. Only a problem is if it wants to drop it after that for some reason and K11 Art Mall does not want to take full responsibility.

Plate 6.1 Art HK 12 plastic bottle installation at the entrance to the fair designed by corporate sponsor, Douglas Young (du Cros 2012)

Plate 6.2 Art HK 12 VIP Lounge sponsored by a bank which is an important partner for the event (du Cros 2012)

Plate 6.3 Interesting synergy between HK ArtWalk and Arts Bus events with appearance of a bus and jazz performers at 2013 ArtWalk (du Cros 2013)

Plate 6.4 Some ArtWalk patrons enjoy the performance and wine (left), while students survey others about the event in the background (du Cros 2013)

Plate 6.5 Over 140 schools took part in the Arts Bus design competition for 2013. A few of the winners are featured here with the actualized designs on the bus in the background (du Cros 2013)

Plate 6.6 Art Basel HK Asia Archive talk for a small group at the fair (du Cros 2013)

Table 6.4 A summary of possible strategies based on the case studies

Event	Issues	Strategies/actions
Hong Kong ArtWalk	1. Hong Kong is becoming a more popular site for arts events that involve private galleries. 2. Ticket sales were a little slower in 2013. Also, need to understand more about whether the inclusion of new activities is attractive to participants.	1. More research needed into impact of the timing of competing events on ticket sales. 2. More research into event participant satisfaction levels to ascertain whether new activities and other changes are still providing pleasurable and affirming experiences that are assisting the event in maintaining its SCA.
Hong Kong Art Fair/Basel HK	The experience of participants from each sector likely differed and requires more research than one page in a seven page online survey to assess fully.	More research needed into impact of the new changes brought on by the advent of the event's sale satisfying all stakeholders for the event's orientation. Continued effort to increase and maintain regional networks in the art world would be appropriate for this new version of the event to maintain its SCA.
Arts Bus: On the Move!	1. This is a much newer event than the other two and is still trying to establish itself. Resources and long-term partnering with key sponsor are still an issue. 2. Monitoring of how effective different kinds of activities are needed on a more regular basis in order to stay true to its educational and community outreach mission. 3. HKIEd staff member organizers need continued support and recognition for their role.	1. Maintain strong communication channels with Citybus and report frequently on successes. Encourage media coverage of the key role of Citybus in the project. Foster cross sector partnering such as K11 Artmall exhibit on the Arts Bus project as K11 has indicated it would prefer a long-term involvement and a greater role. 2.More research needed into impact of the timing of competing events and participant satisfaction levels to ascertain whether new activities and other changes are still providing pleasurable and enriching experiences – assisting the event in maintaining its SCA. 3. Attention needs to be paid to how resources (human and financial) can be more securely dedicated towards the long-term continuation of the event. HKIEd benefitting as much as Citybus from the event's publicity should ensure that staff member organizers continue to receive support.

7   Conclusion

Key areas that have emerged from the analysis of the accumulation of creative capital through repetition of particular events are power, authority and inclusiveness, glocality and its relationship to the health of arts/cultural ecologies. In addition to these key areas, this chapter will address the possible application and assessment of SCA for arts events, and further research that may result from that and exploring new concepts. In summary, the new insights regarding the arts and events throughout the book will be discussed here against a background of understanding and safeguarding cultural diversity, encouraging links to cultural identity or heritage; offering enjoyable recreational, leisure and touristic experiences; and attention to creating opportunities for professional, personal and economic growth.

Power, authority and inclusiveness

The socio-political debates revolving around power, authority and inclusiveness often underlie changes in how the arts and events are developing in the twenty-first century. This is particularly the case when event managers and others pause to reflect on changing nature of many forms of arts events. This section will expand on issues raised earlier in the debates and case studies regarding contemporary public policy, private and not-for-profit initiatives, changes in the nature of curatorship and leadership that are striking in the context of understanding arts events.

Public policy initiatives

There is an increasing trend for government arts and education agencies to work more closely on building more appreciation and understanding of the arts amongst the general public. This also includes access to lifelong opportunities for learning about arts and culture, which means there is a growing focus on arts education quality and inclusiveness in countries where cultural development is considered desirable and not just a needless luxury (UNESCO Arts Education 2013; UNESCO Observatory 2013b). A situation is developing with the recent advent of the *Seoul Agenda: Goals for the Development of Arts Education* in

2010 that encourages a more systematic effort by governments to implements these goals at the macro level. The development of public cultural policy and subsequent actions by government agencies inevitably has a trickle-down effect on arts events (particularly community arts events) in that they need not all be held by the public sector, but still able to reflect aspects of public policy, which can ensure public promotion and/funding. Naturally, there are events that eschew such support, especially most fringe festivals and artist-run events, such as the Burning Man discussed earlier in Chapter 3. These arts events in their truest form are likely anti-authoritarian in essence, hence their attraction to participants who are jaded by or suspicious of overly public policy linked events.

In terms of government assessment of the impact of public policy, arts events of all kinds are a visible measure of how successfully a community is supporting and participating in the arts. Measuring this aspect can be useful for many events organizers concerned about identifying ways a successful and repeatable arts event can presented as being essential to continued public support of the arts. Many arts events oriented chiefly towards the public (see Chapter 3) will be identified as providing continued education opportunities, which are also supported by the general public and arts administrators (especially in public arts/ cultural policies). Some arts administrators have taken this objective further by setting up a specific authority to work closely with creative industry partners and not-for-profit organizations to develop and expand audiences for the arts, such as in Northern Ireland (Audiences NI 2013). As mentioned earlier, this initiative was effective in garnering more support for local festivals.

When applying public policies regarding more inclusiveness and equity of access to the management of publicly run arts events, administrators will need an appropriate arts background combined with the skills necessary to develop events. Applying the sustainable creative advantage (SCA) assessment framework for such events that we postulated earlier in the book would assist in matching them to the goals derived from such policies. Accordingly, Dewey's (2004) observation that a shift towards more self-reflection in cultural administration requires an increase in training opportunities in administering the new arts management and assessment tools, such as SCA, which are likely to then enhance the effectiveness of such administrations.

However, what happens when arts administrations of public arts facilities try to host events that they have had little or no involvement in creating? This is a more common situation for performing arts venues than it has been in the past for visual arts facilities such as public arts museums. Examples were given earlier of how priorities are set by external and privately funded organizers/curators which affect the content as much as the cost and inclusiveness of blockbuster exhibitions in public galleries of developed countries. For large and long-established art galleries who have a mandate in arts education, these blockbuster exhibitions also provide a valuable tool for stimulating an interest in art in students through providing programmes and activities of a more intensive nature than is usually possible with public funding solely. Blockbuster exhibitions held in large public museums have more opportunity to explore and implement forms of inclusiveness for the public (such as interactive activities for all ages, cultural backgrounds and levels of arts knowledge) than temporary exhibitions in smaller institutions, which cannot draw on the same resources and the same level of self-financing.

Private sector initiatives

Whilst travelling blockbuster exhibitions have been a successful initiative for the private sector, other forms of private arts events continue to appear and evolve. For instance, art fair organizers can see a benefit from increasingly the arts discourse between collectors, galleries, curators and critics even when this discourse may be very similar or overlap with that generated by biennales. However, with new arts markets opening up in developing countries, there is pressure on the latter to distinguish themselves further from art fairs and offer something different in terms of arts knowledge and experiences, particularly to those participants who lack a deep knowledge of the visual arts.

Accordingly in the search for new ways of reaching such a new market, digital fairs/exhibitions have been proposed and, in a few cases, undertaken. However, it is too early to say whether private-sector events organizers are seeing much of a benefit from these new forms. It is possible that the sensual nature of visual arts precludes these from being popular with a large section of the public who visit these events, and it may be of more interest to collectors with investment as their goal. The limitations of the digital art fair (on its own without a visit to real event) are that it would preclude any kind of social interaction or opportunity to view artworks from a greater number of perspectives in order to appreciate their aesthetics fully. If both are held simultaneously, maybe digital arts fairs/exhibitions could enhance the real fair experience and be more useful guides than paper catalogues (and use less paper).

Overall, digital fairs, from a participants' point of view, could mean free access to sample works if participants are undecided about attending or unable to attend. It would be preferable to a bad experience because an event is so popular that it is crowded (as many of the current Asian art fairs are). However, there are fewer opportunities to understand the context behind certain artworks and ask questions of gallery owners or artists. Critics and curators would probably prefer broader access than a website in which to evaluate artworks. There are some financial considerations for smaller galleries, as many of these cannot afford high rental fees for the booths of highly popular events. While most have their own website, they would benefit from being associated with larger galleries and viewed by their clientele.

An alternative to this trend are the heavily place-based events that actively use their outdoor setting and its historical context as part of the experience, such as Kabosh, HK ArtWalk and the Summer in the Bight Festival. Such events are unlikely to have a digital component, unless it is something like the two smartphone apps for Kabosh's *Belfast Bred* or an app that improves the experience for the disabled. Downloads of these apps have allowed these events to develop new audiences for their work and diversify income streams through app purchases. Finally, tourists would also benefit from specially designed apps that give them more of the artworks' local cultural context than would be needed by the local community.

Not-for-profit initiatives

One the most ground-breaking initiatives for this not-for-profit group revolve around crowdsourcing by a new kind of not-for profit that is essentially virtual in nature. Starting with sites, such as Fringebacker, easier access to funding is likely to impact on the diversity of arts events and the nature of private patronage. It takes five per cent for a fee towards administrative support and that is only after the project reaches its target amount and can be funded. No fee is taken if the project is not funded and all the donations are returned. It is the first of its kind to do this and hopefully not the last.

Although, there are still some cases of a more traditional style patronage to artists of the type evident over the centuries, artists are relying more and more on other funding sources. Organizations that can provide more conventional project-based funding or mid-career grants are still active and crowdsourcing is more likely to complement these (especially with money-matching grants) than supplant them in the near future.

All sectors

A trend that crosses all sector initiatives is that of the increasing phenomenon of bundling events together tightly around certain dates in the arts scene calendar whether they form one event or not. In terms of visual arts, it is mainly done to attract tourists/serious art collectors over a particular period to a destination, such as occurred recently in Hong Kong with the end of May presenting a very crowded arts calendar with Art Basel HK, auctions, Contemporary Asian Art Fair, Cat Street Gallery Uber exhibition. Rather than compete, sometimes it is case of coordinating two or three separate events to reap the maximum benefits for all. For instance in Sackville, Canada, organizations such as The Struts Gallery and Faucet Arts Centre worked with the organizers of the Music Festival, Sappyfest, to cross-promote their events when these coincided within the timeframe of the larger and more well-known OK.Quoi?! Festival. This increased public awareness of complementary activities such as the roundtable discussions, screenings, artist's talks, installations, performances and workshops. It also ensured that tourists could benefit from the additional activities offered, if they could only afford a short stay at the destination.

Changing nature of curatorship

Curatorship of events is undergoing a revolution in many ways. This revolution is marked by the advent of virtual exhibitions, artist-curated events, the possible demise of specialist curators (or changes in their focus to more providing interaction with the public) in large public institutions and private-sector events. At present, the full impact of these changes and their combined impact on the role of curators is still largely unknown. The commercialization of curatorship can be seen when a company's personnel are used to produce travelling exhibitions as packages that then can be adapted to local conditions in close cooperation with local museum staff. For instance, the 'Wallace and Gromit's World of Invention' and the 'Capture the Moment: The Pulitzer Prize Photographs' travelling exhibitions. The latter by 2013, at the time of writing, had appeared in more than 30 cities internationally, with more than three million people having seen it since opening in New York in 2000. This circulating exhibit is attributed to the Newseum, a Washington DC-based museum of news and visitor attraction. The exhibition was created by Cyma Rubin and is coordinated by the Business of Entertainment Inc. These kinds of events contrast strongly with the early travelling exhibition of the kind curated by the Museum of Modern Art and in-house temporary exhibitions curated only by full-time museum staff.

Also, museums are better able to exploit merchandizing opportunities in conjunction with such events. The visitors benefit as these purchases act as souvenirs which can extend the exhibition experience (Collins-Kreiner and Zins 2013). This means that more research is being conducted into the meaning and use of souvenirs beyond that of examining the issue of demand and supply in a simplistic way. This study and other recent work also reveal a rich vein of inquiry that sets souvenir consumption against the background of societal and transnational contexts (Jolliffe, Cave and Baum 2013).

Arts events and leadership

Increasingly, there are more events being promoted with guest or professional artistic directors (e.g. Belfast Festival, Sharjah and even Art Basel) the justification for which seems to be that the content will be stronger and the event more appealing to the target audience or market. The leadership in deciding the vision for the event has a big impact on the content offered, including possible gaps and biases. However, even with a famous artist as a guest curator, the event still replicates a leadership model that has a member of the arts elite making many of the key decisions about the direction and content of the event. However, the top-down nature of this model has been tested, more recently, by the creation of new art events forms. Often, these are event forms that are more affordable, accessible and inclusive than those in the past, such as pop-ups, PechaKucha evenings and affordable art fairs. There is more evidence of a 'bottom-up' rather than 'top-down' approach as different communities (real and cyber) are becoming more involved in their creation worldwide. The challenge for arts events leadership, overall, is to more consciously aim for one or more of the five arts event categories into which various examples were outlined earlier – inspirational, affirming, pleasurable, enriching and celebratory – that will meet the needs of the event's key audience or orientation.

Changing nature of arts criticism

There is no denying that this shift towards more inclusiveness through increasing use of the Internet for arts event promotion and management is having an impact on the nature of arts criticism. In particular, where, how and when it is offered and how much is now deemed to be formal as against informal aesthetic critiquing. Arts authorities who provide such criticism for a living have tried to move with the times by engaging with online arts criticism, through online arts publications, (and some on Facebook, Twitter) in order to make sure their views on the quality of artworks, performances, art market trends, events management and cultural/ arts ecologies reach as broad an audience as possible. However, remaining well-remunerated in this context is probably only going to get more challenging for those who see themselves as professional critics, if such criticism becomes increasingly viewed as elitist. Accordingly, it is possible that professional art critics could see a diminishing of their role, as the arts community and the arts-consuming public could become more drawn to the views in less formal forums and media that virtual technology is providing.

Glocality and its relationship to the arts ecologies of an event

The twenty-first century may be witnessing a divergence in ways of staging arts events, where local conditions are moulding the content and form of many types of events. From personal observation, fringe festivals in Asia are very different to those in the UK and North America, while outdoor music festivals in Australia, with such a small local market, are likely to be more competitive than cooperative over their headlining acts. Middle Eastern events tend to utilize the cooler evenings to the utmost for both indoor and outdoor activities. The overall differences between the Middle East, Asia, North America, Australia, and so on are likely to be numerous and are more a topic for the future than this book.

Another issue is whether event organizers, particularly for city arts festivals, compare themselves regionally first or internationally and which is more important. In terms of tourism, obviously the potential for regional short-haul tourists to visit is high. Often there is a mix, even when successful aspects of some event forms are not readily transferrable to other locations. Arts leadership can play a role in terms of an event organizer trusting an artistic director from outside the local arts ecology to fulfill a designated mission for the event. The Sharjah case study brought up a number of issues about direction, management and nationalism in a situation where different cultures can clash.

One change in Australia is that museums, such as the Western Australian Museum, have in the last 20 years worked more closely with Indigenous communities. This has included holding arts events that fall in line with new museum outreach policies to form the kind of partnerships that promote this kind of cooperation. Again, there are many other factors working away in the background for each event that require a discussion about cultural and economic conditions when trying to understand the glocal issues.

The role of expatriates or residents with overseas/international perspectives in establishing events also needs further examination. The Bookworm International Literary Festival in China offers an insight into the progression of a themed festival over time, starting with much expatriate interest and later building up a following amongst Anglophone Chinese in the region. Accordingly, the event organizers have been able to develop a creative and yet sustainable programme that is supported by all sectors. Likewise, the Hong Kong ArtWalk was first popular amongst local expatriate residents and as the art market has developed more Hong Kong Chinese residents and mainland Chinese tourists have begun to regularly attend the event. The food and beverage options have changed to accommodate this recent interest, but nothing else major about the event has been altered. Finally, there is the example of the PechaKucha arts event form, which was developed by expatriate artists, Astrid Klein and Mark Dytham, in a Japanese context initially, before it became a worldwide phenomenon.

The examination of glocality has also brought out the role that a diaspora has played in regard to participating in and adapting events from the home country. Most of the discussion in the Caribbean example (Trinidad festivals, Chapter 2) revolved around affirming cultural identity in a way that builds the health of both local and overseas arts ecologies for certain art forms and artists. Such strategies could be examined more by those authorities needing to devise measures for ensuring the survival of intangible cultural heritage (ICH) in this era of high mobility. Also, those concerned about the loss of cultural diversity through such mobility. A recent example from South America in a UNWTO study of ICH found that art activities, such as performing dances for tourists, were useful for reintegrating members of the community, who had moved back to the village from large cities (UNWTO 2012). It may be possible to do more in this line to affirm cultural identity and pass on unique heritage arts to the next generation.

Artists and glocality

Another aspect is the nature of the glocality of artists and their artworks, particularly with regard to place-based events, such as sculpture trails. The Saint John event in New Brunswick, Canada, was inspired by a similar arts event, the Schoodic International Sculpture Symposium (SISS) in nearby Maine, USA. Both the Maine and the New Brunswick symposiums' works build on the local traditions and history of stone masonry. These symposiums in both areas are then contrasted against international sculptures. The event has been promoted as creating a special cultural landscape, while it also provides an opportunity for worldwide artists and a group of young local sculptors to work together. The works of art created are then made accessible to the public and tourists in particular and striking settings. Sculpture by the Sea has used this approach too, however, the sculptures are only exhibited on a short-term basis with the hope that some may be sold. Although, the co-production is not one of its objectives, both local and international artists can benefit financially from this arrangement, as well as having their works publicly exhibited.

There has been some discussion in the arts media in the United Kingdom about how and if artists really benefit much from festivals where there is not much in the way of remuneration. In particular, 'how the arts festival format and place-based commissions might facilitate creative output and extend audience engagement seems ripe for more exploration' (Portland Experiments Collective in Thomas 2013). Proposals for greater artistic engagement with the different sectors of the community also covered how such events could do more in terms of providing arts activities that increase the health and wellbeing of participants (Thomas 2013). The latter aspect of arts events' utility for the public may mean more recognition and remuneration for artists involved. Research is showing that it could become a bigger part of the remit from some artists in the future, while complementing public efforts for a healthier and happier society (Clift 2012; Michalos and Kahlke 2010).

Glocality and the internet

Most event organizers of popular arts events are aware they are walking a fine line in relation to public relations about issues such as ticketing and access to all activities at an event. Recently, the actual usefulness of digital technology in reaching new audiences and also making popular events more popular was evident when Glastonbury 2014 tickets sold out online in one hour and 27 minutes! This was averaging 3,000 tickets per minute after the website had got over the initial shock of so many hits. All this attention occurred without the line-up even being confirmed (BBC News, 2013).

Online ticketing services for arts events generally do not favour local purchases over international ones, so that pre-sales tickets are only available to a local resident, if one is a member of a certain professional group, corporate sponsor or sometimes a cardholder of a particular credit card. For repeatable events, this area requires special attention otherwise it can be grounds for a backlash against the event or result in an increase in counterfeited tickets. More needs to be understood by organizers about what is good for tourists/international arts/cultural ecologies versus the local residents and arts/cultural ecologies and assessing all aspects of SCA could give an indication of how well the event is working for each side.

Social media is increasingly playing a role in the promotion mix for arts events, and is indeed making possible new forms of impromptu events in the arts, by creating a direct channel for sponsoring agencies to connect with their audiences as mentioned in Chapter 5. However, not all netizens are benign in their interaction with others on the web. As observed in certain cases, events became 'compromised' when social media commentary about their organization and purpose turned negative, as in the cases of Stone Music Festival, Sydney and the Dome Festival, Hong Kong. More research into the impacts of their informal avenues of critique on arts events could be of use when trying to understand how successfully such events can generate creative capital and build their SCA, whilst keeping international and local arts/cultural ecologies on their side.

Sustainable creative advantage assessment

The sustainable creative advantage assessment approach is useful for understanding more about new forms of arts events that are spread and adapted (or not) to local conditions. Where potential for an event to be compromised or to lose its appeal to a key group exists, it is hoped that applying the SCA process to analyse its planning and implementation will prevent some of the most obvious problems. It is also possible to apply the SCA approach as a tool to track possible trends by assessing more than the event, as was demonstrated in Chapter 6. For instance, an investigation into whether there is a local emergence of arts events forms that is influenced by global trends, but still retains some essential local features could be undertaken by looking at a number of such events. Possible issues that arts events organizers and others can focus on by applying the SCA approach on a regular basis could include (but are not limited to): awareness of partners' needs and changes in the relationship over time; meeting artistic goals as well as financial goals; and keeping it fresh for repeat visitors/participants (as well as newcomers) each time the event is repeated.

Finally there may be issues that are beyond even the best-made plans and analyses. It is likely that outdoor arts events that are vulnerable to weather changes brought about by climate change will have to take extra care, even when held in summer. This would mean building into the implementation more flexibility, better contingency planning, and, where necessary, risk management. Alternatively, some events known for their atrocious environmental conditions may even witness an amelioration of the experience with a change to more temperate weather. Even so, no mud at Glastonbury would make it less challenging for those participants who expect and enjoy that as part of the event experience.

Relevance of the research

This volume has attempted to fill gaps in the social and cultural context of arts events management by introducing new concepts for categorizing and managing events and which have been illustrated with numerous case studies and examples. Chapter 1 introduced the disciplinary context within which the research was situated and Chapter 2 carried on to examine how event forms have arisen or evolved up to the present. Some of the latest trends raised at the end of that chapter have been explored in others in order to understand the appeal, planning, implementation and ongoing management of repeatable arts events. Finally, discussion of an approach to identify, document and make recommendations to enhance was outlined with examples from Hong Kong in Chapter 6. It is hoped that this approach may be also useful for researchers when comparing events to understand their glocality and sustainability.

Further research

This section has tried to be comprehensive, however, it is definitely not the last word in relation to arts events and associated socio-political debates revolving around power, authority and inclusiveness. In particular, the role of curators and critics in a glocal world needs more examination than was possible in this volume. As does the nature of arts events leadership in relation to whether top-down will give way eventually to bottom-up decision-making, or whether a fringe festival is still fringe, if it is heavily curated or making a high profit which is not equitably shared.

As mentioned above, research is needed on the nature of arts events, in particular geographical regions, especially those with an emerging interest in establishing more repeatable events with or without international appeal. Research on new trends in arts events should not favour the successful ones but also not ignore 'compromised' events in order to understand more about what does and does not work and how difficult issues can be resolved. Using the SCA approach could be one tool, and if it does happen to be applied by other researchers and event organizers on a regular basis, how they refine it and adapt it to their circumstances would be of great interest to the authors of this volume. Also, the emergence of different approaches with the same purpose would be interesting to compare with that of the SCA approach to see which is the most effective at uncovering insights into how and why certain arts events work and can be enhanced where necessary.

Notes

2 Historical context of arts events

1 Most dramatic productions were written in verse so that the authors were acclaimed as poets first and foremost.
2 This event is distinct from the more exclusive Dionysian Mysteries discussed earlier, which included ritualistic dances rather than theatrical performances.
3 The ten tribes or *phylae* involved in the festival's competitions were closer in nature to civic or voting districts after the establishment of Athenian democracy than the old Ionian ones (Goldhill 1987).
4 Framed works that are hung together on a wall from the floor to the ceiling: that is, almost up to the 'sky'.
5 There was a similar event in Hong Kong in the late 1990s where the rents are incredibly high, however, it did not start a trend in the way that the first New York exhibitions did.

3 Understanding arts events

1 Interview with Kin Cheung, Executive Project Officer, 30 September 2013.
2 Interview with Ivana Padovca, Varaždin City Tourist Association, 20 August 2010.

4 Key issues in planning and developing arts events

1 Interview with Bec Millar, Event Coordinator, Zest Festival, 9 April 2013.
2 Ibid.
3 Interview with Diana Alexander, Event Coordinator, Saint John Sculpture Festival, 7 November 2013.

References

Aardman Animations/BBC TV (2010) *Wallace and Gromit's World of Invention.* Aired 3 November, 2010. UK: Aardman Animations/BBC TV.

Affordable Art Fair, (2013) From Battersea and Beyond. Available: http://affordableartfair. com/hampstead/about/ (accessed 30 October 2013).

AIA Memphis (2013) '60th Anniversary Celebration of Architectural Gala'. Available: http://www.aiamemphis.org/celebration-of-architecture-gala/ (accessed 30 October 2013).

Ali-Knight, J. and Robertson, M. (2003) 'Introduction to arts, culture and leisure', in I. Yeoman (ed.), *Festivals and Events Management: An International Arts and Culture Perspective,* Oxford: Elsevier, pp. 3–28.

Allen, J., O'Toole, R., Harris, R. and McDonnell, I. (2002) *Festival and Special Event Management,* Milton, Queensland, Australia: John Wiley & Sons.

Altschuler, B. (2013) *Biennials and Beyond: Exhibitions that Made Art History, Volume II 1962–2002,* London: Phaidon.

Andreasean, A.R. and Kotler, P. (2003) *Strategic Marketing for Nonprofit Organisations,* Upper Saddle River, NJ: Prentice Hall.

Aquino, J., Phillips, R. and Sung, H. (2012) 'Tourism, culture, and the creative industries: reviving distressed neighbourhoods with arts-based community tourism', *Tourism, Culture and Communication* 12(1): 5–18.

Arab Cultural Trust (2013) 'Histories and culture'. Available: http://www.al-hakawati.net/ english/Culture_Traditions/chronology.asp (accessed 30 October 2013).

Art Basel (2013) 'About us'. Available: https://www.artbasel.com (accessed 16 November 2013).

Art Basel Hong Kong (2013) 'Showguide'. Pamphlet provided by Art Basel HK.

Arts Council of England (n.d.) 'Self evaluation framework'. Available http://www. artscouncil.org.uk/selfevaluation/framework/business-management/risk-management/ (accessed October 30 2013).

Asia Hotel Fair Committee (2013) 'Timeline/overview'. Available: http://hotelartfair.kr/ wp/overview/ (accessed 30 October 2013).

ACAF (Asian Contemporary Art Fair) (2013) 'About us'. Available: http://www. asiacontemporaryart.com/about-us/ (accessed 30 October 2013).

Athenian Agora Excavations (2013) 'The ten tribes'. Available: http://www.agathe.gr/ democracy/the_ten_new_tribes.html (accessed 20 October 2013).

Audiences NI. (2013) 'Kabosh create third digital Smartphone app' Available: http://www. audiencesni.com/news/Kabosh-create-third-digital-Smartphone-app (accessed 28 October 2013).

Auerbach, J.A. (2008) 'Introduction', in Auerbach, J.A. and Hoffenberg, P.H. (eds) *Britain, the Empire, and the World at the Great Exhibitions of 1851*, Aldershot: Ashgate, pp. ix–xviii.

Avery, P. (2007) 'Born again: From dock cities to cities of culture,' in Smith, M.K. (ed.), *Tourism, Culture and Regeneration*, Cambridge: CABI Publishing, pp. 151–62.

Bagdadli, S. and Arrigoni, L. (2005) 'Strategic positioning of the Venice Biennial: Analysing the market for periodic contemporary art exhibitions', *International Journal of Arts Management,* 7(3): 22–31.

Bailey, M. (2012) 'Art will cross the line last during the Olympics', *The Art Newspaper,* January 2012, 231: 37–38.

Barlow, M. and Shibli, S. (2007) 'Audience development in the arts: A case study of chamber music', *Managing Leisure*, 12(2–3):102–19.

Barthes, R. (1972) *Mythologies*, Paris: Seuil.

Bartholomew, I. (2013) 'Indelible images'. *Taipei Times*. Available: http://www.taipeitimes. com/News/feat/archives/2013/01/20/2003552950 (accessed 15 October 2013).

Basel Hong Kong (2013) 'Online survey'. Available (between 28 May and 30 June 2013): https://www.artbasel.com/en/Hong-Kong (accessed 30 May 2013).

Bazin, G. (1967) *The Museum Age,* New York: Universe Books Inc.

BBC News (2013) 'Glastonbury 2014 tickets sell out in record time'. Available: http:// www.bbc.co.uk/news/entertainment-arts-24418582 (accessed 24 October 2013).

BBC Northern Ireland (2013) 'Management review for 2012–2013'. Available: http://downloads.bbc.co.uk/annualreport/pdf/2012-13/bbc-management-review-northernireland-2013.pdf (accessed 15 October 2013).

Beechey, M. (2012) 'BBC Last Night of the Proms 2012 – Rule Britannia!' Available: http://www.youtube.com/watch?v=yprh8ElXgbU (accessed 30 October 2013).

Belfast Festival at Queen's. (n.d.) 'Belfast Festival at Queen's'.Available: http://www. belfastfestival.com/ (accessed 1 November 2013).

Bendixen, P. (2000) 'Skills and roles: Concepts of modern arts management', *International Journal of Arts Management*, 2(3): 4–13.

Bihagen, E. and Katz-Gerro, T. (2000) 'Culture consumption in Sweden: The stability of gender differences', *Poetics* 27: 327–49.

Bobić, D. (2011) 'Festival Varaždin Baroque Evenings'. Unpublished report to Concert Agency Varaždin.

Bodick, N. (2013) 'In praise of being lost. Reflections on the March meeting', *Artasiapacific,* July/August 2013, 84:40.

Bookworm International Literary Festival (2013) *The Bookworm International Literary Festival Program,* Chengdu, China: Bookworm International Literary Festival.

Bookworm International Literary Festival (n.d.) 'The Bookworm Literary Festival' Available: http://bookwormfestival.com/ (accessed 15 October 2013).

Bourdieu, P. (1984) *Distinction: A Social Critique of the Judgment of Taste*, London: Routledge and Kegan Paul.

Bowdin, G. (2010) *Events Management*, London: Routledge.

Brooks, A.C. and Kusher, R.J. (2001) 'Cultural districts and urban development', *International Journal of Arts Management*, 3(2): 4–15.

Brown, K.G. (2009) 'Island tourism marketing: Music and culture', *International Journal of Culture, Tourism and Hospitality Research*, 3(1): 25–32.

Brown, K.G., and Geddes, R. (2007) 'Resorts, culture and music: The Cape Breton tourism cluster', *Tourism Economics*, 13(1): 129–41.

Burning Man (2013) 'About us'. Available: http://www.burningman.com (accessed 20 October 2013).

Business of Entertainment Inc. (n.d.) 'Exhibitions'. Available: http://www.bizzent.com/ (accessed 21 October 2013).

Caldwell, N.G. (2000) 'The emergence of museum brands', *International Journal of Arts Management*, 2(3): 28–34.

Campetta, R., Manzoni, B. and Salvemini, S. (2010) 'Value drivers for cultural events: Empirical evidence from Italy', *International Journal of Arts Management* 12(2): 4–16.

Carpenter, G. (2008a) 'Overview of arts and cultural programming', In Carpenter, G. and Blandy, D. (eds) *Arts and Cultural Programming. A Leisure Perspective*, Champagne, IL: Human Kinetics, pp. 3–22.

Carpenter, G. (2008b) 'Special Events', in Carpenter, G. and Blandy, D. (eds) *Arts and Cultural Programming. A Leisure Perspective*, Champagne, IL: Human Kinetics, pp. 143–57.

Cartiere, C. and Willis, S. (2008) *The Practice of Public Art*. London: Routledge.

Catherwood, D.W. and Van Kirk, R.L. (1992) *The Complete Guide to Special Event Management: Business Insights, Financial Advice, and Successful Strategies from Ernst & Young, Advisors to the Olympics, the Emmy Awards and the PGA Tour*, New York: John Wiley and Sons.

Celtic Colours International Festival (n.d.) Online. Available: http://www.celtic-colours.com/ (accessed 10 October 2013).

Chabra, D. Sills, E. and Cubbage, F. (2003) 'The significance of festivals to rural economies: estimating the economic impacts of Scottish Highland Games in North Carolina', *Journal of Travel Research*, 41(4): 421–7.

Chadwick, A.F. (1980) *The Role of the Museum and Art Gallery in Community Education*, Nottingham: Barnes and Hornby Ltd.

Chan, G. (2013) 'Under-fire bands keep cool', *The Standard*, 2 July 2013: 2.

Chang, T.C. and Teo, P. (2009) 'Vernacular heritage in creative Singapore', *Urban Studies*, 46(2): 341–367.

Chang, T.C., Milne, S., Fallman, D. and Pohlmann, C. (1996) 'Urban heritage tourism: The global-local nexus', *Annals of Tourism Research*, 23(2): 284–305.

Cheerbo, J.M. and Peters, M. (1995) *American Participation in Opera and Musical Theater 1992*, Washington, DC: National Endowment for the Arts.

Chengdoo Citylife Magazine (2013) 'Bookworm International Literary Festival Special'. Available: www.chengdoo-magazine.com/pdf/ISSUE_062_WEB.pdf (accessed 15 November 2013).

China Today (2013) 'China City and Province: Chengdu'. Available: http://www.chinatoday.com/city/chengdu.htm (accessed 1 November 2013).

Chong, D. (2009) *Arts Management*, London: Routledge.

Chong, T. (2004) 'Society–state collaboration in Singapore: The Necessary Stage and the Arts Education Programme', in Tan, C.K. and Ng, T. (eds) *Ask Not: The Necessary Stage in Singapore Theatre*, Singapore: Times Publishing, pp. 245–60.

Chong, T. (2011) *The Theatre and the State in Singapore. Orthodoxy and Resistance*, London: Routledge.

Chow, V. and Lo, W. (2013) 'Protest trumps pop as "coincidental" concert subverted', *South China Morning Post*, 2 July 2013: A2.

Christin, A. (2012) 'Gender and highbrow cultural participation in the United States', *Poetics*, 40: 423–43.

CISV (2013) 'About us'. Available: http://www.cisv.org (accessed 30 October 2013).

City of Buenos Aires (2013) International Tango Festival. Available: http://festivales.buenosaires.gob.ar/tango/festivalymundial/web/en/about/index.html (accessed 30 October 2013).

City of Reykjavik (2011) *Tourism Strategy for the City of Reykjavik 2011–2020*, Reykjavik: City of Reykjavik.

City of Varaždin (2013) Spancirfest World Music Festival. Available: www.tourism-varazdin.com (accessed 30 October 2013).

Clift, S. (2012) 'Creative arts as a public health resource: Moving from practice-based research to evidence-based practice', *Perspectives in Public Health*, 132(3): 120–7.

Colbert, F. (2003) 'Entrepreneurship and leadership in marketing the arts,' *International Journal of Arts Management*, 6 (1): 30–9.

Collins-Kreiner, N. and Zins, Y. (2013) 'With the passing of time: The changing meaning of souvenirs', in Cave, J., Jolliffe, L. and Baum, T. (eds) *Tourism and Souvenirs. Glocal Perspectives from the Margins*, Bristol: Channel View Publications, pp. 29–39.

Cultural Olympiad (2012) 'Festival and events'. Available: http://www.london2012.com/about-us/cultural-olympiad/ (accessed 30 October 2013).

Delta Bridges (2012) 'Lusofonia Festival (Macau)'. Available: http://www.deltabridges.com/event/macau-events/lusofonia-festival-macau (accessed 30 October 2013).

Derrett, R. (2009) 'How festivals nurture resilience in regional communities', in Ali-Knight, J., Robertson, M., Fyall, A. and Ladkin, A. (eds) *International Perspectives of Festivals and Events: Paradigms of Analysis*. Oxford: Elsevier, pp. 107–24.

Designing Hong Kong (2013) 'About us'. Available: http://www.designinghongkong.com/v3/?page_id=2 (accessed 30 October 2013)

Dewey, P. (2004) 'From arts management to cultural administration', *International Journal of Arts Management*, 3: 13–23.

Dhar, J. (2009) 'Development of art across the Emirates', *Artmap*, May: 4–5.

Dhar, J. (2013) 'Sharjah Biennale 11 Review', *Artasiapacific*, May/June 2013: 83.

Dicks, B. (2003) *Culture on Display. The Production of Contemporary Visitability*, Maidenhead: Open University Press.

DiMaggio, P. (1991) 'Social structure, institutions and cultural goods: the case of the United States', in Bourdieu, P. and Coleman, J. (eds) *Social Theory for a Changing Society*, San Francisco, CA: Westview Press, pp. 133–66.

DiMaggio, P. (2004) 'Gender, networks, and cultural capital', *Poetics*, 32: 99–103.

Discover Saint John (2013) 'Gallery Hop'. Available: http://discoversaintjohn.com/event/gallery-hop-2/ (accessed 30 October 2013).

Do, J. and Leong, S. (2012) 'Arts, social impact and community development: A case study from Hong Kong'. The 5th International Conference on the Arts in Society 5–7 July, 2012, London.

Drake, G. (2003) 'This place gives me space: place and creativity in the creative industries', *Geoforum*, 34(4): 511–24.

du Bois, W.E.B. (1900) 'The American Negro in Paris', *The American Monthly Review of Reviews*, 22(5): 575–7.

du Cros, H. and Jolliffe, L. (2011) 'Bundling the arts for tourism to complement urban heritage tourist experiences in Asia', *Journal of Heritage Tourism*, 6(3): 181–95.

du Cros, H. and Leong, S. (2011) 'A new approach to arts policy formulation that directly supports the arts and cultural identity in Hong Kong', The Asian Conference on Arts and Humanities, IAFOR, Osaka, Japan 27–30 May 2011. Available: http://iafor.org/acah_proceedings.html, (accessed 20 October 2013).

Dvorjetski, E. (2012) 'Maioumas festivities in the Eastern Mediterranean Basin: Maioumas-Shuni as a case study', *Strata*, 30: 89–125.

Earl, P.E. (2001) 'Simon's travel theorem and the demand for live music', *Journal for Economic Psychology*, 22: 335–8.

Ebrey, P. (1999) *Cambridge Illustrated History of China,* Cambridge: Cambridge University Press.

Edinburgh College of the Arts (2013) 'History'. Available: http://www.ed.ac.uk/schools-departments/edinburgh-college-art/about/our-history (accessed 20 October 2013).

Edinburgh Festival Fringe (EFF) (2013) 'About us'. Available: http://www.edfringe.com/ (accessed 21 October 2013).

Edinburgh International Festival (EIF) (2013) 'History'. Available: http://www.eif.co.uk/about-festival/history-festival (accessed 21 October 2013).

Edventures (2013) 'Vision/Schedule'. Available: http://www.edventures.ca/en/ (accessed 30 October 2013).

Evans, G. (2009) 'Creative cities, creative spaces and urban policy', *Urban Studies,* 46(5): 1003–40.

Evans, G.L. (2007) 'Tourism, creativity and the city,' in: Richards, G. and Wilson, J. (eds) *Tourism Creativity and Development*, London: Routledge, pp. 57–72.

Falassi, A. (1987) *Time out of Time: Essays on the Festival*, Albuquerque: University of New Mexico Press.

Fenich, G.G. (2011) *Meetings, Expositions, Events, and Conventions*, Upper Saddle River, NJ: Pearson, Prentice Hall.

Fernsebner, S. R. (2006) 'Objects, Spectacle, and a nation on display at the Nanyang Exposition of 1910,' *Late Imperial China*, 27(2): 99–124.

FESFOP (2013) 'Presentation'. Available: http://www.fesfop.org/ (accessed 30 October 2013).

Fitzsimons, S. (2013) 'Stone Music defy critics and want Muse for 2014'. The Music – Industry/Festival. Available: http://themusic.com.au/news/all/2013/04/22/stone-music-defy-critics-and-want-muse-for-2014/ (accessed 30 October 2013).

Florida, R. (2002) *The Rise of the Creative Class: And How It's Transforming Work, Leisure, Community and Everyday Life*, New York: Basic Books.

Foley, M. McGillivary, D. and McPherson, G. (2009) 'Policy, politics and sustainable events,' in Stabler, M.J. (ed.) *Tourism and Sustainability: Principles to Practice*, New York: CAB International, pp. 13–21.

France, R.L. (2011) *Veniceland Atlantis. The Bleak Future of the World's Favourite City* (A Web-Enhanced Book), Faringdon, UK: Libri Publishing.

Fredericton Tourism (2013) 'Media release'. Available: http://www.edventures.ca/en/news/edventures2013launch.asp (accessed 30 October 2013).

Frew, E.A. and Ali-Knight, J. (2010) 'Creating high and low art: Experimentation and commercialisation at fringe festivals', *Tourism, Culture and Communication,* 10(3): 231–46.

Fringebacker, (2013) 'Crowdfunding: Learn more'. Available: http://www.fringebacker.com/ (accessed 13 November 2013).

Frith, S., Brennan, M., Cloonan, M. and Webster, E. (2013) *The History of Live Music in Britain, Volume I. From Dance Hall to the 100 Club*, Farnham, UK: Ashgate.

Frost, W., Wheeler, F. and Harvey, D. (2009) 'Commemorative events: Sacrifice, identity, and dissonance'. In Ali-Knight, J., Robertson, M., Fyall, A. and Ladkin, A. (eds) *International Perspectives of Festivals and Events: Paradigms of Analysis,* Oxford: Elsevier, pp. 161–72.

Fusco, C. (2003) '5th and final international sculpture symposium in Changchun', *Craft Arts International*, (56): 107–8.

Galligan, A.M. (2008) 'The evolution of arts and cultural districts,' in Cherbo, J., Stewart, R., and Wyszomirski, M. (eds) *Understanding the Arts and Creative Sector in the United States*, New York: Rutgers University Press, pp.129–42.

Ganga, R. N. (n.d.) 'European cultural institutions as glocalisms. the cases of the Fundacao de Serralves and the Contemporary Art Centre (Porto): 329-342'. Available: http://ler. letras.up.pt/uploads/ficheiros/10364.pdf (accessed 29 October 2013).

GIGA (German Institute of Global and Area Studies) and *China Aktuell* (2012*). China Aktuell* (Journal issue on Africa and China). Available: http://www.giga-hamburg.de/index.php?file=cha_0803.html&folder=publikationen/archiv/ch_aktuell (accessed 30 October 2013).

Getz, D. (1997) *Event Management and Event Tourism,* New York: Cognizant Communication Corporation.

Getz, D. (2008) 'Event tourism: Definition, evolution, and research', *Tourism Management,* 29(3): 403–28.

Getz, D. (2009) 'Policy for sustainable and responsible festivals and events: institutionalization of a new paradigm', *Journal of Policy Research in Tourism, Leisure and Events,* 1(1): 61–78.

Getz, D. (2010) 'The nature and score of festival studies,' *International Journal of Events Management Research,* 5(1): 1–47.

Getz, D. (2012) *Event Studies: Theory, Research and Policy for Planned Events (Events Management)*, London: Routledge.

Glastonbury Festival of Contemporary Performing Arts (2013) 'History'. Available: http://www.glastonburyfestivals.co.uk/history/2001/ (accessed 30 October 2013).

Godfrey, J. (2006) 'Business support for arts festivals in Britain: An exploratory study', *LSA Publication,* 93: 93–106.

Goldbard, A. (2006) *New Creative Community. The Art of Cultural Development*, Oakland, CA: New Village Press.

Goldblatt, J.J. (1998) 'Special events: Best practice in modern event management', *Managing Leisure,* 3: 111–16.

Goldblatt, J.J. (2002) *Special Events: Twenty-first Century Global Event Management,* New York: John Wiley and Sons.

Goldhill, S. (1987) 'The Great Dionysia and civic ideology,' *Journal of Hellenic Studies,* 107: 58–76.

Goodwin, R. (2010) 'Best arts events in unusual London venues'. *London Evening Standard.* Available: http://www.standard.co.uk/goingout/attractions/best-arts-events-in-unusual-london-venues-6479550.html (accessed 14 November 2012).

Gordin, V., and Matetskaya, M. (2012) 'Creative tourism in St Petersberg: The state of the art', *Journal of Tourism Consumption and Practice,* 4(2): 55–76.

Gray, J. (2010) 'Two roads west'. Available: http://www.culturenorthernireland.org/article/2579/two-roads-west (accessed 30 October 2013).

Green, G.L. and Scher, P.W. (2007) 'Introduction', in Green, G.L. and Scher, P.W. (eds) *Trinidad Carnival. The Cultural Politics of a Transnational Festival*, Bloomington, IN: Indiana University Press, pp.1–25.

Guggenheim Museum. (2011) 'The Guggenheim releases its first e-books'. Available: at http://www.guggenheim.org/new-york/press-room/news/4374-the-guggenheim-releases-its-first-e-books (accessed 11 October 2013).

Guth, C.M.E. (2004) 'Takamura Koun and Takamura Kotaro: On being a sculptor', in Takeuchi, M. (ed.) *The Artist as Professional in Japan*, Stanford, CA: Stanford University Press, pp. 152–79.

Hager, M. and Sung, H. (2012a) 'Local arts agency participation in cultural tourism', *Journal of Heritage Tourism,* 7(3): 205–17.

Hager, M.A. and Sung, H. (2012b) 'Local arts agencies as destination management organisations', *Journal of Travel Research*, 51(4): 400–11.

References 159

Haigh, A.E. (1898) *The Attic Theatre,* Oxford: Clarendon Press.
Hall, P.G. (2000) 'Creative cities and economic development', *Urban Studies,* 37(4): 639–49.
Hand, C., (2011) 'Do arts audiences act like consumers?'*Managing Leisure,* 16(2): 88–97.
Hart, M. (2010) *The Art of Ancient Greek Theater*, Los Angeles, CA: The Paul J. Getty Museum.
Hartig, F. (2011) 'Confucius Institutes and the rise of China', *Journal of Chinese Political Science,* 17(1): 53–76.
Harvey, D.C. Hawkins, H. and Thomas, N.J. (2012) 'Thinking creative clusters beyond the city: people, places and networks', *Geoforum,* 43: 529–39.
Hassanien, A. and Crispin, D. (2011) 'Toward a typology of events venues', *International Journal of Event and Festival Management*, 2(2): 106–16.
Hede, A., and Rentschler, R. (2007) 'Mentoring volunteer festival managers: Evaluation of a pilot scheme in regional Australia,' *Managing Leisure,* 12(2/3): 157–70.
Hede, A.M. Jago, A.L, and Deery, M. (2003) 'An agenda for special event research: Lessons from the past and directions for the future', *Journal of Hospitality and Tourism Management*, 10 (supplement): 1–14.
Henderson, J. (2003) 'Government and the arts: a framework for analysis', *Managing Leisure,* 8(3): 121–32.
Hennessy, K. (2013) 'Long hair, tight pants, big grins'. Available: http://www.smh.com.au/entertainment/music/long-hair-tight-pants-big-grins-20130421-2i7za.html#ixzz2aQ5Z51C7 (accessed 30 October 2013).
Herman, A. (2003) *The Scottish Enlightenment. The Scot's Invention of the Modern World*, London: Harper Collins.
HK Clubbing (2009) 'Summer pop live in Hong Kong'. Available: http://www.hkclubbing.com/articles/entertainment/summer-pop-live-in-hong-kong.html (accessed 30 October 2013).
Hobsbawm, E. (1992) 'Mass-producing traditions: Europe, 1870–1914', in Hobsbawm, E. and Ranger, T. (eds), *The Invention of Tradition,* Cambridge: Canto/Cambridge University Press, pp. 11–36.
Holloway, J.C. and Humphries, C. (2002) *The Business of Tourism*, Harlow: Pearson Education Limited.
Home Affairs Bureau HK (2013) 'Cultural policy'. Available: http://www.hab.gov.hk/en/policy_responsibilities/arts_culture_recreation_and_sport/arts.htm (accessed 15 November 2013).
Hong Kong ArtWalk (2010) 'ArtWalk, 2010' Unpublished pamphlet and map, Hong Kong.
Hong Kong ArtWalk (2013) 'ArtWalk, 2013' Unpublished pamphlet and map, Hong Kong.
Hong Kong Companies Registration (2013) *Hong Kong Companies Register*. Available: http://www.hkcomp.info/hkcps-1292080-d16ea366.html (accessed 30 October 2013).
HKIEd (Hong Kong Institute of Education) (2013) 'Arts Bus: On the Move!' Publicly presented PowerPoint presentation, Hong Kong: Hong Kong Institute of Education.
Hornblower, S. and Morgan, C. (2007) *Pindar's Poetry, Patrons, and Festivals. From Archaic Greece to the Roman Empire*, New York: Oxford University Press.
Hui, D. (2006) *A Study on Creative Index*, Hong Kong: University of Hong Kong.
Iceland Naturally. (n.d.) 'Reykjavik Arts Festival'. Available: http://www.icelandnaturally.com/ (accessed May 10 2013).
International Olympic Committee (IOC) (2000) *The IOC and its Cultural Policy Forum*, Lausanne: International Olympic Committee.
Ioannidou, E. (2011) 'Toward a national *Heterotopia*: Ancient theaters and the cultural politics of performing ancient drama in modern Greece', in Gounaridou, K. (ed.) *Text*

and Presentation. Comparative Drama Conference Series, London: Macfarland, pp. 385–403.

Ivakhiv, A. (2005) 'Colouring Cape Breton "Celtic": Topographies of culture and identity in Cape Breton Island', *Ethnologies*, 27(2): 107–36.

Jacobs, A. (2004) 'Wood, Sir Henry Joseph (1869–1944)', *Oxford Dictionary of National Biography*, Oxford: Oxford University Press.

Jepson, A., Wiltshier, S. and Clarke, A. (2008) 'Community festivals: Involvement and inclusion'. CHME International Research Conference, Strathclyde Business School, University of Strathclyde, 14–16 May 2008, Glasgow: The Council for Hospitality Management Education (CHME).

Jolliffe, L., Cave, J. and Baum, T. (2013) 'Lessons in tourism and souvenirs from the margins', in Cave, J., Jolliffe, L. and Baum, T. (eds) *Tourism and Souvenirs. Glocal Perspectives from the Margins*, Bristol: Channel View Publications, pp.189–99.

Jones, A. (2007) *National Theatres in Context. France, Germany, England and Wales*, Cardiff, University of Wales Press.

Jones, N. (2013) 'Huh? Stone Music Festival lawyers up against tone deaf'. Available: http://www.tonedeaf.com.au/features/columns/268219/stone-music-festival-sends-lawyers.htm (accessed 30 October 2013).

Jones, S.T. (2011) *Tribes and Burning Man: How an Experimental City in the Desert is Shaping the New American Counterculture*, San Francisco, CA: CCC Publishing.

Kabosh Theatre Company. (n.d.) 'About Kabosh'. Available: http://www.kabosh.net/aboutkabosh.php (accessed 30 March 2013).

Karp, I., Kratz, C.A., Swzaja, L. and Ubarra-Frausto, T. (2006) *Museum Frictions: Public Cultures/Global Transformations*. Durham, NC: Duke University Press.

Kay, P. and Polonsky, M. (2010) 'Creative industries and experiences: Development, marketing and consumption', *Tourism, Culture and Communication,* 10(3): 181–6.

Keaney, E., (2008) 'Understanding arts audiences: Existing data and what it tells us', *Cultural Trends,* 17(2): 97–113.

Kelemen, K. (2011) 'Everything that makes the town happens during the festival: the construction of the meaning of place through festival practices'. People make places – ways of feeling the world; SIEF 10th International Congress, Lisbon, Portugal, 17–21 April 2011. Available: http://bib.irb.hr/prikazi-rad?rad=511232 (accessed 30 October 2013).

Kickstarter.com (2013) 'What is Kickstarter?' Available: http://www.kickstarter.com/hello?ref=nav (accessed 30 October 2013).

Kidd, S. (2013) 'Lay of the land: Topography of 2013 Chengdu Bookworm Literary Festival. *Chengdoo Citylife Magazine*, Bookworm International Literary Festival Special. Available: www.chengdoomagazine.com/pdf/ISSUE_062_WEB.pdf. (accessed April 15 2013).

Kley, J. (2011) 'Energy in form essay on coherences between geomorphology, human mind and stone-sculptor's effort', DLA Dissertation, Faculty of Music and Visual Arts Doctoral School, University of Pécs, Hungary.

Knelman, M. (2013) 'Toronto's billboard tax set to fund city art and culture'. *The Toronto Star*, 16 January 2013. Available: http://www.thestar.com/ *(accessed 1 November 2013)*.

Kotler, N. (2001) 'New ways of experiencing culture: the role of museums and marketing implications', *Museum Management and Curatorship*, 19(4): 417–25.

Kurlantzick, J. (2007) *Charm Offensive: How China's Soft Power is Transforming the World*, New Haven, CT: Yale University Press.

L'Art Noveau (2013a) 'L'Exposition Universelle de 1855'. Available: http://lartnouveau.com/belle_epoque/paris_expo_1855.htm (accessed 30 October 2013)

L'Art Noveau (2013b) 'L'Exposition Universelle de 1889'. Available: http://lartnouveau. com/belle_epoque/paris_expo_1889.htm (accessed 30 October 2013)

Laws, C. and Beaven, Z. (2006) 'Practice/policy dichotomies in the successful delivery of arts events: an operations management perspective', in Fleming, S. and Jordan, F. (eds) *Events and Festivals: Education, Impacts and Experiences.* Eastbourne: Leisure Studies Association, 109–28.

Lee, T. (2010) *The Media, Cultural Control and the Government in Singapore*, London: Routledge.

Leung, C. C. and du Cros, H. (forthcoming) Confucius Institutes: multiple reactions and interactions. *Journal of Asian Public Policy.*

Liu, J. E. (1972) *Six Yuan Plays*, London: Penguin Books.

Long, P. (2000) 'After the event: Perspectives on organizational partnerships in the management of a themed festival year', *Event Management*, 6(1): 45–59.

Macau Daily Times (2011) 'Lusofonia Festival hits downtown' *Macau Daily Times,* 24 October 2011. Available: http://www.macaudailytimes.com.mo/macau/30800-Lusofonia-Festival-hits-downtown.html (accessed October 2013).

Mackey, E. (2002) *The House of Difference: Cultural Politics and National Identity in Canada*, Toronto: University of Toronto Press.

Maguire, T. (2008) 'Northern Irish drama: Speaking the peace', in Holdsworth, N. and Luckhurst, M. (eds). *A Concise Companion to Contemporary British and Irish Drama*, Hoboken, NJ: John Wiley and Sons, pp. 66–84.

Maitland, R. (2007) 'Culture, city users and the creation of new tourism areas in cities', in Smith, M.K. (ed.), *Tourism, Culture and Regeneration*, Cambridge: CABI Publishing, pp. 25–34.

Mann, T. (2013) 'Stone Music Festival on 2014 headliners: "It could be Muse, Kings of Leon or Pearl Jam"'. Available at: http://m.fasterlouder.com.au/news/35494/Stone-Music-Festival-on-2014-headliners-It-could-be-Muse-Kings-Of-Leon-or-Pearl-Jam (accessed 10 January 2014)

Maughan, C. and Bianchi, F. (2004) 'Economic and social impact of cultural festivals in the East Midlands'. Available: http://www.efa-aef.eu/newpublic/upload/efadoc/11/ Economic%20and%20social%20impact-final%20report.pdf (accessed 30 October 2013).

Mazdon, L. (2006) 'The Cannes Film Festival as transnational space', *Postscript,* 25(2): 19–30.

Mazza, C.M. and Pedersen, J.S. (2008) 'Creativity at work: Who's last? Challenges and advantages for late adopters in the International Film Festival field', Creative Encounters Working Paper 6. Copenhagen: Copenhagen Business School. Available: http:// filmfestivalsummit.com/PDF/IFF%20challenges.pdf (accessed 30 October 2013).

McCabe, H. (1998) 'Contesting home: tourism, memory, and identity in Sackville, New Brunswick', *The Canadian Geographer*, 42(3): 231–45.

McDowell, S. (2008) 'Selling conflict heritage through tourism in peacetime Northern Ireland: Transforming conflict or exacerbating difference?' *International Journal of Heritage Studies*, 14(5): 405–21.

McKercher, B. and du Cros, H. (2002) *Cultural Tourism: The Partnership between Tourism and Cultural Heritage Management*, Binghamton, NY: The Haworth Press.

McNicholas, B. (2004) 'Arts, culture and business: a relationship transformation, a nascent field', *International Journal of Arts Management,* 7(1): 57–68.

McReary, M. (2008) 'Festival future looks bright with £1m deal', *The Belfast Telegraph*, 8 February 2008: 3.

Michalos, A.C. and Kahlke, P.M. (2010) 'Arts and the perceived quality of life in British Columbia', *Social Indicators Research,* 96:1–39.

Miles, M. (2005) 'Interruptions: Testing the rhetoric of culturally led urban development', *Urban Studies*, 42(5/6): 889–911.

Miller, E. (1996) *Edinburgh International Festival 1947–1996*, Menston: Ashgate, Scolar Press.

Mitchell, P. and Fisher, R. (2010) 'From passenger to driver: Creativity and culture in rural communities', *Tourism, Culture and Communication,* 10(3): 187–200.

MOMA (2013) 'The family of man'. Available: http://www.moma.org/learn/resources/archives/archives_highlights_06_1955 (accessed 30 October 2013).

Mommaas, H. (2004) 'Cultural clusters and the post-industrial city: Towards the remapping of urban cultural policy', *Urban Studies* 41(3): 507–32.

Mottner, S. and Ford, J.B. (2005) 'Measuring nonprofit marketing strategy performance: The case of museum stores', *Journal of Business Research*, 58(6): 829–40.

Mulcahy, L. (2005) *Theatre Festival: Best Worldwide Venues for New Works*, New York: Allworth.

Mullens, P. (1995) 'Everyone knows Henry Woods set up the Proms. But who remembers the man who hired him to do it?' *The Independent,* 21 July 1995. Available: http://www.independent.co.uk/arts-entertainment/music/everyone-knows-henry-wood-set-up-the-proms-but-who-remembers-the-man-who-hired-him-to-do-it-by-peter-mullen-1592519.html (accessed 30 October 2013).

Muller, N. (2009) 'Contemporary art in the Middle East', in Sloman, E. (ed) *Contemporary Art in the Middle East*, London: Black Dog Publishing, pp. 12–25.

Murray, K. (2007) 'Hong Kong plays host to talks about place of creative industries in cities', *Planning,* 1721: 26.

Myecopaloosa (2012) 'Oh, the places you'll go at Burning Man!' Available: http://www.youtube.com/watch?v=YIwE-ECjbx8 (accessed 30 October 2013).

NEA (National Endowment for the Arts) (2013) 'initial public art project becomes a landmark'. Available: http://www.nea.gov/about/40th/grandrapids.html (accessed 30 October 2013).

Nelson-Atkins Museum of Art (2012) 'Inventing the modern world: Decorative arts at World's Fairs 1851–1939. Available: http://www.nelson-atkins.org/art/exhibitions/worldfairs/ (accessed 30 October 2013).

NOJHF (New Orleans Jazz and Heritage Festival) (2013) 'History'. Available : http://www.nojazzfest.com/info/history/ (accessed 30 October 2013).

New World First Bus (NWFB)/Citybus (2013) 'Press release 23 January 2013'. Available: http://www.nwstbus.com.hk/en/uploadedPressRelease/5718_20130123_eng.pdf (accessed 18 October 2013).

Newfoundland and Labrador Heritage, (2013) 'Rising Tide Theatre historical background'. Available: http://www.heritage.nf.ca/arts/risingtideprof.html (accessed 30 October 2013).

News 352 (2009) 'The Family of Man'. Available: (http://www.youtube.com/watch?v=HsE-6ZpUo2A (accessed 30 October 2013).

Newstead, A. (2013) 'Stone Music Festival promoters distance themselves from Bikie connections'. Available: http://www.tonedeaf.com.au/news/tournews/280073/stone-music-festival-promoters-distance-themselves-from-bikie-connections.htm (accessed 30 October 2013).

Nickerson, N.P., Kerr, P. and Murray, W.C. (2014) *An Introduction to Tourism,* 6th edition, Toronto: Pearson Canada.

Nip, A. (2013) 'Pull out of July 1 gig, pop stars told', *South China Morning Post*, 20 June 2013: C1.

Nurse, K. (2001) *Festival Tourism in the Caribbean: An Economic Impact Assessment*, Washington, DC: USA: Inter-American Development Bank.

Nurse, K. (2004) 'Globalization in reverse: Diaspora and the export of the Trinidad Carnivale,' in Cozart Riggio, M. (ed.) *Carnival – Culture in Action: The Trinidad Experience*, London: Routledge, pp. 245–54.

Nurse, K. (2011) 'Diasporic visitors bigger spenders than foreigners'. Available: http://www.shridathramphalcentre.org/index.php?option=com_content&view=article&id=832:uwis-dr-keith-nurse-diasporic-visitors-bigger-spenders-than-foreigners&catid=13:src-news&Itemid=100114 (accessed 30 October 2013).

O'Hagan, J. and Harvey, D. (2000) 'Why do companies sponsor arts events? Some evidence and a proposed classification', *Journal of Cultural Economics*, 24(3): 205–24.

O'Sullivan, D. and Jackson, M.J. (2002) 'Festival tourism: A contributor to sustainable local economic development?' *Journal of Sustainable Tourism,* 10(4): 325–42.

Ontario Arts Council (n.d.) 'Ontario ArtsCoucil'. Available: http://www.arts.on.ca/site4.aspx (accessed 8 October 2013).

Orbaşli, A. (2000) *Tourists in Historic Towns: Urban Conservation and Heritage Management*. London: E&FS Spon.

Page, S. and Hall, C. M. (2003) *Managing Urban Tourism*, London: Prentice Hall.

Page, S.J. and Connell, J. (2012) *Handbook of Events*, London: Routledge.

Paglia, C. (2012) *Glittering Images. A Journey through Arts from Egypt to Star Wars*, New York: Pantheon.

Papaioannou, D. and Lykesas, G. (2012) 'The role and significance of dance in the Dionysian mysteries,' *Studies in Physical Culture and Tourism,* 19(2): 68–72.

PechaKucha Barnsley (2013) 'Frequently asked questions'. Available: http://pknbarnsley.co.uk/about-pecha-kucka-barnsley (accessed 30 October 2013).

PechaKucha 20 × 20 (2013a) 'Frequently asked questions'. Available: http://www.pechakucha.org/faq (accessed 30 October 2013).

PechaKucha 20 × 20 (2013b) 'Arts Bus: On the Move!'. Presented at 25 May 2013 Kong Kong. Available: http://www.pechakucha.org/cities/hong-kong/presentations/arts-bus-on-the-move (accessed 15 October 2013).

Pine, J. and Gilmore, J. (1999) *The Experience Economy*. Boston, MA: Harvard Business School Press.

Powerhouse Museum (2013) 'Wallace and Gromit's World of Invention'. Available: http://www.powerhousemuseum.com/wallace-and-gromit/?campaign=fb (accessed 30 October 2013).

Preez, K. and Bailey, J. (2010) *Artistic Reflection Kit: A Guide to Assist Arts Organizations to Reflect on Artistic Vibrancy and Measure Their Artistic Achievements.* Canberra: Australia Council for the Arts.

Putler, D.S. and Lele, S. (2003) 'An easily implemented framework for forecasting ticket sales to performing arts events', *Marketing Letters,* 14(4): 307–20.

Quinn, B. (2006) 'Problematising "festival tourism": Arts festivals and sustainable development in Ireland', *Journal of Sustainable Tourism,* 14(3): 288–306.

Quinn, B., (2010) 'Arts festivals, urban tourism and cultural policy', *Journal of Policy Research in Tourism, Leisure and Events*, 2(3): 264–69.

Quinn, M. (2007) 'Belfast Festival "will close this month" without more funding', *The Stage*, 16 January 2007. Available: http://www.thestage.co.uk (accessed 15 October 2013).

Radbourne, J. (2002) 'Social intervention or market intervention? A problem for governments in promoting the value of the arts', *International Journal of Arts Management,* 5(1): 50–61.

Ray, L. (2010) 'Migration and remembrance. Sounds and spaces of klezmer "revivals"', *Cultural Sociology,* 4(3): 357–78.

Reykjavik Arts Festival (2013) 'Reykjavik Arts Festival'. Available: http://www.listahatid. is/2013/en/ (accessed 1 October 2013).

Richards, G. (2011) 'Creativity and tourism: The state of the art', *Annals of Tourism Research*, 38(4): 1225–53.

Richards, G. and Marques, L. (2012) 'Exploring creative tourism: Editors introduction', *Journal of Tourism Consumption and Practice,* 4(2): 1–11.

Richards, G. and Palmer, R. (2010) *Eventful Cities*, London: Routledge.

Richards, G. and Raymond, C. (2000) 'Creative Tourism', *Atlas News 1,* 23.

Rising Tide Theatre Company, (2013) 'The pageant'. Available: http://www.risingtidetheatre. com/?Content=The_Performances/Pageant (accessed 30 October 2013).

Robinson, M. (2010) 'Just how big is the arts ecology?' Available: http://thinkingpractice. blogspot.hk/2010/07/just-how-big-is-the-arts-ecology.html (accessed 13, October 2013).

Roche, M. (2003) 'Mega-events, time and modernity: On time structures in global society', *Time and Society*, 12(1): 99–126.

Rojnik, R. (2011) Discography of 40 years of the VBE and its significance for the promotion and preservation of the Croatian and European musical heritage. Available at: http://hrcak. srce.hr/index.php?show=clanak&id_clanak_jezik=98132 (accessed 8 January 2014).

Rossabi, M. (2013) 'Mongol support of artisans'. Available: http://afe.easia.columbia.edu/ mongols/history/history6.htm (accessed 30 October 2013).

Saadawi, G. (2011) 'Post-Sharjah Biennial 10: institutional grease and institutional critique', *E Flux,* 26 June 2011: H1–H8.

Safed Israel (2013) 'Klezmer masterclasses and festival'. Available: http://www.safed-home.com/klezmer-festival-in-safed.html (accessed 30 October 2013).

Salem, G., Jones, E. and Morgan, N. (2012) 'An overview of events management', in Yeoman, I., Robertson, M., Ali Knight, J., Drummond, S., and McMahon, B., (eds) *Festival and Event Management*, Oxford: Butterworth and Heinemann, pp. 14–31.

Sanada, H. (2009) 'Artistic competitions at the Greek Olympia Games in the 19th century', *International Journal of Sport and Health Science, 7*: 23–30.

Schoodic International Sculpture Symposium. (n.d.) 'Schoodic International Sculpture Symposium'. Available: http://schoodicsculpture.org/ (accessed 1 November 2013).

Schumacher, E.F. (1989) *Small is Beautiful: Economics as if People Mattered*, 2nd edn, New York: Harper Perennial.

Science Museum (2009) 'Discover a world of cracking ideas'. Available: http://www. sciencemuseum.org.uk/on-line/wallaceandgromit/ (accessed 30 October 2013).

Scott, C. (2000) 'Branding: Positioning museums in the 21st century', *International Journal of Arts Management*, 2(3): 35–9.

Sculpture by the Sea (2013) 'History/Frequently Asked Questions/Tactile Tours'. Available: http://www.sculpturebythesea.com/Home.aspx (accessed 30 October 2013).

Sculptures by the Sea Aarhus, (2013a) 'Information for visitors'. Available: http://www. sculpturebythesea.dk/en/Information.aspx (accessed 30 October 2013).

Sculptures by the Sea, Aarhus (2013b) 'Sculpture by the Sea Aarhus has ended'. Available:http://www.sculpturebythesea.dk/en/Medier/Nyheder/2013/3-kvartal/SxS-2013-slut.aspx (accessed November 15 2013).

Sculpture Saint John (n.d) 'Sculpture Saint John'. Available: http://www.sculpturesaintjohn. com (accessed 10 October 2013).

Selka, E. (2012) 'Leonardo da Vinci exhibition: the queue is an art in itself', *The Telegraph*, 30 January 2012.

Shade, R. (2004) *Communication Breakdowns. Theatre, Performance, Rock Music and Some other Welsh Assemblies*, Cardiff, University of Wales Press.

Sharjah Art Foundation (2013) 'March meeting'. Available: http://www.sharjahart.org/ march-meeting/march-meeting-2013/welcome (accessed 30 October 2013).

Sharjah Biennial (2013) *'Re:emerge, Towards a new cultural cartography'*. Available: http://www.sharjahart.org/biennial/sharjah-biennial-11/welcome (accessed 30 October 2013).

Shaw, T. B. (1867) *A Complete Manual of English Literature*. New York: Sheldon and Company.

Shellenberger, C. (2013) 'Rain dampens Artist Alley event'. *Spoke: The Newspaper of Conestoga College's Journalism Program*. Available: http://spokeonline.com/?p=7632 (accessed 2 October 2013).

Shone, A. and Parry, B. (2004) *Successful Event Management: A Practical Handbook*, London: Thomson Learning.

Sigurðardóttir, M.S. and Young, T. (2011) *Towards Creative Iceland: Building Local, Going Global*. Reykjavik: The Consultative Forum of Creative Industries in Iceland.

Silverman, M. (2013) 'Life tunes up for the Proms' man on the spot'. *South China Morning Post Review*, 4 August 2013: A11.

Simone-Charteris, M.T. and Boyd, S. (2010) 'Developing dark and political tourism in Northern Ireland: An industry perspective', in Gorman, G. and Mottiar, Z. (eds) *Contemporary Issues in Irish and Global Tourism and Hospitality*, Dublin: Dublin Institute of Technology, pp. 106–23.

Simpson, P. (2012) 'My life: Interview with Liam Mullone', *South China Morning Post Magazine,* 12 August 2012: 11.

Sintas, J.L., and Alvarez, G. (2005) 'Four characters on the stage playing three games: performing arts consumption in Spain', *Journal of Business Research*, 58: 1446–55.

Smith, H.P. (2012) 'The art of mini golf OK.Quoi?! arts festival makes the ordinary extraordinary', *HERE Magazine,* 14(29) July: 25–28.

Smith, K.A. and Lockstone, L. (2009) 'Involving and keeping event volunteers: Management insights from cultural festivals', in Baum, T., Deery, M., Hanlon, C. Lockstone, L., and Smith, K. (eds) *People and Work in Events and Conventions: A Research Perspective,* Mongewell, UK: Cabi, pp. 154–68.

Smith, M. (2003) *Issues in Cultural Tourism Studies*, London: Routledge.

Smith, M. (2007) 'Space, place, placelessness in the culturally regenerated city', in G. Richards (ed.), *Cultural tourism: Global and local perspectives,* Binghamton, NY: The Haworth Press, pp. 91–112.

Smith, P.B. and Peterson, M.F. (1988) *Leadership, Organizations and Culture: An Event Management Model,* London: Sage.

Smith, P.F. (1973) 'Urban sculpture: A kind of therapy', *Leonardo*, 6(3): 227–32.

Smith, T. (2012) *Thinking Contemporary Curating*, New York: Independent Curators International.

South China Morning Post (2013) 'March sees storm clouds gather for C.Y.', 2 July 2013: Front page.

Spinnerei. (2009) *Spinnerei: From Cotton to Culture Report 2009*, Leipzig: Leipzig Baumwollspinnerei.

Stanfield, P. (2008) 'Toward a history of the Edinburgh International Film Festival, 1969–77', *Film International* 6(4): 63–71.

Staniszewski, M. (1998) *The Power of Display. A History of Exhibition Installations at the Museum of Modern Art*, Cambridge, MA: MIT Press.

Stolarick, K. and Florida, R. (2006) 'Creativity, connections and innovation: A study of linkages in the Montreal region', *Environment and Planning A,* 38: 1799–1817.

Stone Music Festival Official Facebook Website (2013) 'Responses to "Did we have a good time guys?"' Available: https://www.facebook.com/StoneMusicFest/posts/439311206161616?comment_id=2660428&offset=50&total_comments=142 (accessed 30 October 2013); Boycott HK Dome Festival https://www.facebook.com/Boycott.HK.Dome.Festival (accessed 30 October 2013).

Swain, R. (2013) 'Fringe theatre must tackle its "low pay, no pay" gremlins from within', *The Guardian*: Cultural Professionals Network 11 June 2013. Available: http://www.guardian.co.uk/culture-professionals-network/culture-professionals-blog/2013/jun/11/low-pay-no-pay-fringe-theatre (accessed 30 October 2013).

Thomas, D. (2013) 'What do artists get out of arts festivals?' *The Guardian* Cultural Professionals Network. Available: http://www.theguardian.com/culture-professionals-network/culture-professionals-blog/2013/oct/18/arts-festivals-site-specific-art (accessed 25 October 2013).

Thomas, R. and Thomas, H. (2013) 'What are the prospects for professionalizing event management in the UK?' *Tourism Management Perspectives*, 6(0): 8–14.

Tighe, A.J. (1986) 'The arts/tourism partnership', *Journal of Travel Research*, 24(3): 2–5.

Timothy, D. J. (2011) *Cultural Heritage and Tourism: An Introduction,* Bristol: Channel View Publications.

Toepler, S. (2006) 'Caveat venditor? Museum merchandising, nonprofit commercialization, and the case of the Metropolitan Museum in New York', *Voluntas: International Journal of Voluntary and Nonprofit Organizations,* 17(2): 95–109.

TTCSI (Trinidad and Tobago Coalition of Service Industries), (2013) 'Project ICT innovations for the development of the masquerade industry of Trinidad and Tobago'. Available: http://www.ttcsi.org/repository/library/ttcsi_-_mas_project_abstract.pdf (accessed 30 October 2013).

Tum, J., Norton, P. and Wright, J.N. (2006) *Management of Event Operations,* Oxford: Elsevier.

UNESCO (2013) 'Al-Taghrooda, traditional Bedouin chanted poetry in the United Arab Emirates and the Sultanate of Oman'. Available: http://www.unesco.org/culture/ich/index.php?lg=en&pg=00011&RL=00744 (accessed 30 October 2013).

UNESCO Arts Education (2013) 'Arts education'. Available: http://www.unesco.org/new/en/culture/themes/creativity/arts-education/ (accessed October 15 2013).

UNESCO Bangkok (2013) Second World Conference on Arts Education. Seoul Agenda: Goals for the Development of Arts Education. Available: http://www.unesco.org/new/fileadmin/MULTIMEDIA/HQ/CLT/CLT/pdf/Seoul_Agenda_EN.pdf (accessed 30 October 2013).

UNESCO Creative Cities Network (2006) *Towards Sustainable Strategies for Creative Creative Tourism,* Santa Fe, NM, October 2006.

UNESCO Observatory for Research on Local Cultures and Creativity in Education (2013a) *Cultural Development and Sustainability*. Focus Issues Series 3. Available: http://www.unescohkied.org/ckeditor_assets/attachments/365/fiss_3_publication.pdf?1374475385 (accessed 30 October 2013).

UNESCO Observatory for Research on Local Cultures and Creativity in Education (2013b) *Synergies between Arts Education and Culture*. Focus Issues Series 2. Available: http://

www.unescohkied.org/ckeditor_assets/attachments/372/fiss_2_publication_revised1. pdf?1376038367 (accessed October 15 2013).

UNTWO (United Nations World Tourism Organization) (2012) *Tourism and Intangible Cultural Heritage.* Madrid, UNWTO.

Varaždin City Tourist Association (2013) 'History/programme'. Available: www. spancirfest.com (accessed 30 October 2013).

Velayutham, S. (2007) *Responding to Globalisation. Nation, Culture and Identity in Singapore*, Singapore: Institute of Southeast Asian Studies.

Vogel, H.L. (2011) *Entertainment Industry Economics. A Guide for Financial Analysis*, 8th edn, New York: Cambridge University Press.

Watt, D.C. (1998) *Event Management in Leisure and Tourism,* Harlow: Addison Wesley Longman.

West, S. (1995) 'National desires and regional realities in the Venice Biennale, 1895–1914', *Art History,* 18(3): 404–34.

Wiedenhoft Murphy, W.A. (2010) 'Touring the troubles in West Belfast: Building peace or reproducing conflict?' *Peace and Change*, 35(4): 537–60.

Wilkins, H. (2012) 'Souvenirs: What and why we buy', *Journal of Travel Research*, 51(2): 239–47.

Williams, M. and Bowdin, G.A.J. (2007) 'Festival evaluation: An exploration of seven UK arts festivals', *Managing Leisure*, 12(2–3): 187–203.

Wilson-Goldie, K. (2005) 'Sharjah Biennale. Art, anxiety and autocracy in the Gulf', *Flash Art,* 38 May/June: 89–90.

WOMAdelaide (2013) 'Welcome to WOMAdelaide'. Available: http://www.womadelaide. com.au/ (accessed 30 October 2013).

Xiao, H. and Smith, S.L.J. (2006) 'Case studies in tourism research: A state-of-the-art Analysis', *Tourism Management*, 27(5): 738–49.

Zaremba, A. (2012) 'Comes the time, comes the man', *Art Map Express,* May 2012: 1.

Zest Festival. (n.d.) 'Zest Festival'. Available: http://zestfest.com.au (accessed 10 October 2013).

Index